Film and Fiction

Film and Fiction / The Dynamics of Exchange

Keith Cohen

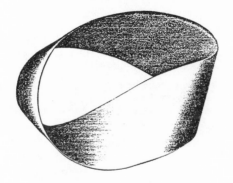

New Haven and London

Yale University Press

1979

Published with assistance from the foundation
established in memory of Henry Weldon Barnes
of the Class of 1882, Yale College.

Designed by Sally Harris
and set in IBM Press Roman type.
Printed in the United States of America.

Published in Great Britain, Europe, Africa, and
Asia (except Japan) by Yale University Press,
Ltd., London. Distributed in Australia and
New Zealand by Book & Film Services, Artarmon,
N.S.W., Australia; and in Japan by Harper & Row,
Publishers, Tokyo Office.

Library of Congress Cataloging in Publication Data

Cohen, Keith
  Film and fiction.

  Includes index.
  1. Moving-pictures and literature. 2. Fiction—
20th century—History and criticism. I. Title.
PN1995.3.C6   791.43   79-64073
ISBN 0-300-02366-9

for my parents
Maxwell Lewis Cohen
Dolores Keith Cohen

Contents

Preface

Personal history is linked to the evolution of this book in an un-usual way. My first real attraction to the movies came in a period of intellectual awakening on many fronts, a period of simultaneous displacement and reinforcement: my enthusiasm for the theatre waned as my interest in film grew, while my own reading and writing seemed constantly invigorated, revalidated. The films of the early 1960s—by Resnais, Antonioni, Fellini, Godard—moved me to a divided allegiance between literary studies and film studies. Work on this book represented a way of doing both at once.

Out of my fascination for cinema developed a steadily stronger notion that modern fiction depends for what it is on a cinematic way of seeing and telling things. Examples were not lacking. All I needed to do was to construct the case, to discover if, when retraced through history, my conviction held. It did. The twentieth century brought new attitudes about artistic creation and the role of technology in art. What was most pronounced, though, was a turning away from artistic purity in preference for artistic exchange.

The turn of the twentieth century was a vantage point for looking backward to the impressionist painters and forward to the *nouveau roman*. I needed focus, and so I chose to concentrate on the period from 1895 to 1925. This is, in any case, the incubation period for what I call the "classic modern." It is the period during which nineteenth-century theorists' tentative ideas about permutations among the arts are put into practice, at times with certitude, and memorably. So great is the change from artistic independence to interdependence that it suggests the positing of a *coupure* in aesthetic development.

I do not argue that cinema is solely responsible for this cut-off or aesthetic swerving, or that it is the exclusive factor in the radically new formulations of the twentieth-century novel. I do argue, however, that, among the many factors brought to bear upon the novel, the movies, that new contraption of dubious artistic status, became a unique source of inspiration for the modern novelist's revamping of traditional form. I have wished to avoid at all cost a deterministic approach; I have tried not to get hamstrung in the mechanics of "influence." I hope nevertheless to demonstrate that the cinema represents not simply another element in the turn-of-the-century *Zeitgeist* but a privileged precedent, aesthetically and epistemologically, to the experiments carried out by the classic modern novel.

An argument subjacent to the whole book is that the very concept of artistic creation has been changed by the advent of the cinema. The movies were the first "invented" art. Machines are crucially relied upon in the cinematic process for a re-presentation which, rather than becoming more complete, more all-encompassing, or more efficient through automation, is full of deletions, ellipses, and partial views. Cinema can be seen as the epitome of twentieth-century relativism for the way in which it cuts up reality, endows these "rescued fragments" with special significance, and combines them in an order at odds with their lived sequence.

The boom years of the classic modern, from World War I to the end of the 1920s, hark back to the period of Wagner and Baudelaire. At both times artists became convinced that their art had reached the limits of its expressive capabilities. Conventional forms were exhausted. And, just as in the 1850s and '60s, there was in the 1920s an unusual willingness on the part of artists to be attentive to the strategies and techniques of other arts. Given this historical tendency, the identification of a cinematic format in the novel points to those areas of traditional form being revamped. In the absence of strict literary conventions for depicting, say, simultaneity, the novelist turns to the cinematic model. Such innovations inspired by the movies, or analogous to cinematic techniques, inform us as well about the longevity and variability of novelistic conventions.

When I first began in 1967 to think through the project which culminated in this book, "literature and film" was scarcely etched out as a field of research, much less an academically sanctioned discipline, as it is in many places today. Development in the field since that time has been staggering; it has become clear to me in recent years, in fact, that it is precisely along the boundaries, the margins around and among the arts, that the most fascinating observations in aesthetic and cultural theory have been taking place. This is another way of explaining, with a mixture of regret and happy resignation, that I have not been able to include any kind of systematic accounting for all of these new developments.

There are many people who deserve special thanks for a study such as this one, which was, in its original format, a doctoral dissertation in comparative literature at Princeton University. My deepest gratitude is to Joseph Frank, who closely advised my thesis writing for over four years with careful and constant wisdom. Others at Princeton who gave unstintingly of their time in reading and commenting on the work at various stages are Robert Fagles and Ralph Freedman. The other scholars and critics whose work I am indebted to are enumerated in the notes to each chapter.

A good deal of rethinking that went into the final book manuscript has been inspired by conversations with colleagues in film here at the University of Wisconsin-Madison, David Bordwell and Russell Merritt, and by participating in the outstanding conferences on film theory and related disciplines sponsored over the past five years by the Center for Twentieth Century Studies at the University of Wisconsin-Milwaukee. Some of the most challenging and most fruitful exchanges have been with students, Maureen Turim, Edward Branigan, John Mowitt, and others.

I wish also to thank Princeton University for the dissertation fellowship which made my initial research possible and the Graduate School of the University of Wisconsin-Madison for its generosity over the last five years in supporting my continued interest in inter-art relations.

A special note of thanks goes to the city of Paris, where I conducted research from 1970 to 1974, to the Cinémathèque Française, and to Hélène Cixous and Jean Gattegno, colleagues at Vincennes, whose ministrations made it possible for me to carry out my work in as unfettered a manner as I could have hoped for.

Some of the material in chapters 1 and 5–8 has appeared, in different form, in *Film Reader* 3 (February 1978): 150–68 and *Film Reader* 2 (Winter 1976): 42–51. It is used here with permission. For their help with film and photo processing for the illustrations in the book, I wish to thank Great Big Pictures, Inc., Madison, Wisconsin.

Throughout this long process by which a conviction becomes a book, my wife Paula has been an invaluable source of encouragement and emotional support.

Finally, I wish to thank Ellen Graham at Yale for her sound editorial advice over the past year and Barbara Folsom for her excellent job of copy-editing.

Madison   K.C.
April 1979

Introduction: Debatable Affinities

The twentieth century began in a flurry of artistic hybrids, everything from calligrams to tone poems. The mood in this period of *contre-décadence* was to change significantly after the First World War, but the gesture of drawing on one art for the enrichment of another—a gesture that Europe had become familiar with since Wagner's generation—was repeated over and over and has come to be an essential characteristic of twentieth-century art. This is not to say that ours is a century of bastard art forms. Quite the contrary: our century has put more rigorously into practice than ever before certain theories concerning the interrelatedness of the arts which were formulated in the nineteenth century, in an effort precisely to strengthen the specific effects of single arts. Today we can speak, without metaphor or exaggeration, of musicians learning from painters, writers learning from dance, and dramatists learning from cinema.

Cinema, it might in fact be argued, has been the most active catalyst in this process of convergence and exchange. Cinema was first evaluated as an art form in terms of a fantastic amalgamation. Phrases such as "a powerful synthesis" and "an extended expression" of all the arts[1] echoed important aesthetic platforms of the nineteenth century. The theory of the arts' interrelations had an early

---

1. "Naissance du cinéma," in *Intelligence du cinématographe,* ed. Marcel L'Herbier (Paris, 1946), p. 118; introduction to Moussinac's book of the same title. All translations are my own unless otherwise indicated.

1

implicit spokesman in Hegel. His *Aesthetics* (1801) corrected, among other things, a tendency among philosophers to think of the arts in terms of limits and restrictions, as had been polemically maintained by Lessing in *The Laocoön* (1766). Hegel searched instead for the underlying similarities, just as Wagner would when he described his great *Gesamtkunstwerk*, the *Musikdrame*. Thus, it was not surprising to hear Georges Méliès, one of the first movie-makers, speak of the cinema's capacity for combining the arts in equal doses: dramatic art, drawing, painting, sculpture, architecture, mechanics, manual labor.[2]

If the cinema could, and still can, be seen as a hodgepodge of various artistic impulses, its finished product has at the same time been capable of shocking the other arts into an awareness of their own potentials. Here I am thinking of the cinematic inspiration of the staging decor of Meyerhold and Brecht, the juxtapositional methods common to both the movies and surrealistic art—but most of all, the techniques of discontinuity and montage in the modern novel. It will be the primary objective of this study to trace this exchange of energies from the movies, an art originally so thoroughly informed by nineteenth-century sensibility, to the modern novel, whose major innovations will be seen as closely patterned after those of the cinema.

Such a view is by no means new. In a sense, the demonstration of the cinematic quality of the modern novel has been available ever since the first reader of *Ulysses* noted the montage technique of "The Wandering Rocks" or since Dos Passos included the "Newsreel" and "Camera Eye" sections in *U.S.A.* In other words, certain modern novels proclaim themselves cinematic.

The need for the present study arises, then, not so much from the lack of insight among general readers of the modern novel, but rather from the dearth of discussions of novel and cinema that seek, at a theoretical level, an explanation for the cinema's impact. The basic conviction of a relation between the two media has most often led to a search for the "laws" governing and limiting each medium[3] or to juxtaposing *grosso modo* the two arts in order to deduce,

2. "Les Vues cinematographiques," in ibid., p. 180; from Méliès's book of the same title, first published in 1907.
3. Etienne Fuzellier, *Cinema et littérature* (Paris, 1964).

largely at the level of production history, superficial similarities.[4]

On the other hand, the earliest and probably most influential American work on novel and cinema not only skirts the theoretical problems at stake but also concentrates its efforts on one particular practice: adapting novels into films. Such a focus leads to the regrettable conclusion that "The great innovators of the twentieth century in film and novel both have had . . . little to do with each other, have gone their own ways alone, always keeping a firm but respectful distance."[5] By insisting, without further investigation, on the notion of a strict, unalterable *difference* of communication in novel and film, word against image, this view ignores the very real, observable phenomenon of *mutation* among such signs, which has been documented since the early nineteenth century.

A great number of books have been written on the movies qua movies. The scope of the present study is such that the discrete development of cinema and the methods of individual masterpieces cannot be given any more than cursory consideration. From a methodological vantage point, however, I have taken much from recent studies of the cinema. For example, a basic assumption I make is that both words and images are sets of signs that belong to systems and that, at a certain level of abstraction, these systems bear resemblances to one another. More specifically, within each such system there are many different codes (perceptual, referential, symbolic). What makes possible, then, a study of the relation between two separate sign systems, like novel and film, is the fact that the same codes may reappear in more than one system.[6]

From the moment visual and verbal elements are seen as component parts of one global system of meaning, the affinities between the two arts come into focus. Eisenstein, who was deeply sensitive to the cinema's indirect ancestors among the other arts, compares literature to the movies because it, too, is an "art of viewing—not only the eye, but *viewing*—both meanings embraced in this term."[7]

---

4. Robert Richardson, *Literature and Film* (Bloomington, Ind., 1969); Edward Murray, *The Cinematic Imagination* (New York, 1972).

5. George Bluestone, *Novels into Film* (Berkeley, 1961), p. 63.

6. Christian Metz, *Langage et cinéma* (Paris, 1971), pp. 20-21.

7. Sergei Eisenstein, *Film Form*, trans. Jay Leyda (New York, 1957), p. 233.

The modern semiotician adopts the view of Eisenstein and, with a new vocabulary, goes further than ever before in breaking down the barrier that has existed, in theoretical terms, between the verbal and the visual. The very mechanisms of language systems can thus be seen to carry on diverse and complex interrelations: "one function, among others, of language is to name the units segmented by vision (but also to help segment them), and . . . one function, among others, of vision is to inspire semantic configurations (but also to be inspired by them)."[8]

Eisenstein provided one of the earliest practical explorations into the relation between novel and cinema in a famous essay entitled "Dickens, Griffith, and the Film Today." His main point is to demonstrate the manner in which Griffith's montage techniques are indebted to Dickens's use of close-up details, as in the opening pages of *The Cricket and the Hearth*. This is part of Eisenstein's more general enterprise to show that montage composition is not unique to the cinema but a fundamental technique of all art. In this light, the observations he makes are mainly instructive in what they reveal about Dickens's sophisticated practices. The analogy with Griffith has always seemed weak to me.

The essay points in passing, however, to another kind of indebtedness that characterizes early films: the more or less blatant appropriation of the themes and content of the nineteenth-century bourgeois novel. Herein, certainly, lies the more fundamental connection between Dickens and Griffith. Like most of his contemporaries, Griffith raided the nineteenth century in search of a certain sort of adventure and a certain brand of sentiment. The melodramatic and sentimental motifs characteristic of Dickens's fiction, along with the themes of the sacrosanct homogeneity of the family, the privileges of owning property, the primacy of the individual, can be seen to be lifted intact into the early films of Griffith, those of the Biograph years. The reliance of early films on a predigested, tried-and-true content remains one of the most important defining characteristics of this period of film history.

8. Metz, *Langage et cinéma*, p. 24.

The details of such a comparative content analysis need to be worked out on a full scale. Similar parallels have been suggested, such as that of historical analogy. The cinema develops as a mass medium through stages that are roughly analogous to the novel's development, so that one might speak of a parallel sequence of sensibilities in passing from Fielding to Richardson and from Porter to Griffith.[9] Such parallels have their pertinence in a discussion of this sort, but the present study locates the primary nexus elsewhere.

This is not to say that I wish to avoid the dynamics of history. In fact, the novel's liability to a massive technical reorientation that cinema fostered was due in large measure to the decline of the bourgeois novel toward the end of the nineteenth century. An important argument to be expanded in the course of this study concerns the type of basic remodeling the novel underwent during the "impressionist" era. Bored with the prevailing trend of an inflexibly omniscient, authoritative narrator, innovative novelists, beginning with James and Conrad, sought to lay bare the process of fiction by inserting a highly self-conscious narrator as first-person teller or third-person "central reflector." The emphasis, as a result, was on *showing* how the events unfold dramatically rather that recounting them, from an aloof position, as already having taken place; on conveying richly complex experiences through a shifting narrative perspective; and on opting for a potential energy required from the reader to reconstruct into a cohesive whole what often came across in fragmented bits.

What I anticipate, actually, on the part of readers familiar with the modern literary tradition, is not a reservation regarding the importance of history, but rather a skepticism regarding the unilateral manner in which I argue for the impact of the cinema. Some may respond that it is mere coincidence that the earmarks of modern fiction share so many technical and ontological qualities with the movies, that these earmarks must be located first and foremost within the evolution of the novel as literary genre. For me, the two perspectives are not mutually exclusive. There is no doubt about the modern novel's responsiveness to an inner dynamic;

9. Susan Sontag, *Against Interpretation* (New York, 1961), pp. 242-43.

Flaubert foresaw with uncanny acuteness many of the directions the new novel would take. But to deny the impact of the cinema would be like denying the importance of science to Romantic poetry; beyond the constraints felt by the writers as coming from their specifically literary forebears, a new cultural phenomenon was forcing itself into their awareness and into the way in which their generation saw the world.

A further point should be made in order to bring into sharper perspective the historical encounter between the novel and the cinema. As the movies cultivated their built-in potentials for narration and emerged as the dominant form of mass entertainment during the 1910s, the novel encountered a crisis of survival unknown to it since the early eighteenth century. The attitude of contemporary observers—an attitude that persists today—was that the novel was likely to disappear altogether: " 'The pictures' are driving literature off the parlor table." [10] The novel faced a fate similar to that of figurative painting when photography preempted the field of pictorial verism in the late nineteenth century. It was not really a question of struggling to win over an audience in either case, but rather of discovering new methods of handling more or less traditional material. Degas disarmed the adversary (in this oversimplified schema) by taking up and putting to use devices that were peculiar to photography. In a similar way, the innovative novelist, the novelist sensitive to the vast areas of narratable experience that had been either emptied of relevance or recharged through new manners of seeing, was to exploit to his or her own advantage the techniques of fragmented vision and discontinuity peculiar to the movies.

Cinema has a special relation to the twentieth century and to the development of modernism. It might easily be argued that every avant-garde movement since 1900 owes something to the new visions afforded by the movies. Cubism and futurism both bear resemblances to cinema insofar as they emphasize an analytic, even mechanical, way of viewing the world. Surrealists, who were among

10. Reported by the director of the Denver Art Association in 1922 and quoted in George William Eggers's foreword to Vachel Lindsay, *The Art of the Moving Pictures* (New York, 1922), p. xiv.

the first to suggest the similarity between dream work and film work, use methods of collage and discontinuity that recall similar methods in cinema. Indeed, surrealists like Picabia, Man Ray, and Buñuel were the first to experiment with the medium and apparatus of the movies in a dynamic way.

The reasons for this close alliance between the principles and special capacities of cinema and the general aesthetic development of the twentieth century are difficult to explain in detail. A point of departure in such an investigation, however, could very well be the amazing similarity between the potentially disorienting capabilities of cinema, in terms of space and time, and the principles of Einstein's new physics. One of the basic premises of the theory of relativity is that phenomena can no longer be measured exactly and absolutely within a model of static spatial relations and clock time. The simple interdependent yet mutually exclusive relation between space and time posited by Newtonian physics is no longer tenable. Cinema, as is well known by the average movie-goer, has unique capabilities of compressing and expanding time, confining or en-larging the space of vision and the sharpness of its precision. Cinematic articulation, in fact, as will be further discussed below, depends on a special interrelationship between the spatial and tem-poral dimensions. It seems almost as though Minkowski were speaking of the cinematic experience when, in 1908, he proclaimed, "Henceforth, space by itself, and time by itself, are doomed to fade away into mere shadows, and only a kind of union of the two will preserve an independent reality."[11]

Modern social and psychoanalytic theory has often formulated its tenets in ways surprisingly analogous to a cinematic framework and the cinematic apparatus. Jean-Louis Baudry has explained in some detail the manner in which both Marx and Freud took re-course in cinematic metaphors to explain some of their most funda-mental doctrines.[12] Ideology, for Marx, is that which forces the subject to see social relations in a precisely inverted order—just as if

11. "Space and Time," in H. A. Lorentz et al., *The Principle of Relativity*, trans. W. Perrett and G. B. Jeffery (London, 1923), p. 75.
12. "The Apparatus," trans. Jean Andrews and Bertrand Augst, in *Camera Obscura, A Journal of Feminism and Film Theory* 1 (Fall 1976): 104-26.

one were looking through the aperture of a camera obscura. This image of the world upside down has, of course, persisted in Marxist sociological analyses, and contemporary discussions of film and ideology have investigated the implications of the ironic fact that the camera, a modern version of that camera obscura used during the Renaissance to perfect vision with "correct" perspective, can thus be considered bound, historically, by a limited, essentially bourgeois manner of representation.[13]

Freud's description of the subject's dream process, similarly, bears an uncanny resemblance to the process of viewing a film. As the subject sleeps, images are projected onto the "dream screen" of his perceptual apparatus.[14] These images originate in the unconscious, and so the subject is never aware of the manner of functioning of this projection.

But while social and psychoanalytic theory may resort to cinema mainly as a convenient metaphor, the general aesthetics of modernism can be seen to rely more and more on a notion of art and artistic production that would have been untenable within the cultural context prior to the advent of the movies. Here, still, cinema is not exactly touted, as music was in the nineteenth century, as some sort of ideal art. (It is nevertheless often referred to as the "typical" art of the twentieth century.) Rather, the technological constitution of the cinematic process—from recording to editing to projecting—becomes a model for the relation between the configurating signifiers of art and the signifying apparatus.

The dominant informing characteristic of representational art is the transparency of the mode by which the fictional world is created. It is as though we were to become oblivious, in a realistic novel or a figurative painting, to the materials that produced the world or the figures. Modernism reverses this aesthetic. Art becomes interesting, captivating, compelling precisely when attention is called to the apparatus of production. For the Russian Formalists,

---

13. Cf. Jean-Louis Comolli, "Technique and Ideology: Camera, Perspective, Depth of Field," trans. Diana Matias, *Film Reader* 2 (Jan. 1977): 128–40.
14. Because of the awkwardness of the joint pronouns *he/she, his/her,* I have used *he* and *his* throughout the text. The reader should, however, understand that the feminine pronoun is included in this generalized usage of *he, his,* etc.

for example, one means of producing the effect of "defamiliariza-
tion" they considered essential to great art was to bring into the
foreground of a fiction not the action of the characters but the
action of the scriptor writing. While such a device can be found as
early as Sterne's *Tristram Shandy,* often called for this reason an
uncannily modern work, we find it with greater frequency and
regularity as we enter the twentieth century.

Any modern view that values this foregrounding of the apparatus
must at some point hold its underlying tenets over against the
cinema. In cinema, more than in any previous art, the production of
a fiction is entirely dependent on the tools of modern technology. It
can be asserted without exaggeration that the cinematic experience
is impossible without a simultaneous experience of its apparatus—at
least of the projector. It is true that cinema includes a strong representational tradition, that of Hollywood in the 1930s and 1940s.
But it is just as pertinent to mention the countertrend of Russians
like Eisenstein and Vertov, the surrealists during the 1920s, and the
explicitly anti-Hollywood avant-garde European films and underground American films of the 1960s. In these works not only do the
conditions of projection remind the spectator of the film's apparatus,
but the techniques of montage and camera movement insist that the
spectator pay at least as much attention to the film's process of production as to its unfolding fiction.

It is for this reason that I will consider as extremely pertinent to
the development of a modernist narrative the theories and practice
of Eisenstein, in particular the notion of montage. By the same
token, I see very little relevance in the theories of "invisible editing"
propounded by Bazin and others. Those films which seek to transport the spectator entirely into their fictional world have more in
common, formally and ideologically, with the realist novel of the
nineteenth century, whose bankruptcy had already been attested to
by the James-Ford-Conrad group. It should come as no surprise,
therefore, that I draw few examples from the Hollywood film. Instead, two levels of self-consciousness in film production will be
insisted on as seminal in the development of an aesthetic of modernism: the intrinsic dependence of cinema on recording, editing, and
projection machinery to achieve its net effect, and the more specialized foregrounding of the cinematic apparatus in the montage
tradition of film-making.

It is not, then, in terms of a vague *Zeitgeist* that the basic parallels between novel and cinema will be argued. I perceive the impact of cinema to be precise and describable. Although there may be no statistics and little documentary evidence to bear out this thesis, I maintain that the contours of modern narrative would not be what they are without the precedents set by the movies.

Everyday experience in modern civilization, with its bombardment of visual and aural signs of all sorts, demonstrates, it seems to me, in a practical and immediate way, the constant interference taking place between diverse language systems and suggests both the theoretical affinities of these systems and the means by which mutual illustration and reduplication has taken place in practice. What is necessary today is not to take these interferences for granted but to return to that golden era of metamorphosis and massive cultural change at the beginning of this century, when modernism first discovered itself and, in particular, learned with surprise the pleasure of calling attention to itself.

The line of argument developed in the following pages begins with a careful consideration of the informing principles of cinema itself in the domains of the plastic arts, popular media, and technology. On the basis of this background, an analysis is made of both inherited and inherent traits of cinema. Part I, "Convergence," ends with a comparative study of film and novel techniques, with an aim toward discovering the mechanisms by which literary narrative could be exploded by the cinematic example. Part II, "Exchange," details the specific ways in which the modern novel registered the impact of the cinema. This part includes detailed analyses of five modern novels treated not in succession but as a constant body of exemplary material that can be left and then returned to when needed.

The overarching rationale for this organization is as follows: given the origin, informing traits, and nature of the cinematic medium, aspects of modern literary narrative such as radical temporal and perspectival distortion and discontinuity must be seen in rigorously analogous terms. Replaced in a general cultural framework, this study seeks not an origin but simply a first solid example of how powerful the precedent of one art could be for the practitioners of another, how one set of codes became the common tools of artists working in widely disparate fields.

PART I / CONVERGENCE

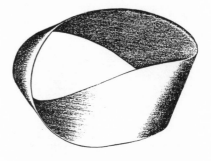

1 Impressionism

But just as painters, unable on a flat canvas to represent equally well the diverse faces of a solid body, choose a principal one, which they position toward the light and, leaving the others in shadow, make them appear no more than they could be seen when being looked at; in the same way, fearing the inability of putting into my discourse everything I had in my mind, I undertook only to lay out with any amplitude therein that which I understood about light, then, in this regard, to add something about the sun and the fixed stars, because light proceeds almost entirely from them; something about the skies, because they transmit light; something about the planets, the comets, and the earth, because they reflect light; and something in particular about all the bodies on earth, because they are either colored, transparent, or luminous; and finally something about man, because he is of all this the spectator.

Descartes, Discourse on Method, *V*

Without light, in a strict empiricist sense, the external world ceases to be. Given light, the world—the whole universe, as Descartes movingly and understatedly points out—appears instantly open to description. The impressionist painters were more keenly aware of this than most of their predecessors. That is not to say that the impressionists were the first artists to study the effects of light: Rembrandt, Vermeer, La Tour all studied light more dramatically. Here light must be understood in a very specific (though most

obvious) sense:[1] outdoor illumination produced by the sun and reflected against and through the earth's atmosphere. The impressionists forsook the light of the atelier, set up their easels outside, and,
unlike the Barbizon painters who also sketched outdoors, applied
their oils and completed their composition *en plein air.*

There is an important difference, however, between Boudin, who
was thankful "that the Creator has spread here, there, and every-
where his splendid light and that it is less this world than the eternal
envelope that we reproduce,"[2] and his disciple Monet, who
probably inaugurated the impressionists' consideration of light as a
physical phenomenon.[3] Such an insight was, no doubt, a wholly
experimental one that can at best be extrapolated from the paintings
of Monet and others.

H. Helmholtz, one of the leading theoreticians of optics at the
time the impressionists were working, emphasized the need to
understand visual sensations as produced by "luminous vibrations
of the ether."[4] Light was no longer a nondescript donnée assumed
in nature, but rather a material process that could itself be examined, analyzed. Unlike their immediate predecessors and teachers
(for example, Boudin), who were content with Descartes's principles
as well as his metaphors, the impressionists were eager to discover
how the "eternal envelope" is made up and how it is really illuminated. The divide between Boudin and Monet becomes a great one,
not only for the history of art, but for the place of science in art as

1. The metaphorical sense of light as "truth" or "reason," as in the
En*light*enment, might nonetheless be operative in the impressionists' struggle
against romantic obscurity. "Apart from its obvious scientific elements, this
technical idea (of open-air painting) also has a political and moral content and
seems to be trying to say: Out into the open, out into the light of truth!"
Arnold Hauser, *The Social History of Art,* trans. Stanley Godman (New York,
1951), 4:69.
2. Cited in Louis Hautecoeur, *La Littérature et la peinture en France du
XVIIe au XXe siècles* (Paris, 1942), p. 148, and commented on by Ruth
Moser, *L'Impressionisme français* (Geneva, 1952), p. 66.
3. Pierre Francastel, *L'Impressionisme* (Paris, 1937), p. 134. Cf. Hauser,
Social History of Art, 4:170–71.
4. *Optique physiologique,* trans. Emile Jeval and H. Th. Klein (Paris, 1867;
orig. Leipzig, 1856, 1860, 1866), p. 264. As a physiologist, Helmholtz was less
concerned with the properties of light (the domain of physical optics: p. 43)
than with the reception of light by the human eye.

well. If not actively engaged in scientific pursuits, the impressionists were at least imbued with what Francastel calls "the scientific spirit" and shared with the physical scientists this materialistic and ultimately atomistic view of light.

The impressionists' first important achievements, then, were to have opted for experimentalism in their *en-plein-air* method and, in their analysis of light, to have brought the art of painting into line with the scientific and technical advances of the century. This latter achievement was recognized rather early by art critics and led to a temporary assimilation of the impressionists, or L'Ecole de Paris, into the school of "Réalisme."[5] What is of principal interest to us here, however, is the special technical innovations that proceeded from these initial achievements.

Light was seen to have a double effect. It both decomposed and recomposed the unity of the object. In the first case, outdoor sketching and composing had demonstrated to the impressionists that a constant change in the angle of source light (i.e., the movement of the earth around the sun) resulted in a constantly changing angle of shadow, and that an irregular source light (e.g., as the result of clouds) went along with this first effect to produce a constantly changing color tone. Monet's series on *Haystacks* and the *Rouen Cathedral* are the most systematic record of such observations. The hour-to-hour changes in the angle of source light can be seen consistently to alter the total form of the object. Where a constant source of light had to be postulated, the objects represented would be nonetheless dramatically subjected to the absence and presence of light. One of the earliest examples of this is Monet's *Les Femmes au*

5. One of the first defenses of the impressionists (though often in pseudo-scientific terms) was E. Duranty's *La Nouvelle Peinture* (A propos du Groupe d'Artistes qui expose dans les Galeries Durand-Ruel), ed. M. Guérin (Paris, 1946; orig. 1876). Duranty was one of the chief *animateurs* of the realist movement, which flourished through the 1850s and thereafter.

The impressionists' radical change in topoi was not accompanied by a radical change in ideology, and in this respect they differ quite manifestly from *réalistes* like Courbet, Millet, and Daumier. Though the impressionist artist of the 1860s and 1870s was outwardly alienated from the bourgeois ideology that had nourished him, he had no means of incorporating this alienation into his art. Cf. Meyer Schapiro, "Nature of Abstract Art," *Marxist Quarterly* 1, no. 1 (Jan.-Mar. 1937): 83.

Claude Monet, *Rouen Cathedral, West Façade.* Courtesy of the National Gallery of Art, Washington. Chester Dale Collection.

Claude Monet, *Rouen Cathedral, West Façade, Sunlight.* Courtesy of the National Gallery of Art, Washington. Chester Dale Collection.

jardin (1867).[6] Here the folds of the one young woman's dress fall half inside and half outside the shadow of the wide central tree. The dress (along with the woman) is neither sculpted with undulating shadow not cast in several overlapping degrees of light and dark (chiaroscuro). Instead, a sharp line cuts across the dress, separating the area in shadow from the area receiving direct sunlight. The object, thus literally split in two, loses its traditional unity (of treatment) and focuses attention less on how it is illuminated, less on its own isolated form than on the interrelated forms around it.

In the other case, when diffused through water, the other natural element fundamental to impressionist art,[7] light had a unifying effect. Harbor and coastal scenes lent a new dimension to light studies because the sun, in most cases hidden from view, dispersed its rays through each tiny drop of water in the air, leaving its mark, however, on each of these drops, giving body to what normally went unseen. Thus, a new, *apparently* immaterial, foreground was set up that acted like a theatrical scrim to reunite the disparate objects of the scene onto a single plane. The unity of the individual object was assured by the evenness of illumination produced by dispersion of sunrays. The more important unity, that of the whole scene, was produced by the now visible (and perhaps exaggerated), monolithic humid atmosphere that enveloped it. One wonders, in fact, if these early studies of sea-spray, fog, and mist did not provide a kind of paradigm for later work in full sunlight where the background and foreground nonetheless seem to be united into a single plane and together produce a foreground that duplicates, and then becomes, the two-dimensional canvas. (Cf. Monet's *Gare Saint-Lazare.*) Such a reduction to two dimensions is, of course, the basic mimetic process of all painting; but here the important difference is that external elements—light, mist, and air—being perceived for the first time as material, appear to be the true agents of this flattening process. "Ideal" conditions, just like "ideal" perspective (as perfected during the Renaissance), no longer existed. The abstract principles applicable

6. Cf. analyses of this painting in both Francastel, *L'Impressionisme,* and Moser, *L'Impressionisme français.*

7. Note the importance of the Normandy coast in the early development of Monet and Pissarro, as well as the influence of the thick atmosphere of London and the Thames.

Claude Monet, *La Gare Saint-Lazare.* Courtesy of the Art Institute of Chicago.

to painting, rather than being based on lines and planes or on full studio light, were now, rather, based on the atomistic nature of elements previously regarded as evanescent effects and on some theoretical "aerial perspective"[8] that might take these as yet dimly understood material variables into account.

I have insisted on this material view of light, even though it may have an anachronistic or otherwise confused relation to the development of optical theory, because it best explains, however prophetic or rehashed it may have been, the impressionist idea of sensation. The first aesthetic evaluations of impressionism emphasized the modern ideational connotation of "impression" rather than its primal sense of impressing (from *imprimere*)—that is, making a mark. Accordingly, the impressionists, in much the same manner as the romantics, were to have seized not so much on the objects of their

8. M. E. Chevreul, *De la loi du contraste simultané des couleurs* (Paris, 1839), p. 171; Helmholtz, *Optique physiologique,* pp. 799-800. It is interesting that both these theoreticians make explicit statements concerning the value of their research to painters. A more detailed discussion of point of view is taken up below.

perception as on the emotions that the impressions of these objects produced. Sensations, that is, were to have been a kind of two-way transmission of impressions, first pure (as transmitted from the object to the artist), then mixed with the artist's innermost feelings and transmitted, slightly transformed, onto the canvas. The objects represented on the canvas were thus the combined product of the external source objects and the artist's subjective reaction to them.

There is no doubt that the impressionists *felt* their work as much as any other artists and that they perhaps even had a self-indulgent attitude toward their objects of inspiration—what Cézanne was to refer to as "*la petite sensation.*" But to identify the artistic impulse primarily in the impressionist's internal feelings is, it seems to me, a confusion. It is, most of all, a confusion of processes. The impressionist artist had, no doubt, the same dynamic relation to the phenomena he described that all artists have. The important advance (or simply change) is that there is a greater interest in the *process* going on entirely *outside* the artist. Light, the most important example of this, is considered not as some naturally achieved product laid across the surface of the object but as a dynamic process in a constant state of flux. The impressionist perceives the *effect*[9] of natural processes, but this effect goes no further than the perceptual field of the artist. It never becomes an *affect*; it is the mark made on his perceiving faculties—a mark that can be analyzed independently of the artist's subjective reactions, however strong.[10]

Sensations were like documents: the primordial human data in the new experiment of painting. Since the human eye is the only instrument that can determine the aspect (height, length, depth, color) of the external world, the artist had to cultivate and pay close attention to the impressions it receives. Again, the word *impression* is open to multiple interpretations, according to a quite paradoxical etymology. Helmholtz considers "impression" to be the simplest type of notion

9. Cf. Mallarmé, apropos of his *Hérodiade*: "I'm inventing a language that of necessity springs from a new poetics, which I would define in two words: Depict not the thing but the effect that it produces." Quoted in Moser (see n. 2 above), p. 87.

10. Cf. Eliot's description of the modern poet as impersonal mediator: "the poet has, not a 'personality' to express, but a particular medium, which is only medium and not a personality, in which impressions and experiences combine in peculiar and unexpected ways." "Tradition and the Individual Talent," *Selected Essays* (London, 1932), p. 19.

(*Anschauung*): it "contains nothing which does not proceed immediately from the sensations of the moment."[11] According to his research, sensations are produced by light hitting the retina, the "sensate part of our nervous system" (p. 43). Once the sensation passes along the optic nerve to the brain, that is, once the external effect is transformed into an internal effect, perception takes place. Perception is necessary for any type of *Anschauung*. Thus, the critical point (for this study) is in distinguishing between impression, the moment-to-moment application of human perception to sensation, and representation (*Vorstellung*), "the *idea* or image that our memory furnishes us of an absent object" (p. 571; Helmholtz's emphasis). The impressionists, by keeping the object of their sensations constantly before them (especially in the case of landscapes) and by relying less and less on their conditioned memory of objects, were able to take advantage of the experimental or documentary quality of their sensations. Like Helmholtz, they realized that all perception is influenced by past impressions and by academically conditioned ideas; at the same time, they acknowledged that the reproduction or imitation of nature by a means entailing human intervention is bound to be an approximation. Hence, they concentrated on that part of perception which was most closely related to the object: on their sensations and the immediate impressions they gave rise to.

In this sense, the impressionist painter optimally became a kind of recording instrument of the external flux. He relied less and less on subjective reactions that originated internally so as to seize all the better on objective, external phenomena. This sharpening of the impressionist's powers of objectivity goes hand in hand with the new interpretation of light to minimize the importance of subject matter. Francastel has gone a long way to show that "the mythic space of art," as inherited from the Renaissance and the neoclassics, had already been significantly reshaped by Romanticism.[12] But, though the classic imagery was changed, the hierarchical system of values and the tendency toward allegory remained constant (David and Delacroix, for example). It was only with the impressionist's radically new vision of matter and space that the notion of "subject

11. Helmholtz, p. 571. (Cf. n. 25 below.)
12. *Etudes de sociologie de l'art* (Paris, 1970), pp. 197–201.

matter" underwent the greatest modifications. The romantics may have successfully abolished the *lieu privilégié*, but the impressionists abolished all subordination between species, genre, and kind. Since the sun casts its rays evenly, equally, and without discrimination on all the elements of the universe, the impressionist considers these elements equally, without predilection for any one part. All is reduced to one and the same level of phenomena, as background fades into foreground, the near into the distant, the exalted into the mundane. Not only is the mythical, imaginary landscape gone from the horizon, but man, the inventor of such a myth, loses his old hegemony.

It is not surprising that the impressionists, being taken up so seriously with the varying *intensities* of light, should also examine the varying *qualities* of light—that is, color. Duranty remarked, as early as 1876, that the new painters' discovery "consists in having recognized that sunlight *discolors* tones."[13] Even before this time, Chevreul had outlined his theory of "simultaneous contrast": when two colored objects are seen next to one another at the same time, "the color of each appears not as a single unmixed tone, that is, the way it might appear if it were seen in isolation, but rather as a tone resulting from the native color combined with the complimentary color of the other object. . . . In a word, colors, when juxtaposed, will appear different from what they really are."[14] These two conclusions—that light changes ("absolute") color and that in a given context one color changes another—were arrived at experimentally by the impressionists and thereby led them to perfect the technique of divisionism, by which the form of an object was subordinated to or rather defined by, the play of colors that composed that form. As with the representation of light as refracted through tiny globules of water in the air, here again a technique of discontinuity (discrete, unblended brush strokes on the canvas) resulted in an effect of continuity in the object depicted. Preference for the *tache* over the line, already evident in a predecessor like Courbet,[15] was brought to its apogee in the shimmering scenes of Monet, Pissarro, and Sisley, where objects were no longer filled-in drawings but, rather, com-

---

13. *La Nouvelle Peinture* (see n. 5 above), p. 39. Duranty's emphasis.
14. Chevreul (see n. 8 above), p. 190. See also pp. 148ff. for the effects of variously colored light.
15. Francastel, *Art et Technique* (Paris, 1956), p. 134.

posed conglomerations of separate and apparently independent
brush strokes.

It can now be seen that, for the impressionists, light was not
simply the revealer of the external world but the founder of spatial
relations as well. In order to render the precise effects of light,
otherwise whole objects must be divided, cut apart, according to the
change in intensity of the light source (*Les Femmes au jardin*). At
the same time, subtle changes in color (the quality of light) that result from adjacent complementaries can best be rendered by *building
up* the represented object in a series of detached or overlapping
units of pigment. Extension, therefore, is rendered less by lines leading to the vanishing point of traditional perspective than by simple
juxtaposition. Objects are related to one another less by virtue of
their individual contoured wholeness than with regard to the light
and color values they share. The omnipresent outline around principal figures (still evident in Manet) disappears; arms and branches,
faces and facades, fields and passers-by—all grow together; patterns
of colors among heterogeneous objects become as fundamental to
the relation of those objects as physical proximity.[16]

The *en-plein-air* method, which, as we have seen, answered to the
impressionists' experimental needs, was carried to a curious extreme
by Daubigny. Not content simply with setting up his easel outside,
he bought a small houseboat and painted from this unique position
the scenes along the banks of the Seine. In this case, the painter became more critically subject to the flux outside him, participating,
by virtue of the instability of his own spatial coordinates (whether
actually moving in the stream or anchored and simply rocking), in
the constantly changing scene before him. Daubigny's boat might
thus be considered an emblem of the impressionists' desire to capture nature *dans le vif*, to put themselves on the same level as those
dubious or ambiguous natural elements which, like light, mist, and
air, define the space of other objects while resisting precise spatial
definition themselves, and, by recording the effects of these elements to reembody in their paintings both nature and its processes.

Even more important, Daubigny's exaggerated mobility of perspec-

16. Cf. *Les Coquelicots* by Monet, in which the repetition of red in both the
field of flowers and the small (distant) mother and child passing by, leads to a
blurring of the separate forms.

tive points to a fundamental corollary of *en-plein-airisme*. The experiments of placing the easel up and down, to one side or to the other in a given landscape, led to the abandonment of fixed point of view.

> The real innovation was, first, to have often given up placing the unitary eye one meter up from the ground, according to the Alberti Rule, and to have placed it instead in any position, at any height whatever. The consequential discovery was that, depending on the distancing and the angle of viewpoint, the world takes on very different aspects.[17]

The plane represented by the canvas no longer stood necessarily for the plane of one particular postulated viewer of the scene. The artist could move himself within the scene; the frame, therefore, could correspond to any of these points of view. Most important of all: the frame no longer stood for the proscenium of a discrete, cubed section of space. The Renaissance scenographic conception of space was now entirely forsaken.[18] Whether or not this technique proceeded from the impressionists' enthusiasm for the (non-Euclidian) juxtaposition of unrelated fragments of space in Japanese art, its gradual development corresponds, as Francastel points out, to the prevailing analytic and relativistic preoccupations of the time. Manet had already painted his Dead Toreador on a ground whose plane was not perpendicular to the plane of the viewer. In other words, a point of view was postulated that theoretically could never be maintained in the moment-to-moment process of painting. The impressionists took up this shocking uniqueness of point of view but applied it to more ordinary objects. This is where selection and combination became so important. Since the "eye" was eminently mobile, it could survey in such a way as to take in and cut off exactly where it wished. It could linger on a previously unnoticed detail and make of it an entire composition (Francastel gives this aspect perhaps an exaggerated importance), or it could take in a normal or large space in which the individual objects have the most tangential relation to one another.

The pleasure of total randomness of framing reaches its climax with Degas, in paintings like *Place de la Concorde* (around 1873). It

17. Francastel, *Etudes de sociologie de l'art,* p. 211.
18. Cf. ibid., pp. 211–13.

Edgar Degas, *Place de la Concorde (Count Lepic and His Daughters)*. Formerly, Gerstenberg Collection, Berlin; destroyed during World War II.

was Degas, in fact, who seems to have most successfully combined the technique of unusual point of view with that of arbitrary framing. In his *Place de la Concorde* no single figure or object plays a dominant role. Each object is cut off—so much so that the foreground figures seem to be growing out of one another: the girl to the far right out of the man's umbrella, the dog out of the central girl. The point of view has been placed in such a way as to seem too close to the foreground figures and too far away from the background (the carriage, the buildings, and the park). Furthermore, the various planes of movement of the foreground figures seem to have been all compressed onto one frontal plane (like the "scrim" of Monet's harbor scenes) before the actual space of the painting. And this central space—the *Place* itself—is only noteworthy by virtue of the absence of all substance save the street.[19] The figures, foreground and background alike, lead the vision outside the confines of the frame. Even the look of the fragmented man on the far left, aimed at the other foreground figures, is just short of being left out altogether. There is no centrifugal force in the composition: no

19. "Degas is one of the few painters to have stressed the importance of the *ground*. . . . The ground is one of those factors essential to our viewing of things." Paul Valéry, "Du sol et de l'informe," in *Degas danse dessin* (Paris, 1965; orig. 1938), p. 91.

Henri de Toulouse-Lautrec, *The Ringmaster at the Cirque Fernando.* Courtesy of the Art Institute of Chicago.

rallying point at which the lines converge. All is centripetal. the looks of the two girls, the man with the umbrella, and the dog, the direction of their actions, and the "logical" continuation of the moving carriage and standing men.

Relativity of point of view led the impressionists to pose some fundamental questions of motion. If all appeared to be in a state of permanent flux, as the analysis of light revealed, then how, in the purely spatial art of painting, could this motion be arrested yet implied as a continuing process just the same? Could motions, such as the breaking of waves, the horse's gallop, the ballerina's twirl, be broken down into their component parts in such a way as to record once and for all the *instant fugitif*? Leading photographic experimenters and harbingers of the cinema, Muybridge and Marey, were revealing some of the secrets of motion for the first time, but could such perceptions be transposed to the painter's medium?

Chevreul and Helmholtz had been aware of the differences of color and form produced by varying distance and angle of point of view, but they also laid stress on the painter's inherent fixity of vision once the desired point of view is chosen.[20] More particularly, the impressionist painter, no matter how much he could move within the

20. *Du contraste simultané* . . . , pp. 172–74; *Optique physiologique*, pp. 568–69 and 806.

Edgar Degas, *The False Start.* The John Hay Whitney Collection. Reproduced by permission.

scene being painted, could never offer the spectator more than a single angle—unless the painter was willing to go back to medieval triptychs or to wait for the advent of cubism. Speed of sketching[21] was the only device that could attenuate these conditions implicit in the art. We know that Monet experimented in this manner, catching in a few seconds the light values present in a given moment.

But Degas, who was always less interested than the other impressionists in pure landscape painting, went directly to an analysis of the movements of specific external objects. Basing his studies on the experiments made in photography, a medium he was one of the first painters to praise and frankly to use,[22] Degas achieved, perhaps

21. Chevreul, *De la loi . . .* , pp. 202 and 215–16. Hauser notes the tremendous surge of technological activity corresponding to this "new feeling of speed and change" in impressionism (*Social History of Art*, pp. 167–68).

22. Valéry, *Degas danse dessin*, p. 79. Cf. André Bazin: "It is Degas and Toulouse-Lautrec, Renoir and Manet, who have understood from the inside, and in essence, the nature of the photographic phenomenon and, prophetically, even the cinematographic phenomenon. Faced with photography, they opposed it in the only valid way, by a dialectical enriching of pictorial tech-

better than even the most baroque painters who preceded him, the impression of movement.[23] He realized that, as with the primordial processes in nature, the discrete unities of duration of an action could be perceived. The artist had, more than ever, to observe closely and sharply. And, without any intervention whatsoever in the external process, he had to select and seize on that fraction of duration that contained within it the suggestion of the movement as a whole.[24] Here, the artist is one step removed from the objective on-the-spot observer of early Impressionism. There is no model (even the landscapes with ever-changing light and atmosphere were a sort of model): only the glimpsed perception and, possibly, the mechanical artifact (photo). The artist has stepped in, so to speak, and stopped the process, arrested the action he hopes to imply. Yet even here, the action goes on outside the creating subject and there is no subjective distortion beyond that implicit in the limitations of human perception: the reliance on the senses and the interception of their data.[25]

The discontinuous brushwork functions not only as a sign of permanent impermanence, of the artist's hesitancy to confer anything so definite as an unbroken line or contour to an object outside himself. It also functions as a medium by which the creative process is extended far beyond the individual artist who applies the paint. The spectator is charged, more than ever before, with composing dabs of pigment in order to extrapolate the objects represented.[26] The spectator becomes the active receiver of the "message"—with

---

nique. They understood the laws of the new image better than the photographers and well before the movie-makers, and it is they who first applied them." *What is Cinema?*, trans. Hugh Gray (Berkeley, 1967), p. 119.

23. Unlike Rubens, Rembrandt, Fragonard, or Delacroix, Degas never considered external motion as "the manifestation of an internal drive." Francastel, *L'Impressionisme*. p. 133.

24. Cf. Degas's sculptures of horses in action.

25. Cf. Helmholtz, pp. 579–81. Helmholtz is very much concerned with the problem of lag (both temporal and philosophical) necessarily intervening between the moment of impression (reception of sense datum through the sense apparatus, such as the optic nerve) and the moment of epistemological perception (or *Anschauung*).

26. Once the painting has been completed, conditions of exhibition and gradual wearing away of the colors carry on the mobility of subject and object (here, spectator and canvas) initiated by the painter: "object and subject are thus irremediably in motion, elusive and impalpable." Jules Laforgue, *Oeuvres complètes*, (Paris, 1903), 3:141.

the important difference that now the message does not depend on any predetermined code, such as Christian symbolism or classical mythology. The emphasis is thrown onto the very form and substance of the objects of perception and on how they are known. The message is neither in the topoi nor in the fact they they have changed; it resides now in the process of seeing, of visually constructing and hence of becoming cognizant. The need for decoding becomes an integral part of the artistic act, the spectator a direct accomplise of the artist in the seizing of nature. These two subjects, artist and spectator, bring their visions together on the canvas, which, in spite of everything else, is not an end in itself but a mediator and, like the phenomena it supposedly imitates, is constantly being created and re-created by successive viewers.

It is well known that the public, at the time of the first impressionist exhibitions, was far from able to decipher what seemed to be random dabs and splotches of color. The fact carries with it an implicit comment on the enormous role that habit and visual conditioning play in plastic art. From a purely physiological point of view, Helmholtz noted this influence of habit, experience, and other "unconscious inductions" in the process of perceiving, placing these at the top of his list of contingencies to be considered in all optical studies.[27] In the same way, it took some time before the public could rid itself of the prejudices and assumptions established by centuries of academic art, especially conventional lighting and perspective.[28] It was only by adapting his vision to the new code that the spectator could begin to engage in the dynamic process of exchange being offered. The fact of the gradual assimilation of Impressionism into the traditional canon—both popularly and academically—bears witness to the efficacy of the impressionists' visual reeducation. This same pattern will be seen repeated in other arts: a break with traditional ways of seeing or reading, followed by a period of instituting new codes of perception.

It is difficult to say if those writers who are often called impressionists managed to tear down and renovate the conventions of their craft with as much vigor and thoroughness as the painters. Ruth

27. Helmholtz, pp. 565–566.
28. Cf. Laforgue, pp. 135–36 and 138–39.

Moser in *L'Impressionisme français* (see note 2) includes an interesting study of French prose writers who might be considered impressionists. Her main remarks focus on the minute descriptions of fleeting sensations in the prose of the Goncourt brothers, Loti, Daudet, Colette, and the Contesse de Noailles (pp. 100-35). "La prose de la sensation" covers a wide range of effects not usually encountered in prose fiction, such as painterly details and musical sonorities. In this appeal to nonliterary art-forms, it seeks a Baudelairean or Wagnerian synesthesia, in which the separate sense impressions are always at the command of one all-embracing atmosphere.[29] The *phrase type* of this impressionism was suggested in 1928 by Leo Spitzer: "avec sur la figure grave un bon et doux sourire" (Goncourt, *Les Frères Zemganno*). This leads Moser to postulate a basic impressionist modus operandi, linguistic and compositional, whereby the result of an action precedes the enunciation of the action itself: "depict the sensation, the effect," she writes, recalling Mallarmé's words, "before the cause that produces it" (p. 115). And this procedure is found abundantly in the works of Proust (pp. 117-18).

The pictorial and musical (rhythmic, phonic) components of prose can be seen frankly put into effect early in the nineteenth century. Chateaubriand, in whom Proust recognized an early forebear, presents many examples of a prose reduced purely to the elements of sensations (e.g., *Atala; Mémoires d'outre-tombe*). Aloysius Bertrand patterns his "fantaisies" on the etching of Rembrandt and Jacques Callot. Maurice de Guérin achieves strange prose rhythms by the use of Greek mythological names. In fact, the whole development of prose poetry in France tends to refute any strict classification of literary impressionism in terms of sensorial vividness. The criterion of the effect-before-the-cause, being more closely connected with the structural and linguistic patterns of the work, may be more justifiable,[30] but even here one finds

29. Proust is quoted (p. 111) as having written that what he liked most in the Comtesse de Noailles's *Visage émerveillé* is that "it is not composed of parts, it is a whole, bathed in a single atmosphere, bathed through and through where colors are organized in terms of each other, complementary to one another."

30. Moser does study a kind of structural impressionism in the Goncourts' *Renée Mauperin*, pp. 128ff. It is possible that even in this respect the prose poets, particularly Baudelaire, may have laid some of the foundations for

an impressive number of isolated examples rather than an overall pattern. From a historical point of view, Hauser remarks that what is generally considered literary impressionism is, from the beginning, "hardly recognizable within the total complex of naturalism, and its later forms of development are completely merged with the phenomena of symbolism." Unlike impressionism in painting, it "becomes almost from the outset the champion of that idealistic reaction which finds expression in painting only after the dissolution of impressionism. The main reason for this is that the conservative élite plays a much more important rôle in literature than in painting."[31]

Thus, literary impressionism—in France, at least—shuttles between two other movements so as to have itself a dubious existence. The various "-isms" cloud the picture considerably, but one thing is clear: artists of the 1860s and 1870s turn, with more or less deliberateness, to the crutch or panacea afforded by science.[32] "That's what is so fine about the natural sciences," Flaubert had already written, "they don't wish to prove anything." "When literature has the precision of results of an exact science, that's going some." "In the present day when the Novel has undertaken the studies and obligations of science, it can demand the liberties and freedom of science," wrote the Goncourts in their preface to *Germinie Lacerteux* (1865). Zola reports, in the preface to his first novel, *Thérèse Raquin* (1868): "I have simply done on the living bodies the work of analysis which surgeons perform on corpses."[33] Indeed, it was Zola more than any other who, in *Le Roman expérimental* (1880) summed up these aspirations and perhaps overstated the goals.[34] In applying the experimental methods of Claude Bernard's "experimental medicine" to the novel, he notes that the new naturalist

---

formal experiments in the novel. The questions of form and point of view in the Anglo-American novel of this period are treated below.

31. Hauser, *Social History of Art*, 4: 177.

32. Hauser states that this is mainly due to the general sense of defeat following the 1848 revolution: "After the failure of all ideals, of all Utopias, the tendency is now to keep to the facts, to nothing but the facts" (4: 65).

33. All quoted in *Documents of Modern Literary Realism*, ed. George J. Becker (Princeton, 1963), pp. 92-93, 119, and 159.

34. Hauser makes this important distinction: "Hitherto the representatives of naturalism had regarded science as the handy-man of art; Zola sees art as the servant of science" (4: 86).

novelists both observe and experiment: "their whole task begins in
the doubt which they hold concerning obscure truths, inexplicable
phenomena, until an experimental idea suddenly arouses their genius
and impels them to make an experiment in order to analyze the facts
and become master of them." "There is an absolute determinism for
all human phenomena." Yet in this vast program that includes studies
of heredity, physiology, and environment, "the method is only a
tool; it is the workman, it is the idea which he brings which makes
the masterpiece."[35]

Ironically, the greatest proponent of scientism ends up with an
escape-clause of unilateral control, "mastery." After an attempt to
lay what appears to be the foundations for a new scholastic reduc-
tionism, Zola skirts his own determinism by appealing to craftsman-
ship and the idea. The man who first praised the impressionist painters for embracing a method rightly scientific sows the seeds of the
decadence that will prove his own destruction.[36] In fact, in his
fascinating apotheosis of the impressionists (*L'Oeuvre*,[37] the four-
teenth volume of the Rougon-Macquart chronicle), Zola has his
naturalist spokesman, Sandoz, predict (after the fact) the slippage
toward aestheticism. While the new painting and new literature
each take off from a scientific analysis of nature (pp. 54-55), neither
can maintain this attitude, since, "after a hundred years, science has
still not given us absolute certitude, perfect happiness. . . . It's the
bankruptcy of the century, pessimism twists people's entrails, mysti-
cism fogs their brains; for we've chased after fantoms in vain, misled
by the brainstorms of analysis; the supernatural has taken up arms
again, the spirit of legends rebels and wishes to conquer us once
more, in this impasse of fatigue and anguish" (p. 498).

Outside of France, however, a decade or so later, the impressionist
method had different effects. While all of Europe was in the throes
of the symbolist and decadent movements, certain British and

35. *Documents of Modern Literary Realism*, pp. 169, 172, and 183.
36. The masking of patronizing aestheticism in the robes of scientific
documentation can be seen most flagrantly in the Goncourts: see Erich
Auerbach's essay on *Germinie Lacerteux,* in *Mimesis* (Garden City, N.Y.,
1957).
37. Originally published 1886; page references are to the Fasquelle edition.

American novelists, such as Stephen Crane, Henry James, Joseph Conrad, and Ford Madox Ford, without reneging the "intellectual-ization" of their age, strove to apply to their medium the techniques of fragmentation and changing perspective we associate with the impressionist painters. In fact, they began by looking beyond the painters to the earlier "realist" literature as written by Flaubert and Maupassant. Here they recognized the material analysis of the out-side world that was to be more concretely perceived in the impres-sionists' canvases. With Flaubert, the narrative was not so much a conveyor or representation of nature as a thing in itself: an integral structure of fragmented scenes whose temporal coordinates have been subordinated to the textual, or spatial arrangement of these scenes. In "La Légende de saint Julien l'Hospitalier," for example, discrete, discontinuous sequences of action are juxtaposed in the manner, as Flaubert himself says, of medieval stained-glass windows. The narrated segments, like the painters' divisionist application of pigment, function so as to present a continuity made up of discon-tinuous units.[38] Stephen Crane conceived of the novel in somewhat similar terms: a "succession of sharply-outlined pictures, which pass before the reader like a panorama, leaving each its definite impres-sion."[39] Such is, indeed, the effect of *The Red Badge of Courage* (1894), though Crane has gone beyond an analysis of the material world (apparently extrapolated from Mathew Brady's Civil War photographs) and of his hero's sense impressions to present a narra-tive constructed around sometimes flimsy symbols.

The question of fragmentation becomes more complicated with James, Conrad, and Ford. Mainly interested in the totality of effect and the "progression d'effet," they sought an indirect method of presenting objects to the reader's perception. James realized that, above all, the novel was an "illusion of life" and that to create this illusion the novelist "competes with his brother the painter in *his* attempt to render the look of things, the look that conveys their

38. And perhaps, too, to signify a disintegrating world. In this case, the novelist's attitude was historically as different from the painters' as his med-ium—see below. The idea of continuous discontinuity will be seen to play an important role in the development of "film sensibility."

39. Quoted in R. W. Stallman's introduction to *The Red Badge of Courage* (New York, 1951), p. xxiii.

meaning, to catch the color, the relief, the expression, the surface, the substance of the human spectacle.[40] To create this "look," the novelist is obliged to select, cut out, and reassemble the details of experience—the impressions which "*are* experience," "to give the image and the sense of certain things while still keeping them subordinate to his plan, keeping them in relation to matters more immediate and apparent, to give all the sense, in a word, without all the substance or all the surface, and so to summarise and foreshorten...."[41]

James acknowledges that the technique of "foreshortening," by rendering the all-important "effect of compression, of composition and form," poses automatically the "time-question"; and Ford extends the implications of this technique in the device he calls "time-shift." Here, the various chosen segments of experience are to be arranged not according to chronology but according to their dramatic impact—just as in detective fiction,[42] or, as Ford always insisted in his flamboyant version of "impressionism," just as in life, which "did not narrate, but made impressions on our brains. We [Ford and Conrad] in turn, if we wished to produce on you an effect of life, must not narrate but render impressions." Hence, for a given "story" or preferably "strong situation," "if you carefully broke up petunias, statuary, and flowershow motives and put them down in little shreds, one contrasting with the other, you would arrive at something much more coloured, animated, lifelike and interesting...."[43]

Conrad employs this oblique approach with great success. In his preface to *The Nigger of the "Narcissus"* (1897), he states that the novelist's appeal (to the reader) is "an impression conveyed through the senses" and that, consequently, the task (like James's in *The Ambassadors*) is "by the power of the written word to make

40. "The Art of Fiction" (1884), in *The Future of the Novel*, ed. Leon Edel (New York, 1956), p. 14.

41. *The Art of the Novel*, ed. R. P. Blackmur (New York, 1934), p. 14. Cf. p. 278, where James speaks further of the "particular economic device" called "foreshortening."

42. "Time-shift" [*It Was the Nightingale* (London, 1934)], in *Writers on Writing*, ed. Walter Allen (London, 1948), pp. 192-93.

43. *Joseph Conrad, A Personal Remembrance* (Boston, 1925; orig. London, 1924), pp. 194-95 and 203.

you hear, to make you feel—it is, before all, to make you see." But since this "rescued fragment" of reality depends on the novelist's (or on the narrator's) own sense apparatus, the final impression risks being a composite of disconnected data. This is most evident in *Heart of Darkness* (1899) when Marlow overhears a conversation between the manager and his uncle: "Make rain and fine weather—one man—the council—by the nose'—bits of absurd sentences that got the better of my drowsiness. . . . "[44]

The indirect approach of these novelists is not fully comprehensible without reference to their unconventional handling of point of view. *Heart of Darkness* offers again a clear example. The narrative concerns Marlow's gradual awareness of Kurtz's nature. But this central process is not presented directly. First, we have the narrator, the anonymous "I" who describes the frame scene of the ship, Marlow, and the other sailors. Then, we have Marlow's account of his mission to Africa. Finally, within this quoted story, we have a series of remarks, conversations, impressions about Kurtz on the part of minor characters. The central object of the narrative, Kurtz, is thus presented by means of at least three distinct points of view or angles of perspective, which, far from being consecutive as the above account leads one to believe, overlap and take effect simultaneously. The reader, one might say, is constantly forced to pass through several foregrounds before he can make out clearly what is looming in the background.[45] Or better, the reader, like Marlow and like the narrator, is forced, by this insistence on the relativity and fragmentation of point of view, to reconstruct the figure of Kurtz from the position of one yet further removed.

The same basic mechanism is operative with James's "central reflectors" through whom all or nearly all the action takes place. "I never see the leading *interest* of any human hazard but in a consciousness (on the part of the moved and moving creature) subject to fine intensification and wide enlargement."[46] This consciousness

44. *Heart of Darkness* (New York: Washington Square, 1970), p. 182.
45. Cf. Ramon Fernandez, *Messages*, trans. M. Belgion (New York, 1927), pp. 147-48.
46. *The Art of the Novel*, p. 67.

serves "to record . . . dramatically and objectively." Its use differs from the first-person narrative in that the reflections of the central agent are presented in the third person and are thus constantly mediated by the narrator.[47] James transforms the subjective, perceiving self into an (apparently) objective recorder, the direct, unmediated "I" into a *cogito* whose perceptions are worked out in the third person. The reader sees in *The Ambassadors* (1903), for example, the same threefold structure as in Conrad: narrator, central reflector (Strether), auxiliary characters (Waymarsh and Maria Gostrey, the "ficelles") whose points of view act directly on Strether's—with the important difference that James consistently lays greater stress on the second level, on the "reflecting and colouring medium" of consciousness.

Finally, the reader's job of assembling these diverse points of view, what might be called "reader participation"—like the "spectator participation" required by the impressionist painters, plays a fundamental role in the works of the James-Conrad group. The multiplication of point of view carries in itself the notion of epistemological relativity characteristic of the end of the nineteenth century. What seems incomplete or unlikely from one perspective may gain full validity from another. In the novel this unreliability of narrative point of view places on the reader the burden not only of composition but of judgment as well. James exploited to the fullest this means of engaging the reader: the central consciousness should not by any means be a double of the narrator's omniscience. It should not be "*too* acute—which would have disconnected it and made it superhuman: the beautiful little problem was to keep it connected, connected intimately, with the general human exposure, and thereby bedimmed and befooled and bewildered, anxious, restless, fallible. . . ."[48] The perceptual apparatus of the central reflector is imperfect because it is fully human and no more than human; it

47. Ibid., p. 321, apropos of Strether. Ford, it should be said, used the first-person narrative in *The Good Soldier* (1915) without hampering the multi-perspectivism he sought and without failing to make "certain precious discriminations."

48. Ibid., p. 16.

is at once the medium of the reader's information and the image of the narrated events beyond.

These structural or compositional techniques are the only valid links between the novelists and the impressionist painters; they served to break down and render supple the classic nineteenth-century form of the novel, preparing for the more daring remoldings of the twentieth century in much the same way that the impressionists' "destruction" of Renaissance plasticity paved the way for cubism. But here the comparison ends. The novelists did not posit a firm distinction between subject and object in the manner of the early impressionists. In spite of the Flaubertian-Jamesian "impassibility," James's copious note-taking, and the potentially documentary quality of his inspection of consciousness, the literary artist consistently tends to pass beyond the immediate sense data to a realm of intuition and subjectivity. As is most clear in Crane and the early Conrad, the fidelity to surface, shape, and aura is less a means of giving an impression of reality than a means of revealing some deeper, hidden essence: in brief, the mechanism of the symbol.

James ends up in nearly the same position, even though he is always more interested in the *process* of perception and cognition. In the penultimate scene of *The Ambassadors*, where Strether goes for a day in the country, the hero is not content simply to partake of the rich landscape that has often been compared to an impressionist canvas.[49] Instead, like the dreamy romantic whom James and company would disapprove of, he lets his physical sensations fuse with the objects that give rise to them:

> Strether sat there and, though hungry, felt at peace; the confidence that had so gathered for him deepened with the lap of the water, the ripple of the surface, the rustle of the reeds on the opposite bank, the faint diffused coolness and the slight

49. Most recently by Viola Hopkins Winner in *Henry James and the Visual Arts* (Charlottesville, N.C., 1970), pp. 77ff. Invoking Ian Watt's notion of James's "multiple Impressionism," Winner concludes that James stands to Impressionism as the Mannerists stood to the Renaissance, that his tendency to spiritualize the material world is merely a slight tilting of the impressionist "interrelatedness of all experience," and that from this adventitious position stems critics' difficulty in classifying him (pp. 89-91).

rock of a couple of small boats attached to a rough landing-place hard by. The valley on the further side was all copper-green level and glazed pearly sky, a sky hatched across with screens of trimmed trees, which looked flat, like espaliers; and though the rest of the village straggled away in the near quarter the view had an emptiness that made one of the boats sugges-tive. Such a river set one afloat almost before one could take up the oars—the idle play of which would be moreover the aid to the full impression.[50]

In concluding, it must be reiterated that comparisons among the arts are often vain unless based on clear distinctions among media, among the signs used to communicate. Compared to the painter's pigment, the written word has a less sensuous and only hypothetical relation to the material world. At once more precise and more abstract, it rarely seeks to represent or to evoke *through its own materiality* the objects of the outside world. The greater abstraction of the literary sign[51] leads, by its very nature, to a propensity on the writer's part to forgo any rigorously materialistic rendering of its referents. Furthermore, this is the only way to explain why the flattened effect often noted in impressionist canvases, which results from the attenuation—if not rejection—of Renaissance perspective, has its parallel effect in the novelists' deemphasis of temporal pro-gression and multiplication of point of view. Traditional perspective in space as in time is dealt a roughly similar blow. Secondary, per-haps contradictory, effects of this strategy—the banishment of the anecdote in painting and the pictorial and musical aspirations of written prose—point toward the increasing pace of mutation in each sign. The cinema offers a thoroughly new spatiotemporal sign, whose nature, as will be seen in the next chapter, epitomized the preoccupations of the impressionist era.

50. *The Ambassadors* (New York: Norton, 1964), p. 307.
51. Cf. Hegel's *Aesthetics*: poetry (and the written sign in general) is not perceived directly by the senses but entirely by the mind, under the "aspect of ideal *universality* characteristic of reflective thought." Chinese and other ideographic writings, being exceptions to this, have consistently provided, on the one hand, artistic inspiration and, on the other, critical reservation in formulating such distinctions.

2 Inheritance and Synthesis in the Cinema

The birth of the movies in 1895 and their rapid rise to popularity must be considered from several different viewpoints in order to account for the revolution they fomented in taste and perception. Even before taking stock of the aesthetic and philosophic significance held within this new art, it is necessary to examine three ways in which it functions as a watershed of nineteenth-century intellectual development: (1) to synthesize disparate arts, schools, attitudes, and trends; (2) to reclaim and sublimate vast areas of second-rate, "subcultural" art; (3) to incorporate in itself and galvanize the fruits of modern technology.

The first and, for our purposes, most important function of the movies was to synthesize the goals of impressionism and naturalism, the two literary and artistic schools predominant during the preceding three decades. Most closely related in a material way to photography (etymologically "writing with light"), the motion picture was immediately able to register with a high degree of fidelity the changing light values, natural or artificial, on the objects around us. There was no need for the movie-maker to break down and analyze the process of illumination in the external world, since the camera is itself a highly perfected mechanical tool for doing just this. The degree and quality of illumination by the source light on an object is directly registered by the celluloid treated with light-sensitive silver bromide.

39

Since the sun was the only available source of light in the first years, the movies were by necessity an *en-plein-air* art. (Studios came about as the result not so much of powerful artificial lights as of Méliès's sophisticated needs.) The camera could be brought to the raw material itself. It stood amidst nature, from the polar ice-cap to the poverty-stricken streets of large cities, always on the point of conducting an "experiment" in the naturalist manner. The portability and apparent ubiquity of the camera, responsible, in fact, for the experimental air of those first essentially documentary film-clips (e.g., *La sortie des usines Lumière, Fire Rescue Scene*), represented the complete reduction of external events to mechanically gathered data. From this point, the "art" would depend more and more on the ways in which the camera was manipulated and the shots assembled.

The relationship between the movie frame and the space it defined underwent in a few years an evolution roughly similar to that of impressionism. Just as the painters gradually forsook the traditional unique point of view and the Renaissance scenographic conception of space, culminating in the unusual *encadrages* of Degas,[1] so it became clear almost from the beginning that the specificity of cinematic art was arrived at not by recording a stage play but, rather, by choosing that angle of vision by which the moving figure defined most dynamically its field of activity.[2] It is tempting to carry the comparison even further and to see a correspondence between the impressionists' dissolution of the Renaissance laws of perspective and the cinema's dynamization of the static visual relationships in the still photograph. Such a comparison is all the more compelling in view of the fact that Leonardo da Vinci and Piero della Francesca based their theories on the same camera obscura

1. "His startling series of compositions of women in the bath, *modistes* and *blanchisseuses*, is the best school in which to acquire training in ideas about space composition within the limits of a frame. . . . " Eisenstein, "The Dynamic Square" (1930), in *Film Essays*, ed. Jay Leyda (New York, 1970), p. 56.

2. Jean Mitry, discussing point of view in the very first Lumière clips, claims that "*from the very first days, the narrow frame of scenic representation was shattered.* Space had replaced the stage" (Mitry's emphasis). *Histoire du cinéma* (Paris, 1967), 1:113.

that was, materially, the matrix of the modern photographic camera.[3] The power of the movies to present diverse viewpoints of the same object or action brought to an end—more definitively than impressionism ever could—the reproduction of the "circumscribed space" associated either actually or hypothetically with the stage. (Only cubism sought to achieve the multiplicity of viewpoint—perceived all at once, globally—which the movies automatically presented through time.)[4] André Malraux points out that cinema as a means of expression (and not of reproduction) dates from the time a movie was grasped as a series of shots and not as the recording of a real or fictional event.[5] This succession of diverse viewpoints, part and parcel of the montage process, led to the spatial and temporal simultaneity that was to become the epitome of cinematic experience. The cinema did not simply endow the still photo with motion; it raised to a new, decidedly visual level the investigation of change and mobility, which, with more or less urgency, had preoccupied the European mind since the end of the Renaissance.

One might be led at this point, along with Malraux and Herbert Read, to place movies (or what I have called the cinematic experience) alongside all the baroque, mannerist, "non-naturalist" styles of art—the Egyptian friezes, the statues of Bernini, Diderot's *clavecín*. But this would be to neglect the fact that the images in the movies bear an unprecedented resemblance to their "models,"

3. See ibid., p. 30. Analysis of this parallel between the camera lens and the Renaissance postulation of an ideal viewing-field has led to provocative controversies over the history of perceptual coding and the ideological thrust of such coding. See, in particular, J.-P. Oudart, "L'Effet de réel," *Cahiers du Cinéma* 228 (Mar.-Apr. 1971), J.-L. Comolli, "Technique and Ideology," *Film Reader* 2 (Winter 1977), and Stephen Heath, "On Screen, In Frame: Film and Ideology," *Quarterly Review of Film Studies* 1, no. 3 (August 1976).

4. The relationship between the movies and cubism, coterminous developments linked in the present discussion through the figure of Cézanne, requires a whole study in itself. Some valuable remarks along this line have been made by Elie Faure, *Fonction du cinéma* (Paris, 1964), esp. pp. 52-53, and Francastel, *Art et technique* (Paris, 1964), pp. 164-65.

5. "Esquisse d'une psychologie du cinéma," in L'Herbier, ed., *Intelligence du cinématographe* (Paris, 1946), p. 375; orig. in *Verve* (1941) and later in book form (Paris: Gallimard, 1946).

that historically and aesthetically the movies are a highly "naturalistic" medium—in Worringer's sense of an art that engenders delight by giving us a vivid impression of participating in the organic.[6] The movies did not have to renounce the photograph to achieve its dynamization. They did not reject the set line of photographic harmony, but, as in El Greco's paintings, put it to work in a new way. In fact, the movies can claim recognition as both "naturalistic" and "non-naturalistic": their paradoxical character of actual flatness and experiential depth bears this out. According to most theorists, it is movement within the frame which, dynamizing the still photographic image by conferring a deeper sense of corporeality on the objects filmed, makes them appear to stand out in slight, even if illusory, relief. In Edgar Morin's words: "Movement is the decisive power of reality: it is in and through movement that time and space are real."

Rudolf Arnheim explains this stereoscopic effect as resulting from the juxtaposition of the two-dimensional frame of reference, the actual filmed image, with the three-dimensional frame of reference to which the moving figures constantly allude and which corresponds to the spectator's own everyday experience. Movie-goers of the early days, unaccustomed to the new and unusual effects of moving images, experienced the impression of depth to an exaggerated degree, as is clear from Vachel Lindsay's description of the "dumb giants" in the foreground of the movie screen, whose bodies "are in high sculptural relief." As in impressionist painting, a certain apprenticeship of the eye was necessary, first for the spectator to seize the fact of the motion picture, then for him to neutralize those

6. Joseph Frank, "Spatial Form in Modern Literature," *Sewanee Review* 53 (1945):646–47.

The "impression of reality," so much expounded by film theoreticians, is based, first, on the resemblance of the film images to the events filmed, but also on the high degree of participation that this resemblance encourages. Cf. Christian Metz, "A propos de 'l'impression de réalité' au cinéma," in *Essais sur la signification au cinéma* (Paris, 1968), 1:13–24.

J.-P. Oudart, taking off from Foucault's commentary on the inclusion of the spectator in Velasquez's *Las Meninas* (*Les Mots et les choses*, chap. 1), shows that an essential factor in the production of "l'effet de réel" since the Renaissance has been the perceiving subject's *inscription* in the pictorial or, in the case of the novel and cinema, the narrative frame of reference. "L'Effet de réel," *Cahiers du Cinéma* 228 (Mar.–Apr. 1971):19–26.

extreme first reactions to its diverse effects. British audiences failed to follow G. A. Smith's early montagelike combination (1901) of long and close shots of the same action. D. W. Griffith's first close-ups (1908) were met with shock and disapproval at the chopping off of human bodies.[7]

Regardless of the exaggerated quality of some of these early reactions, they do tend to bear out the physiological argument that a depth-effect is created. Once again, out of this combination of actual flatness and experiential depth, the cinema represents a synthesis of two fundamental, contradictory world-views that have given rise to art throughout history: the "naturalistic" and the "non-naturalistic."

The movies came equipped, then, to respond to the aspirations of the most recent exemplars of these tendencies, the naturalist and the impressionist. Their power to seize the external world directly and with a high degree of objectivity satisfied the "realist" exigencies of both schools. On the one hand, since there was virtually no lag between the phenomenon and its recording, nature was caught *sur le vif*: each shot was potentially a miraculous preservation of the "instant fugitif." On the other hand, the mechanical nature of this recording and its subsequent projection was a reminder of the scientific means by which the image was captured.

The second important function of the movies was their sublimation of subgenres and miscellaneous forms of entertainment generally refused the status of "art" and their "cultural reclamation" of art-forms that had degenerated in the course of the nineteenth century. Erwin Panofsky has suggested a tentative list of subcultural phenomena—widely appreciated forms of expression that were not to survive their fleeting popularity—which inspired a great deal of early film-strip and movie content.[8] It is not difficult to recognize the transpo-

7. Edgar Morin, *Le Cinéma ou l'homme imaginaire* (Paris: Gonthier, 1958), p. 99; Rudolf Arnheim, *Film as Art* (Berkeley, 1957), pp. 58–59; Vachel Lindsay, *The Art of the Moving Picture* (New York, 1915), p. 84; Mitry, *Histoire*, 1:227. Cf. also Lewis Jacobs, *The Rise of the American Film* (New York, 1939), p. 103, and Béla Balázs, *Theory of the Film* (London, 1952), pp. 34–35.

8. "Style and Medium in the Motion Pictures" in Daniel Talbot, ed., *Film: An Anthology* (Berkeley, 1967), p. 17; orig. in *Critique* 1, no. 3 (Jan.–Feb. 1947).

sition of the leading motifs of pop songs, pulp magazines (including the newspaper's "human interest" stories), and dime novels into early films like *The May Irwin Kiss* (close-up of May Irwin and John C. Rice), *Morning Bath, Bains de Diane à Milan, Interrupted Love Affair,* and *Seminary Girls* (1895-97).

From the comic strip, "a most important root of cinematic art,"[9] early movie-makers borrowed gag mechanisms based on the simplest forms of discontinuous or fragmented succession, as in *L'Arroseur arrosé* (1895). Finally, bad nineteenth-century paintings, sentimental picture postcards, albums, and waxen *tableaux vivants* provided inspiration for countless film-strips, which, far from aiming at any dramatic development, satisfied the viewer by presenting lifelike, often romanticized, decors. The emphasis in many of these popular forms of entertainment on both historical events (as in the *Théâtre optique* at the Musée Grévin) and current events (as in the periodical *Lectures pour Tous)* led to such spectacular successes as *La Passion* (composed "on the basis of rather academic paintings"),[10] *L'Assassinat du Duc de Guise* (1897), and *Tearing Down of the Spanish Flag* (1898). It is difficult to ascertain to what extent the movies really sublimated these sub-cultural forms. In one sense at least, they merely corresponded to and advanced enormously the mass-production and "wholesale industrialization of art and literature" which characterized the period.[11] Yet if we look at the work of Georges Méliès, who was a magician before coming to the movies, we see an excellent example of sublimation in his adaptation of magicshow devices to the technical possibilities of the cinema. Here, the original process or material has been used in such a way as to transform the cinema, shock it into an awareness of its own most vital properties. Furthermore, the wholly make-believe world of Méliès's films point, if in an exaggerated manner, to an experiential quality of all these early films: the pleasures of anonymous escape sought in the dark movie houses by the ever-curious fin de siècle public.

9. Maurice Bardèche and Robert Brasillach, *The History of the Motion Pictures*, trans. and ed. Iris Barry (New York, 1938), pp. 14 and 16.

10. Mitry, *Histoire*, 1:123.

11. Balázs, *Theory of the Film*, p. 23.

In sum, one might say that the movies dynamized previously downgraded entertainment interests, such as eroticism, slapstick, current history, and magic into a widely popular medium and that these same interests, though just as escapist in the early movies as in their other forms, were to become central to the development of the art throughout the twentieth century. The movies galvanized into a myth-making "folk art" the tawdry elements of cheap entertainments.

The same sort of mechanism generally holds true for the cinema's reclamation of certain garish forms of nineteenth-century spectacles and theatricals. In this case, however, there is a dynamic relation between the dying forms and the brand new one: a perfect instance of Hegel's view that the seeds of a new mode are sown in the decay of an old one. The simplest example can be seen in the American penny arcades of the 1880s and 1890s. Commercial exploitation of precinematic inventions was quicker and more widespread in the U.S.A. than in Europe, mainly because store-front "parlors" filled with phonographs and other penny machines were already favorite centers of leisure. The new kinetoscope (1894), which in many cases fit right into the cabinets of the old hand-cranked peep-shows (i.e., various types of animated photography machines), was a highly popular and easily stocked addition to the penny arcades. Even more significant, several years later, when projection had become a familiar reality, "parlors and arcades were remodeled at moderate cost into nickelodeons [the first permanent movie houses, 1905] by removing the peep-show cabinets and the partition across the back end of the room, and filling the entire store with kitchen chairs."[12] In France, the *café-concert*, a well-established, low-cost institution, incorporated short film-strips into its programs, thus contributing vitally to the cinema's popularity during the years 1899 to 1904.[13]

Taking more of a long-range view, we can see that the movies,

12. Benjamin Hampton, *History of the American Film Industry* (New York, 1970), p. 45; orig. *A History of the Movies* (New York, 1931). Before this, films were generally shown as part of a "variety bill" in vaudeville houses; in Europe they were integrated into the music-hall shows.

13. Mitry, *Histoire*, 1:107.

while only requiring a gradual and short-lived accommodation by these established forms of popular cultural and variety show, exploited by their very nature the main trends of, in particular, the music-hall tradition. Legitimate theatre in France had, from the time of Romanticism, witnessed numerous attempts to undermine its classical stodginess and its predilection for the *parole*. Hugo's advocacy of a *mélange des genres* was, among other things, a plea for splendor and contrast of a more visual nature, for more optical pleasure. This sentiment corresponded to the advent of, on the one hand, the *spectacle oculaire*, made popular at the Cirque Olympique and later at the Boulevard theatres, and, on the other hand, a new aesthetic code formulated by Théophile Gautier: "The time has come for purely visual spectacle. . . . It is certain that the spoken word is today tiresome and boring." Gautier relates the growing interest in the admittedly mindless *spectacle oculaire* to three phenomena: the extremely poor quality of spoken drama, the current mental fatigue resulting from "one idea . . . worked out twenty times a day," and the general, semihistorical interest in the grandiose exploits of Napoleon (scenic by their very nature).

"In such a mental attitude," he continues, "what is more amusing than to see, as one reclines in a loge, the whole creation, cut up and arranged in *tableaux*, parade by as in a procession, picking up here and there, as though in flight, between a firing squad and a fanfare, just enough words in order not to have to understand the pantomime.

"While watching *Murat, you make, without moving, an immense voyage*. There are Egypt and the pyramids . . . the mysterious Sphynx . . . the Arabs . . ." (my emphasis).

According to Hassan El Nouty, as early as 1811 the French public "demands more powerful devices and can now be satisfied by nothing short of an action-packed drama that presents heroic or extraordinary actions in all their pomp and circumstance."[14]

Together, the Hugo manifesto and the popular cry for the spectacle led, well after the mild boldness of *Cromwell* and *Lorenzaccio*,

14. Théophile de Gautier, *Histoire de l'art dramatique* (Paris, 1859), 2:175-76; Hassan El Nouty, "Littérature et pré-cinéma au XIXe siècle," *Cahiers de l'Association Internationale des Etudes Françaises* 20 (May 1968):203.

to the widespread popularity of the Meyerbeer opera under the Second Empire, accompanied by the increasingly empty, mechanical quality of bourgeous theatre and its *pièce bien faite.* "The Meyerbeer opera was a great variety show, the unity of which consisted more in the rhythm of the moving spectacle on the stage than in the absolute predominance of the musical form."[15] Like it, the Boulevard plays, most notably those designed by Cicéri, made use of techniques developed by the earlier optical shows (diorama, panorama, etc.), seeming to hasten the realization of Théodore de Banville's dream of an "ideal theatre in which the dramatist would wield space and time at his will."[16]

In the Anglo-Saxon world, a similar evolution took place. Two opposite tendencies developed, both designed to circumvent the limitations of the moribund theatre: one was the American version of the *spectacle oculaire*, which culminated in the lavish productions of David Belasco; the other was the English closet drama which, from Byron's *Manfred* to Hardy's *The Dynasts*, sought "to control point of view, and to direct our attention to great panoramas or to minute detail with complete ease and freedom. . . . And both the desire to present spectacle and the wish for a form that would allow the spectator's viewpoint to change rapidly were to find their most successful expression in the new art of the film."[17]

15. Arnold Hauser, *The Social History of Art* 4:103.
16. El Nouty, "Littérature et pré-cinéma," pp. 204–95. Cf. the importance of pantomime in Diderot's and Beaumarchais's work and, above all, the enormous role played by the magic lantern from the eighteenth century on (pp. 336-37: open discussion on El Nouty's paper).

Gautier praises the verisimilitude of one of Cicéri's sunsets in *Histoire de l'art dramatique*, 2:142.

For more details on the relation between experimental nineteenth-century theatre and the cinema, see Mitry, *Esthétique et psychologie du cinéma* (Paris, 1965), 1:217ff.

17. Robert Richardson, *Literature and Film* (Bloomington, Ind., 1969), pp. 22 and 24.

Russia offers a striking contrast to Europe and America precisely because its theatre was witnessing a brilliant renaissance at the same time young artists were learning cinematic art. "Modernism" seems to have hit Russia at about the same time film production became possible, and both yielded their important first fruits shortly after the 1917 revolution. Meyerhold's hostility to naturalism and to Stanislavskyan "method" acting, along with his interest in

What all these subcultural art-forms had in common was the desire
on the part of their creators to appeal to broader masses of people.
The bankruptcy of bourgeois theatre had led by midcentury to
widespread acclaim by the lower classes of music-halls, operettas,
and circuses. Here was the beginning of a direct, dynamic relation
between artistic creation and public consumption, for as the spectacle grew more lavish and more heterogeneous in an effort to appeal
to greater numbers of people, the production costs correspondingly
grew, making it imperative for the showmen to interest more and
more paying customers.[18] Yet it need hardly be added that the
quality of this art went constantly downhill. The movies quickly
assumed the place left vacant by the teetering variety show. Besides
using and sometimes bettering its content, they also prepared to
play its worn-out social role: and there is no doubt that the movies
provided an exciting, vitally new form of entertainment for the
average working man.

Unlike the telegraph and telephone, which for many years were
reserved for members of the high bourgeoisie and ruling class,
the movies were immediately and designedly within the reach of
the proletariat.[19] It should be noted that only in America did this
process of "democratization" take place automatically and spon-
taneously. In France, for example, the early cinema public was
composed chiefly of petitbourgeois employees; thus, the tremendous
hegemony of the American movie industry during the early 1900s
has been attributed to the unique relation there between producers
and public—films responding to specific proletarian needs and
desires.[20] Indeed, the titles of these films alone (*Ten-Cent Lodging
House, Panoramic View of the Ghetto, A Non-Union Paper-Hanger*),
along with their familiar motifs of the working man as unconscious

---

"constructivist" stage setting and "bio-mechanic" (Pavlovian) acting, can be
seen carried over into Kuleshov's experiments proving that spectator emotion
is aroused according to the sequence of shots, and, of course, in the work
of Meyerhold's disciple, Eisenstein, whose first play resembled a circus or a
music-hall production. Cf. Peter Wollen, *Signs and Meaning in the Cinema*
(London, 1969), pp. 16-46.

18. Cf. Hauser, *Social History of Art*, 4: 250.

19. Hampton (see n. 12 above), p. 13.

20. Mitry, *Histoire*, 1: 145 and 179.

adventurer and the dignified rich as unwitting blunderers, testify to the proletarian character of American movies from about 1900 to 1908. Progressivism was not, however, a constant force; in fact, progressive content of any kind must be seen in light of the producers' need to interest precisely that segment of the population that attended the movies in the greatest numbers. As soon as the middle class "discovered" what, until then (around 1914), they had not deigned to enjoy, movie content and its implicit values made a series of sharp reversals.[21]

Everyone knows that the cinema, besides being the first totally new art for several thousand years, is also the first art to be collectively arrived at and the first artistic brain-child of modern industrial science. As the other arts, such as writing, painting, and music, are generally considered to be creative activities whose origins are untraceable except to myth (hence, practically données of the human spirit) and whose developments are inseparable from the history of man's understanding of himself, one might go further and say that the cinema is the only truly *invented* art. The third important function to be examined, then, is the nature of this unusual birthright: the movies' unique exploitation of the scientific and industrial insights that marked nearly every aspect of nineteenth-century expression.

From the "episodic" cave paintings of Lascaux and Altamira to the Egyptian friezes, from the Greek metope sculptures to the medieval tryptichs and "Stations of the Cross," from the camera obscura to the magic lantern (which, coming as it does from ancient China, suggests an entirely different catalogue), men have always had what may be called the cinematic desire—the desire to reproduce artificially forms in motion. We know that Eisenstein not only traced an informal history of "pre-cinematic" literature and theatre but also went so far as to consider the montage principle—his own unique "dialectic montage" capable of generating ideas—as essential to the very condition of art. For such speculations, however, it seems most reasonable to postulate some historical cut-off point

21. See Jacobs, *Rise of the American Film* (see n. 7 above), esp. pp. 138–68.

that marks the inauguration of what Hassan El Nouty has called the
"project du cinéma."[22] Not to be confused with the cinematic
desire or *dream*, the beginnings of the cinema project must correspond to a time when the two essentials of motion pictures were at
hand: the pictures (i.e., the photographic principle) and the motion
(i.e., the means of mechanically synthesizing the discrete part of
any action).

While extensive experimentation throughout the eighteenth
century was conducted on the basis of light sensitivity in silver
chlorides and nitrates, no single process was discovered that could
retain images for more than a few hours (and how ironically fitting
is this series of brilliant but ephemeral images in the *siècle des
lumières*!). It was in 1816 that Niepce achieved the first successful
photographic fixation of images and in 1829 that he went into
business with Daguerre to promote this process. While the effect
known as "persistence of vision" appears in the works of Ptolemy
and Lucretius and was revived during the eighteenth century, there
was no way of putting it to work until controlled experiments had
demonstrated how and why the phenomenon is produced. It was in
1824 that the English doctor and mathematician Roget conducted
experiments with turning wheels and vertical grooves, and in 1829
that Plateau enunciated the law governing the "persistence of
vision" and constructed the first motion-synthesizing machine,
the *phénakistiscope.*[23]

My purpose here is not to detail the history of cinematography,
but simply to set down a few key dates that suggest the time when
men first had the theoretical and material means of realizing the
cinematic desire. Clearly, it was during the 1820s that the cinema
project first got under way. Even more clearly, it was the scientific
know-how and creative inventiveness of this period that made
such a project possible. Phenomena that had been observed and
toyed with by ancient and "modern" thinkers alike, in particular by
the founders of most nineteenth-century scientific tenets and meth-
odologies, Galileo, Descartes, and Newton—phenomena that had
been philosophized practically out of existence by enthusiastic

22. "Littérature et pré-cinéma" (see n. 14 above), p. 197.
23. Mitry, *Histoire*, 1:30–31 and 24–25.

amateurs during the eighteenth century—these phenomena were now being analyzed, described, and synthesized with the aid of a relative newcomer: the machine.

The gradual perfection of the photographic medium, including tests on chemicals and gelatins and the development of a sufficiently supple (eventually celluloid) film base, has relatively little importance for us, apart from the obvious implementation of scientific expertise. The final achievement of motion, on the other hand, has enormous importance, as it links ancient, if not prehistoric, ambitions to the movies and to certain concerns of other arts as well.

The pleasure of seeing objects in motion is a primordial one and, according to some commentators, may sometimes correspond to the pattern or form that human thought takes: that is, succession through space provides a concrete embodiment of that vaguely felt process of mental succession.[24] Edgar Morin has pointed out that what differentiated Lumière from Edison was his realization "that people would be amazed, before anything else, at seeing that which doesn't amaze them: their houses, their faces, the setting of their everyday life."[25] He adds that modern primitives, such as the Moroccan Berbers, experience the same joyful astonishment at seeing familiar objects brought to life.

Western man's comprehension of motion was more or less the same from Aristotle's time to the seventeenth century. Movement through space was generalized into one or another *quality* in an attempt to grasp the action as a form of repose. Scholastic thinkers still used Aristotelian logic to crush Galileo's new ideas of a universe based on mathematically precise movements.[26] As soon as mathematics had been accepted as a valid tool for interpreting the world, Leibniz, who once envisaged a multimedia entertainment with "Magic Lanterns . . . flights, trick meteors, all sorts of optical marvels,"

24. "Our ideas do, whilst we are awake, succeed one another in our minds at certain distances, not much unlike the images in the inside of a lantern, turned round by the heat of a candle." John Locke, *Essay Concerning Human Understanding*, bk. 2, chap. 14, p. 9.

25. *Le Cinéma ou l'homme imaginaire* (see n. 7 above), p. 16.

26. Siegfried Giedion, *Mechanization Takes Command* (New York, 1948), p. 14.

could start speaking of *progress*.[27] From this time on there was at least one project in the air that occupied most theoreticians, that of man's eventual domination, by mechanical means, of nature.

But though the methodology became either more mechanistic, as in La Mettrie's casting aside the soul Descartes had reserved for man and describing him as just another locomotive machine (*L'Homme-machine*), or more materialistic, as in Diderot's prophetic but as yet unprovable theories of molecular motion (*Le Rêve de d'Alembert,* 1769), the means of analyzing movement with precision was still a long way off. There was still too great a gap between science and technology, between the abstraction of progress and its material fruits. It was not until around 1860 that E.-J. Marey invented a way of charting movement in graphic form. Before this, the most advanced means of tracing a moving body had been by representing a series of Cartesian conic sections. Marey discovered that movement could be translated into a curve and demonstrated for the first time mechanically that movement can only be accurately described by movement.[28]

As for the analysis and reproduction of movement, quite the opposite was true. When Leland Stanford, founder and president of the Central Pacific Railway and ex-governor of California, asked the photographer Eadweard Muybridge to demonstrate that a horse has all four feet off the ground at one point in his gallop, Muybridge had to use a serial method. He lined up twelve still-cameras in a row and tied trip-strings from them across the path of a running horse. These key experiments, later expanded to include twenty-four successive shots, resulted in the projection of discontinuous, sequential photographs that, for the first time, gave a totally convincing impression of movement (1877). Later experiments and inventions, in particular Marey's "photographic gun" which used the principle of the revolver to take in a few seconds a large number of pictures of a "sighted"

27. Yvon Belaval, "Une Drôle de pensée de Leibniz," *Nouvelle Revue Française* (1959), pp. 757 and 759. See descriptions by Descartes of universal applications of the machine, by which men would become "masters and possessors of nature," in Alexandre Koyré, "Les Philosophes et la machine," *Critique* 4, nos. 23–26 (Apr.–July 1948). This article is excellent, besides, for all the background on scientific theory and technology merely skimmed over here.

28. Giedion, *Mechanization Takes Command*, pp. 18ff.

object (1882), led quickly to the perfection of the motion picture camera and projector more or less in the form as we know it today.

Increasing mechanization throughout the nineteenth century made the final realization of the movies almost inevitable. In a world where progress was for the first time truly "palpable," "the awe and reverence once reserved for a Deity and later bestowed upon the visible landscape was directed toward technology or, rather, the technological conquest of matter."[29] As the idea of movement and of its reproduction changed, artistic form, goaded by technological advances, underwent a similar and correspondent metamorphosis.

Until now a form had always been engendered by rest; henceforth it arises *also* from movement. . . . Dynamism is the golden rule of our era. Everything rolls, everything flows and is transformed. Societies as well as objects and forms. Equilibrium is no longer in immobility but in movement. We have a direct, intimate experience of movement. When we watch a film as well as when we move about through the world, or when we look at those matter-generating or matter-destroying machines. It was inevitable that art would come to express, by appropriate means, this new experience that man posesses of the external world.[30]

It is not surprising that the movies express best of all the arts man's "new experience" in the technological world. Their popular name itself ("movies," more appropriate than a metonymic name such as "the film") stresses at once their mechanical attributes and the fundamental mobility that distinguishes them from other arts. Motion, conceived of as the basic phenomenon whereby space is delineated through time, is at the essence of the movies' form as much as it is emblemed in their name. The term used to describe a film's compositional process, "montage," is the French word originally referring to the industrial assembly of finished products from individual parts. This is likewise not so surprising a metaphor, since all cinematographic activities, particularly the recording and the subsequent "re-activating" of motion, depend on highly developed machines; and film production, often compared to the collective

29. Leo Marx, *The Machine in the Garden*, (New York, 1964), p. 197.
30. Francastel, *Art et technique* (see n. 4 above), p. 211.

construction of a medieval cathedral, is more akin to the assembly-line process than to painting a picture or writing a poem. At every juncture of production, whether between director and actor or between actor and spectator, between cameraman and celluloid or between celluloid and editor, a machine significantly intervenes.

But if the movies represent the most important artistic exploitation of technological progress, they also stand as a response to a struggle that was growing throughout the nineteenth century between the arts and the sciences. In the eighteenth century, before the practical fruits of machine technology were available on a large scale, there was little or no contradiction between artistic and scientific endeavors: the Cartesian dream of possessing nature was still tenable. In fact, science, from Aristotle on, had always been a main arm of philosophy, a set of *technai* no more threatening to ethical man than artistic techniques. But even by the end of the eighteenth century, a cleavage set in that was coterminous with, because in many ways indistinguishable from, the spirit of Romanticism. The very machine that was to liberate man from ancient modes of production and give him maximum leisure, turned out to chain him to a new, unnatural monster that spread misery, dullness, and ugliness. Diderot was probably the last of the Renaissance-type universal achievers who could yoke scientific investigation with aesthetic creation, rationalism with sensibility. And it was a fairly shaky union at that. With Rousseau, the artist, the man of feeling, rediscovered a world and a register of emotions that had seemingly been neglected by art for centuries. As eighteenth-century rationalism marched on and was transformed into the concrete forms of industrialization of the nineteenth century, the artist and the philosopher became newly aware of the nature and the "natural man" that machine culture would seek to regiment.

One of the first to make a cogent indictment against the machine was Friedrich Schiller in his *Letters upon the Aesthetical Education of Man* of 1795. Schiller describes society in a process of disintegration and man in a process of fragmentation due to the increasingly mechanistic nature of the individual's relationship to himself and to others. "Having nothing in his ears but the monotonous sound of the perpetually revolving wheel, [man] never develops the harmony of his being."[31] Like many of the German romantic philosophers, Schiller had a tremendous impact on the English thinkers of the early nineteenth century, particularly, according to Leo Marx, on Carlyle. Taken aback by the rampant success on all fronts of empiricist philosophy, Carlyle feared that machine culture would bring an end to man's inner life: "Not the external and physical alone is now managed by machinery, but the internal and spiritual life also."[32]

The contradictions between man's spiritual nature and the demands of increasing technological progress, just as those between art and the machine, intensified from this time till the end of the century. No resolution appeared in view, and antimachinism became one of the leading social myths of the century.[33] The implications of these unresolved contradictions are no more dire for the artist and philosopher than they are for the average working person. The millions of individuals who now bend over the machines of industrial capital, compared to the artisans and craftsmen who preceded them, have a less and less organic connection to the objects they produce, which are usually parts of wholes they never see. Marx referred to the complex of working conditions that thus became prevalent in a technological culture as "alienated labor." "The *alienation* of the worker in his production means not only that his labour becomes an object, an *external* existence, but that it exists *outside him*, independently, as something alien to him, and that it becomes a power on its own confronting him; it means that the life which he has conferred on the object confronts him as something hostile and alien."[34]

Even though Marx, like Carlyle, never suggests scrapping the machinery altogether, as the Luddites had before his time, the notion of alienation was to be generally transformed, as today, into a caricature of the machine as depriving the human being of all

31. Quoted in Marx, *Machine in the Garden*, p. 169.

32. Ibid., p. 171.

33. Francastel, *Art et technique*, pp. 27 and 97. See pp. 20-27 for a discussion of the main propagators of this myth, from the Comte de Laborde to Ruskin.

34. *Economic and Philosophic Manuscripts of 1884*, in Robert Freedman, ed., *Marxist Social Thought* (New York, 1968), p. 69; Marx's emphasis.

will, emotion, imagination. The owners of the means of production, in any case, had no interest in helping to resolve this essentially psychological or aesthetic conflict, as a greater share for the workers in the material and cultural benefits of technological progress might very well have led to the owners' loss of economic control. There is no doubt that "scientific management" procedures around the end of the nineteenth century led decidedly toward a dehumanization of the working man. The efficiency pioneer, F. B. Gilbreth, for example, made plastic models of ordinary actions in order to determine which parts of a movement were unnecessary. Such experiments resulted in "that type of phenomena in which the motion means everything, the object performing it nothing."[35]

The challenge for art developing in the late nineteenth century and thereafter consisted in discovering a means of transforming the deleterious social effects of the machine age into pleasurable aesthetic effects. Experiments like those of Gilbreth had done precisely the opposite: in the name of greater efficiency, they allowed the new principles of mechanization to intrude into the very stance and gestures of workers on the job. The antimachine bias of artists going back to the romantics prevented them from depicting images of urban industrialization in any but the most oppressive terms. Social dehumanization, in other words, became an overdetermined factor in the artistic depiction of dehumanization.

It is interesting that the locomotive, the first major invention of the steam age, the first object whose "meaning" lay entirely in the fact of its motion through space, was a prime target of the romantic poets' anti-industrial pleas. John Stuart Mill pointed out that the locomotive is a "perfect symbol" of the invading technological society "because its meaning need not be attached to it by a poet; it is inherent in its physical attributes."[36] Hence the "tristesse" of Hugo's Olympio and Vigny's *berger*, who witness the ravaging of the memory-filled, tradition-bound countryside by the new "iron horse." Hence, too, Hawthorne's more composed dismay when the sounds of the steam engine burst in on his solitary contemplations at "Sleepy Hollow." Leo Marx has gone a long way in

35. Giedion, p. 104.
36. L. Marx, p. 192.

showing how this apparently trivial incident has its literary rever-
berations throughout the nineteenth century and into the twentieth,
becoming a *topos* for the complex of attitudes and reactions summoned up in the American who is faced with the machine's sudden
appearance onto the landscape.[37]

Something similar is true for the French, though a poet like
Baudelaire, while detesting the ugliness of the industrialized city,
is still rather attached to the power and the artificial splendor that
technology is capable of producing. Rimbaud and, most especially,
Apollinaire, will be even more attached to such productions. The
pastoral ideal was never as great or as deeply felt in France as in
America, a nation founded around and dedicated to the idea of
virgin spaces. England, however, had always cherished its countryside, and poets from Blake to Matthew Arnold consistently mourned
its gradual disappearance as the result of technological expansion.
Arnold, even more than Hawthorne, recognized the complexity of
the problem. The same set of objects and conditions which represents a climax of intellectual skill and inventiveness also marks the
definitive attenuation of "sweetness and light" forever.

But it could not be totally forgotten that the locomotive, whose
name is no less precise an indication of its essential nature than
that of the movies, also afforded a new kind of artificial motion.
Popular writers never tired of proclaiming that man "has almost
annihilated space and time" by yoking "to his car fire and water,
those unappeasable foes, and flying from place to place with the
speed of thought."[38] It was also noted that movement through
space was essential to the precise apprehension of comparative
distances and, hence, of perspective.[39] Now man could be propelled
through space and concentrate on the changing perspectives that
passed by him. The "passing by" of scenery, similar in its subject/
object reversal to the "rising" and "setting" of the sun, became a
powerful image for even the most recondite of romantic inheritors.

Accordingly, around the turn of the twentieth century, there
seems to be an important reversal of attitude toward the locomotive

37. Ibid., pp. 3-16 and passim.
38. From the *Democratic Review* of March 1845, quoted in L. Marx, p. 194.
39. Helmholtz, *Optique physiologique* (see chap. 1, n. 4), pp. 805-06.

and, by extension, toward mechanization in general. Amidst sill
fervent cries of spiritual fragmentation and general dehumanization,
there appears to be a change of heart on the part of many. Villiers
de L'Isle-Adam had already apotheosized the modern inventor in
the figure of Edison himself and presented a world in which the
machine not only conquers all but even incarnates a woman (*Eve
future*, 1886). The feeling grows that all this automation, fragmentation, and compartmentalization may actually be valuable—even
artistically valuable. It need hardly be added that both French
and American pioneers of the movies which correspond to this
period of "contre-décadence" began their careers with dramatic
shots of locomotive trains.[40] Indeed, the locomotive is central to
early masterpieces like Porter's *The Great Train Robbery* and
Griffith's *The Lonedale Operator*, both as subject and as fluid
means of endowing the camera with motion.

Coterminous with the movie experimenters, certain literary
experimenters were curiously drawn to the locomotive and its
unique motion—artificial propulsion said in 1845 to correspond to
"the speed of thought!" Is it possible, then, that artificial locomotion too, like the motion of animated objects across our field
of vision, has some secret affinity with the process of thought? We
have noted that the "passing scenery" is an unconscious quid pro
quo for the subject's automated motion, so that the two movements, object-animation and subject-locomotion, are at least aesthetically complementary, two sides of the same spinning coin.

In Gide's *Les Caves du Vatican*, Lafcadio commits his "acte
gratuit" on a moving train. The continuous, persistent motion is
necessary to get himself into the proper mental state. A similar
hypnotic effect of a moving train puts Clyde Griffith in the right
mood to commit a crime in Dreiser's *An American Tragedy*. Brief,
imagistic, parenthetical sentences in italics suddenly appear in the
text (book 2, chapter 46), representing, through fixated images,
Clyde's inner struggle. The moving train and random passing scenery
similarly cause Mauriac's Thérèse Desqueyroux to fall into a kind of
preconscious state. Memories of her past, details that had never

40. Mitry, *Histoire*, 1:88.

occurred to her with such precision, rush in on her and force her to put together and face up to the fact of her attempted murder. Thus, the mechanized motion of the locomotive has become a literary device used as a means of releasing the innermost parts of consciousness. Far from inhibiting the development of spiritual recognition, as does the motion of many machines, it has the power, according to these novelists, to eddy the mind further on in its reflective processes.

The moving-train *topos*, then, is one means by which the reality of industrial technology was seized on and, in a manner totally different from that of the romantics and their Victorian descendants, presented positively, as a catalyst to reflective thought. It represents a tentative bridge across the nineteenth-century gap between art and technology. Many other examples, from the *contre-décadence* on, come to mind, in particular: Apollinaire's poetry of industrialized Paris, Marcel Duchamp's "ready-mades" and his time-lapse paintings, dadaist and surrealist collages and "machines," Léger's paintings of factories and other huge industrial complexes. A whole history of "modern sensibility" could, in fact, be based around the growing presence of the technological object in works of art.

But the most striking example of a material link between art and technology is, as may be gathered by now, the movies. Unlike the writer's typewriter, the painter's acrylics, or the architect's prefabricated materials, the camera, film, and projector of the movies represent the formal and indispensable dependence of this new art on the machine age from which it sprang. Again, unlike most technological innovations of the nineteenth century, which acted as substitutes for human parts of actions (e.g., the cotton gin, the steamboat), the movies replace nothing. They do satisfy a desire, however, as witness the innumerable optical gadgets leading up to their inception. Far more than the locomotive or the airplane, whose effects of shrinking space and automating motion fulfilled many century-old dreams and thus proved highly suggestive to man's imagination, the movies offer a total, all-involving aesthetic experience capable of producing not simply movement, vicariousness, and intellectual configurations, but also a unique combination of the real and the unreal that gives flight to the imaginary faculty. "Cinema . . . is the mother-machine, generator of the imaginary, and, reciprocally, the imaginary determined by the machine."[41]

This does not mean that the cinema, through its recreation of "the spatial unity and dynamic continuity of the world . . . reintegrates us into the very heart of the 'spiritual.'"[42] The cinema does not need to make this claim. It shows, and the spectator does the rest. If the primitive insists there is a demon in the camera or somewhere else in the filming process, and if the 1920 theoretician maintains that the filmic image will restore the life of the spirit to art, each has his reason for doing so. Walter Benjamin has explained that, in the latter case, the only way to establish the movies' status as art seemed to be, in the early days, to discover in them the ritualistic, or cult, values that art had actually been abandoning consistently over the past century. He goes on to show that the cinema offers not a neat resolution of the problem of art's relation to technology but rather the necessary mingling of the two in an age of extraordinary technical advance." For the first time in world history, mechanical reproduction emancipates the work of art from its parasitical dependence on ritual. To an even greater degree the work of art reproduced becomes the work of art designed for reproducibility."[43] Thus, the movies are the first art in which mass reproduction is not, as with lithography and book printing, simply a means of widespread diffusion, but rather, as with industrial production, a financial and aesthetic condition essential to their process of expression. They transform systematically into art even the most stultifying or potentially dehumanizing qualities of machine culture. Born of the machine, they have taught the machine to use its very own materials and principles as means of artistic creation.

41. Morin, _Le Cinéma_, pp. 177–78.
42. Faure, _Fonction du cinéma_ (see n. 4 above), p. 134.
43. "The Work of Art in the Age of Mechanical Reproduction" (1936) in _Illuminations_, ed. H. Arendt, trans. H. Zohn (New York, 1969), p. 224.

3 Inherent Form in the Cinema

So far I have dealt, primarily from a historical point of view, with the material of the movies. In this chapter I shall deal with the inherent rather than inherited form of the movies, their mode of existence, not as detached from their various materials, but as generated onto an aesthetic plane from which the material causes will be viewed only as the inevitable foundations of a less specific, highly abstract configuration. This section is thus entirely synchronic; there will be no attempt to trace the chronological development of film aesthetics either within the medium or without. Rather, the cinema will be treated as a complex artistic phenomenon momentarily arrested, taken out of its evolutionary process, so as to be examined in essence.

A. *Space and Time*

Film presents a new, highly dynamic spatiotemporal form that at once links it to and separates it from the other arts. It is, first of all, endowed with the spatiality of the plastic arts. Like painting, it reduces the experiential three-dimensionality of architecture and sculpture to two-dimensionality; yet film constantly gives rise to the impression of a referential three-dimensionality in its final result (cf. above, chap. 2, n. 7). If it shares with painting the same raw material (the objectively real world outside of consciousness), film nonetheless renounces almost entirely gross matter in its final product: whereas the configurating matter in painting, the various pigments on canvas, constitute an essential part of the artist's creative act, the corresponding matter in film, silver bromide particles on celluloid,

61

is formed entirely by automatic processes and taken for granted, subsumed in the mechanical rather than aesthetic part of creation.

So great is the effect of mechanization in the film-maker's creative task that even to compare the "raw material" with that of painting is misleading. The painter, like the sculptor and writer, even when drawing from models or still lifes, compositionally starts at zero, whereas the film-maker organizes "material things and persons, not a neutral medium, into a composition that receives its styles ... not so much by an interpretation in the artist's mind as by the actual manipulation of physical objects and recording machinery."[1] (Elaboration of this paradoxical production of the image is in section B, below; elaboration of the consequential shift in the artist-object relation is in section C.) Furthermore, while film makes use of the frame, as in painting, to compose its "ready-made" objects, the space referred to is never constrained, restricted, or even organized by the frame. We experience space in the process of being structured at the same time we experience, from moment to moment, its finished structure.[2] Each photogram presents a set spatial configuration composed in terms of the frame, yet the film projects, as it moves from reel to reel, a fluid, developing space; it is constantly alluding to the space outside the frame.

Thus, the film is composed of a plastic material which, when projected by means of a strong light against the screen, is experienced as immaterial shadows like those of Plato's cave; yet at the same time, this evanescent image refers to and gives a fairly complete illusion of a fully material, constantly unfolding space. This tension between perceiving the intangible and conceiving the tangible cannot be fully understood without reference to time.

A film operates fundamentally in terms of two times: abstract, chronological time and psychological, human time—Bergson's

1. Erwin Panofsky, "Style and Medium in the Motion Pictures," in Daniel Talbot, ed., _Film: An Anthology_ (Berkeley, 1967), p. 31. Arnheim (see above, chap. 2, n. 7) has added that the recording instruments, in turn, share a basic quality with the objects recorded, viz., movement: thus "the motion picture is . . . based on a recording process that is as continuous and unitary as the movement of the photographed objects" (p. 179).

2. Cf. Jean Mitry, _Esthétique et psychologie du cinéma_ 1:27 and 198.

"scientific time" and "durée."[3] The celluloid passes through the projector at a fixed rate of twenty-four frames per second. Thus, the actual duration of a film, its succession of images, is a constant, entirely congruent with abstract, chronological time. The time referred to, however, within the film's edited sequences shows no such congruence. On the contrary, as is well known, the diegetic time is constantly deleted, skipped through, and reversed for dramatic purposes. Thus, we must distinguish, on the one hand, *narrative time*, the signifying time that coincides with projection, and on the other hand, the *diegetic time*, the signified time of what is narrated.[4]

Yet there is a third time in cinema (as in literature): the time involved in experiencing the work. The spectator shares in both the abstract and the psychological times: he enters the movie house, say, at two o'clock and leaves at four o'clock, but as a result of following the jumps of the montage, the experience has been not of the two hours passing on the clock but of the hundred-year stretch of diegetic time possibly alluded to in the movie. The same is true for a novel-reader, except that here the outside, chronological time has not the same set influence. One may pick up and put down a novel, read it at several sittings, while a movie is always seen all at once, during a length of time entirely dependent on its spatial length (of celluloid). Thus, narrative time in the movies is, like scientific time, a nonvariable, beyond the spectator's control, whereas in the novel it depends on the volition of the reader. The pacing of a movie is relatively intense, then, like that of a lyric poem or of a symphony. It is at once dictated by the projecting mechanism and liberated by the effects of montage.

Here we approach the specificity of the cinematic experience. While film shares a basic temporality with music, dance, mime,

3. See Hans Meyerhoff, *Time in Literature* (Berkeley, 1955), pp. 4-5, 10, and 14-15.
4. Cf. Christian Metz, "Pour une phénoménologie du film narratif," *Essais sur la signification au cinéma* (Paris, 1968), 1:27-28. The same is basically true for the novel, with certain crucial differences. This usage of "narrative" and "diegesis" proceeds from Gérard Genette's *récit* and *histoire* (or *diégèse*) in *Figures III* (Paris, 1972), pp. 71-76.

poetry, and narrative literature, its unique combination of three distinct kinds of time makes it as different from these as from the spatial arts. Its discrete temporal unities, for example, are far less regular, less preordained than those of music, dance, and traditional verse. It is not the regularity of the film's mechanical passage that, like a metronome, creates its rhythm, but rather the cuts from shot to shot: montage. It is a narrative rhythm, hence roughly similar to that of mime and drama in that the events referred to correspond (or seem to correspond) exactly in time to the perception of these events: experiential and diegetic time appear to coincide.

But the experiencing of time passing is yet fundamentally different in the theatre and in the cinema, due to the different *space* that separates the spectator from the mimetic object. On the surface of it, it would seem that the distance between spectator and stage is fixed in the same manner as between spectator and screen. The stage, however, *contains* mimetic objects, and the spectator, with only minor exceptions, trains his gaze on this space from a set, unvarying distance and angle. The screen, on the other hand, as its name implies, cuts off the spectator at the same time it let him pass through. The film spectator, assuming he follows the *enchaînement* of images, is transported beyond the set distance between him and the screen and, unconsciously associating his own gaze with the registering lens of the camera, assumes a constant variability of distance and angle with respect to the mimetic objects. (This is further elaborated below in section D.)

Thus, for the theatre spectator, excepting the conventional lapses between scenes accompanied or not by a drop of the curtain, chronological and experiential time coincides with the diegetic time elaborated on stage. The film spectator's experience is similar to this only so long as the camera remains focused on one and the same space without a cut, that is, without any change in distance or angle, and only on condition that the continuous piece of film in question has been registered at the standard rate of twenty-four frames per second. Once two pieces of film, which represent disjunct portions of time and space, are spliced together, the chronological time that has ruled over projection and experiencing for the duration of any single shot, now no longer coincides with the diegetic time. The narrative time (simply, the sequence of images) carries on as dictated by the regular, unchanging speed of the projector, while the montage causes leaps and bounds in diegetic time. And the spectator is carried along by both: his external existence continues at the same rate as the narrative and the projector, while his imagination follows the elaboration of the diegesis, the course of the cutting.)

Filmic space and time are synthesized with one another, each losing any absolute claim to independence or integrality: each is experienced no longer separately but in terms of the other.[5] The dynamic structuring of filmic space requires the dimension of time. In other words, perception of the three-dimensional (referential) space cannot take place without the moment-to-moment changes (i.e., movement) introduced by duration. One need only think of the film-clips posted outside movie houses to advertise the movie being shown. In these blown-up photograms, space is two-dimensional, static. But when the same photograms are perceived as part of the projected film, when mere chronological elaboration has been added, space is perceived in its very development and assumes the illusory third dimension. The establishment of spatial relations in film is thus radically different from that in a real, experiential frame of reference. What we apprehend instantaneously by means of our innate stereoscopic vision must be elaborated temporally, and often from various points of view, in the movies.

By the same token, the dynamic organization of filmic time requires the spatial dimension, or at least takes on a spatial character. To begin with, the experiential time of each shot and each scene is determined by the spatial length of the piece of film in question. In this way, spatial length can be seen, entirely outside the film's diegetic content, to measure abstract, chronological time. The spatial length of the celluloid has nothing to do with the space of the diegesis, but everything to do with narrative duration.

This purely physical fact of the moving celluloid is necessary to

5. For background to and variations on the following discussion, see Herbert Read, "Towards a Film Aesthetic" (1932), in R. D. MacCann, ed., *Film: A Montage of Theories* (New York, 1966), pp. 167–68; Faure, *Fonction du cinéma*, pp. 60–61; Panofsky, "Style and Medium," pp. 18–19; Arnold Hauser, *Social History of Art*, 4:239-43; and Edgar Morin, *Le Cinéma ou l'homme imaginaire*, pp. 50-57.

understand the more important, if less precise, spatial quality of film's diegetic time. Each shot in a movie seems to be given in the present tense: in spite of the effects of flashbacks and jumps forward in time, it is inscribed in a here and now that seems capable of being brought back at a moment's notice. Unlike the photographic image, which seems to say, "That was a fine ship," the most static of filmic equivalents would always have to be, "This is a fine ship," even if the image made up part of a sailor's recollection.[6] In passing from one action to another action that we know is diegetically prior to the first, the continuous present is preserved and we have the sense of moving through a medium that no longer has the indomitable forward movement that characterizes chronological time. We pass backward and forward through the compartments of time as though it were an infinitely long, stationary railroad train. Time was never so concretely spatialized, nor so plainly visible, before the movies: not only do we *see* time passing before our eyes, but we also see where it has been and where it may go: we perceive as externality what in all other cases—including certain moments of the cinematic process itself—must be assumed or intuited from within.

The best way to explain this effect is to recall the film's compositional process at its most critical point: the editing. It is then that the spatial hardware and the spatial referent are exactly the same. The editor has before him each shot cut and separated from the spool on which it was taken. Each strip of film hanging in the long row represents a different here-and-now that may ultimately figure in the film's assembly. In putting together these diverse pieces, the editor holds time, so to speak, in this hands. He may situate one shot of the climactic action near the beginning of his footage, or he may, at the end, insert key images from earlier sequences. The editor's job, or the fact of montage—which every film spectator is more or less aware of—provides the clearest emblem

6. Cf. Roland Barthes: "In the photograph, an illogical conjunction is produced between the *here* and the *bygone*. . . . Its reality is that of the *having-been-there*. . . . It would not do to consider the cinema as animated photography; here the *having-been-there* gives way to a *being-there* of the thing. . . ." "Rhétorique de l'image," *Communications* 4 (1964):47.

of the spatial nature of filmic time.

(Space that cannot be perceived without development in time, time that cannot pass without embodiment in space: these are seemingly paradoxical coordinates that define the contours of cinematic experience. It will yet be necessary to elaborate the specific techniques that the film arrives at within this "space-time continuum," so as to gauge its impact on the other mainstay of modern narrative art, the novel. Such effects as expansion, compression, and negation of time, simultaneity, discontinuous continuity, ubiquity of point of view, and restrictive framing will be taken up in chapter 4.)

B. *Mimesis*

The notion of "space-time continuum," seized on by commentators, especially art critics like Herbert Read and Elie Faure, as defining the film's basic mode of existence, seems, as such, to raise more questions than it answers. If film is articulated through space and time indivisibly woven together, then how is it different from life, which is indisputably itself a space-time continuum? If we grant that in the film, partly as the result of its referential movement that engenders depth, the *impression* of reality is produced, then what is the precise relation of the filmic image (whether considered externally as light through celluloid or internally as a perception registered first by the cameraman and then by the spectator) to the reality it mimes? And finally, if film seems to be, in one sense the modern exemplar of those flickering shadows in Plato's cave, then how would its mimetic process fare in comparison with that of other arts banned from the Republic?

(The "iconicity"[7] of the film is far greater than that of other

7. See Metz, "Au-delà de l'analogie, l'image," and Umberto Eco, "Sémiologie des messages visuels," both in *Communications* 15 (1970), where the starting point of analysis is C. S. Peirce's distinction between icon (high degree of perceptual likeness between two members of analogy), symbol (arbitrary relation between the two), and index (causal relation between the two).

Eco (p. 14) demonstrates best the extent and the limits of the analogy between the iconic signs (film images) and the mimetic objects that give

mimetic arts. The retinal image produced within the spectator by the filmic stimulus is extremely similar to that produced by the same "natural" stimulus. (We experience, as Barthes would say, no longer what *has been there*, as with a photographic image, but what *is here*. No mediating terms are necessary: time and space are both immediate. And once the referential movement of the filmic image is taken into account, we can say that we experience *what is becoming here*. Unlike the photographic image, then, to which in other ways it is so similar, the filmic image posits objects in their material essence and adds to this their process of becoming.

In great part this is due, as Panofsky has shown (see above, note 1), to the fact that the mimetic object is the primal cause of its own mimesis. Here I am speaking not of the expressive procedure involved in cinematic recording—which calls into question the status of the creating subject, the film-maker—but simply of the means by which filmic iconicity is achieved. As Jean Mitry has said, the representation is entirely identified with the object it represents—to the point of disappearing behind it:

Reality is thus no longer "represented," signified by a symbolic substitute or by some graphism. It is *presented.* And it is reality now that serves to signify. Caught in the trap of a new dialectic of which it becomes the very form, reality serves as an element in its own confabulation.[8]

Before ever being a question of the confabulating artist, the mimetic object has, by automatic processes, left its iconistic mark. In this sense, the production of the filmic image begins and ends with the mimetic object itself.[9] While the image of the Mona Lisa is produced

---

rise to them, when he notes that "the signs do not 'possess the properties of the object represented' but reproduce some of the conditions of common perception, on the basis of normal codes and by selecting those stimuli which . . . can permit me to construct a perceptual structure that possesses—with regard to the codes of acquired experience—the same signification as the real experience denoted by the iconic sign."

8. *Esthétique*, 1:52; Mitry's emphasis.

9. Cf. Gilbert Cohen-Séat: "That which produces and that which is produced are identical." *Essai sur les principes d'une philosophie du cinéma* (Paris, 1958), p. 149.

by Leonardo, the image of Joan in *The Passion of Saint Joan* is produced not by Dreyer but by the actress Falconetti.

(Film doubles reality, presents an entirely faithful image of its model, what Plato would have called an *eikōn* (*Sophist* 236a).[10] And hence, *iconicity*. To continue in Platonic terms, the filmic image can nonetheless turn into the opposite of *eikōn*, into *phantasma*, that which fools the eye of the spectator by pretending to be an *eikōn*. The fantastic is dominant, for example, in the films of Méliès—not simply because he uses artificial decors, but because the succession (montage) and overlaying (superimposition) of different shots lead the spectator to believe in the existence of what is not and never was)(cf. *Sophist* 2372-242a). In fact, the isolated shot of a "painted" rocket ship or of a miniature (super-imposed) ballerina is still iconistic in that in each case the object retains the same proportions it had when shot. (In cinema, then, the difference between *eikōn* and *phantasma* is not really the difference between good and bad mimesis, but rather that between mimesis and montage.) It is when the editor begins to cut and to juggle the pieces of (doubled) reality that the *trompe-l'oeil* effect seriously intervenes. Film avoids Plato's "machine logique" with the

10. Cf. Jacques Derrida, "La Double Séance," in *La Dissémination* (Paris, 1972), pp. 211-13, n. 8. Derrida briefly demonstrates how Plato's "machine logique" manages to reject mimesis of every type—even when the model imitated is good. The point maintained here is that, apart from the criterion of goodness or badness of the model (a serious exception, but the one which trips up many other arts and art-works), film side-steps the problem of truth in art by assigning to imitation a subordinate role (in that it is taken for granted).

For a differently oriented discussion of mimesis in the cinema, see Gerald Mast, *Film/Cinema/Movie* (New York, 1977), pp. 39-53. Mast takes the term not as it pertains to the relation between model and representation, but rather as it relates to the sense of actual presence of the spectator, the feeling of direct witnessing. He thus raises the question of mimesis in the way it has traditionally been raised with regard to literature, as by Erich Auerbach, by invoking notions like the "willing suspension of disbelief." As such, his remarks make for an interesting contribution toward understanding the various means of effecting verisimilitude in the cinema.

craft of the Sophist insofar as *mimesis is subsumed in the automation of the medium itself.* Expression (which would include many
of the Platonic don'ts: visual trickery, logical ellipsis, apparent
anonymousness) comes thereafter.

C. *The Creating Subject: Artist*

The anonymity of the creating subject is only one porthole through
which to view the problem of authorship as raised by the movies.
A film has at once no creator and hundreds of creators: hence
Claude-Edmonde Magny speaks of the absence, or at least the
effective ellipsis, of an authorial voice[11] with as much validity
as Panofsky when he compares the film to the medieval cathedral
on the basis of "a co-operative effort in which all contributions have
the same degree of permanence."[12] This seeming paradox can be
explained—without being wholly resolved—by distinguishing between the production and the manipulation of the filmic image. As
seen above, production of the image originates in the mimetic object
and retains the highly iconistic imprint of that object regardless of
subsequent manipulations of its context. In these terms, there is
no author, creator, or producer of the image other than the mimetic
object itself.

But even at this initial step in recording, an important qualification must be made. It is true that film-making results in an autonomous, apparently untouched rendering of something "out there,"
the consummate example of an art in which "the artist, like the God
of creation, remains within or behind or beyond or above his handi-
work, invisible, refined out of existence, indifferent, paring his
fingernails." Yet if the will of the artist is at no point *explicitly*
broached, it is also true that the mimetic object no more seeks its
cinematic recording than a fern branch seeks its millennial fossiliza-
tion. (There is no author, but there is an authorizer.) From the moment the camera is called into action, the film-maker's will is *implicitly* broached,) for it is his creating consciousness that delves
into *de rerum natura* to choose, discard, and arrange as wished.

11. *L'Age du roman américain* (Paris, 1948), esp. pp. 60-61.
12. Panofsky, "Style and Medium," p. 29.

Hence, the artistic act of selection must be posited from the very outset.

Here we encounter, though from the opposite end of the viewfinder, something akin to the traditional description of the impressionist painter, supposed to be constantly indulging his subjective sensations, while actually more interested in documenting changes in external reality. The stance of pure objectivity so often attributed to the film-maker is only apparent and never an entirely accurate description of the creative task: consider the narrow line, from a formal point of view, between the documentary and the propaganda film. As in every other art—and most clearly in recent "minimal" arts where this principle seems to exist to the exclusion of any other aesthetic concern—selection implies attitude, commitment, and other forms of internal resolution.[13]

"The mere fact of projecting the image already qualifies the object, which becomes spectacle."[14] At the moment the framed lens is trained upon its object, all the expressive variables—such as distance and point of view—are brought to light. The creating subject is thus, from this moment on, inherently split. The camera lens, an artificial, manmade extension of the film-maker's eye, is endowed with the restrained objectivity, if not indifference, of the machine. It is the silent witness that transmits its "findings" to the spectator. It is certainly not the author of the film. In fact, no one, no thing in a film says "I" in the manner, say, of one of Thackeray's narrators. Yet it is the film-maker who has chosen the mimetic object, its spatial *découpage*, and the angle of vision from which the spectator sees it. At a later point it will be the film-maker—or one of several surrogates, such as the editor—who further manipulates the object by choosing its context, by ordering its syntagmatic development. Long before we come to the question of the "creating spectator," phenomenological clouds gather and blur the line between the creating machine and .the creating film-maker. The distinction that optics would probably like to maintain between

13. Herbert Read (see n. 5 above) maintains that selection is the very principle by which film achieves the status of art (p. 166).
14. Fernand Léger, "Essai critique sur la valeur plastique du film d'Abel Gance, *La Roue*," in *Fonctions de la peinture* (Paris, 1965; orig. in *Comédia* [1922]), p. 162.

visual *sensations* recorded and transmitted by a machine and the visual *perception* directed by the film-maker, simply does not hold up either at the moment of recording the image or during its ulterior manipulation. In the end, the film-maker can say, not simply along with Rimbaud that "Je est un autre," but also along with Mitry that "'I' is projected onto an other. This is then no longer, strictly speaking, an act of consciousness, but the act of a conscious participation. . . ."[15] Thus, the creating subject participates in the object, perhaps even becomes immersed in it, and in so doing charges the object with an "attitude," a visual configuration that reaches out to meet the consciousness of the spectator.[16]

D. *The Creating Subject: Spectator*

Though film viewing is often considered a prime example of passive art consumption, the spectator actually plays a crucial role in the passage from reality to its apprehension. His main task is the *construction* of a referential "real" world on the basis of the fragmentary images provided in the film. For this reason it is best to consider the spectator at the opposite and more or less qualitatively equivalent end of the creative process initiated by the creating artist—hence, the "creating spectator."[17] Among the perceptual activities included in the task of construction are: cognition of the spatial forms alluded to by each image; apprehension of the referential depth that arises from the movement within each shot; connection of sequences of images by mentally supplying what they skip over or by grasping the "idea" that their conflict engenders; and decoding of what might be called "immediate" visual messages, from signs of time passing (e.g., fade) to sociocultural symbols (e.g., a white hat for the "good guy" of classic westerns). These

15. *Esthétique*, 1:134.

16. See Eisenstein, "La Non-indifférente Nature: De la structure des choses," in *Cahiers du cinéma* 211 (Apr. 1969):13-16, for greater elaboration of the creating subject's "attitude."

17. Cf. Eisenstein: "In fact, every spectator . . . creates an image in accordance with the representational guidance suggested by the author. . . . This is the same image that was planned and created by the author, but this image is at the same time created also by the spectator himself." "Word and Image," *The Film Sense*, trans. Jay Leyda (New York, 1957), p. 33; cf. Morin, *Le Cinéma ou l'homme imaginaire*, p. 87.

functions can be considered prerequisites of the cinematic experience; we know that, historically and psychologically, a certain
apprenticeship of the eye preconditioned some of them. They
operate in the same vital way for filmic expression as do the prerequisites of linguistic communication; in other words, the emission
of a message remains impotent and in a way incomplete until it has
been taken in by a receiver.

The creating spectator is, like the film-maker, a *subject* in the
sense that he apprehends the artificially produced spatial configurations with the same perceptual, cognitive apparatus and conditioned
frames of reference that he would use to apprehend nature. Though
at a greater remove and with a different thrust, we find the same
objectification of self-consciousness in the perception of filmed
reality as in its realization. Totally committed apprehension of the
filmic image requires that the spectator direct his perceptual faculties entirely toward the outside. Cinematic apprehension is thus
an intensified instance of the general perception of externality:
"That object *of which* I am conscious does not exist *within* my
consciousness; it is a *donnée of* my consciousness, which is none
other than the perception itself, completed, realized."[18]

The spectator's self-consciousness practically disappears, then, in
the process of perceiving. It is important, however, to pinpoint
what is peculiar to cinematic perception. In the theatre, for example,
such a reduction of self-consciousness does not seem to occur.
Subject and object are part of the same living and playing space;
the distance, as well as the angle of vision, between the two remains
static, while in the film these spatial relations are extremely dynamic. "When living person is set before living person—actor before
spectator—a certain deliberate conventionalising is demanded of the
former if the aesthetic impression is not to be lost";[19] in the cinema,
the absence of an existential vis-à-vis reduces self-consciousness and
breaks down the conventional barriers associated with scenographic
representation. The disintegration of scenographic space in general,

18. Mitry, *Esthétique*, 1:114; Mitry's emphasis.
19. Allardyce Nicoll, "Film and Theatre," in R. D. MacCann, ed., *Film:
A Montage of Theories* (New York, 1966), p. 123; excerpted from *Film and
Theatre* (New York, 1936).

as in painting, tends to integrate the spectator into the creative process by the simple fact of alluding to the (imaginary) space outside the proscenium (or frame).

Furthermore, within the context of a live performance, mimetic objects of the theatre retain their essential differences (actors vs. props, or living consciousness vs. dead matter), while filmed actors and filmed objects become parts of the same permanently etched "performance," reminding the spectator that they are *not* present but absent. The presence/absence effect in cinema goes back to the basic ambiguity of distance separating subject and object. On the one hand, there is an obliteration of the static distance experienced in the theatre by virtue of the camera's ubiquitousness. But on the other hand, there is a fundamental, unalterable distance—like the aquarium glass that separates the observer from the fish—which, guaranteed by the existential absence of the mimetic objects, permits the spectator to observe without being observed. While in the theatre the spectator is basically a witness, in the cinema he is more of a voyeur.

It follows from these differences that the psychological processes of projection and identification are encouraged to a much greater extent in the cinema than in the theatre. "The psychological thrust of drama is not the identification of the spectator with the hero; on the contrary, it is indispensable to the aesthetic effect that the distance between them be kept as great as possible."[20] Projection and identification, which, Morin explains, should be considered as two complementary modes of a vast affective complex originating in the psychology of everyday life, are specifically "motorized" by the film.[21] The spectator *projects* his own aims and desires onto the hero of the film and, conversely, *identifies* with the motives and values embodied by the hero. These two processes quickly blend together in the dynamic system of "affective participation."

But apart from the high degree of affective participation that it gives rise to, we have yet to determine what is specifically cinematic in the eclipse of the spectator's self-consciousness. If we distinguish,

20. Magny (see n. 11 above), pp. 15–16.
21. Morin, *Le Cinéma*, pp. 74 and 87. For a thorough discussion of affective participation, see the whole of Morin's chap. 4: "L'âme du cinéma."

as Mitry does, between mental image and filmic image, the problem is clarified. The mental image exists *within* consciousness, independent of the stimulus object—or, in Mr. Ramsay's formulation, it's the image "of a kitchen table . . . when you're not there." Memory is, by its very nature, composed of mental images. The filmic image is the working double of a real object *outside* consciousness, the real object minus the substance.[22] As we have seen, when perception takes place, subject and object become mingled in such a way that consciousness is indistinguishable from the achieved act of perception. In other words, the mental image is indistinguishable from the retinal image until perception ceases and the image is stored away in the memory.

Now, in the movies the retinal image is constantly being furnished by the filmic image itself. The filmic image *becomes* the retinal image, insofar as the spectator's eye is identified with the lens of the camera. Hence, at every moment of filmic perception, but particularly at moments of high affective participation, *the filmic image replaces the mental image.*[23] By the same token, the subjectivity invested by the film-maker in the filmic image becomes indissolubly mixed with the subjectivity projected by spectator into that same image. A highly dynamic exchange of affectivities is thus established, whereby the cinema becomes "a system that tends to integrate the spectator into the flux of the film. A system that tends to integrate the flux of the film into the psychic flux of the spectator."[24]

From this point it is only a short step to making the further observation that the filmic image not only records the reality that was at one time before the camera: it also *imitates the process by which this reality is apprehended.*[25] In other words, the pattern of objects "perceived" by the camera automatically becomes the pattern

22. Mitry, *Esthétique,* 1:109-10.
23. Ibid., pp. 74-75 and 191. Hugo Münsterberg: "It is as if that outer world were woven into our mind and were shaped not through its own laws but by the acts of our attention." *The Film: A Psychological Study* (New York, 1970), p. 39; orig. *The Photoplay: A Psychological Study* (New York, 1916).
24. Morin, p. 87.
25. Cf. Morin, p. 102, and Mitry, *Esthétique*, 1:109. Cf. also Münsterberg, p. 41: "The photoplay [i.e., film] obeys the laws of the mind rather than those of the outer world."

perceived by the spectator. Narrative literature, of course, sometimes aims toward a similar effect of representation; we construct a mental image of such and such a character performing such and such an action. In the novel, however, the mental image (signified) is elicited by a verbal sign (signifier), itself an obvious abstraction far removed (in the present terms) from the filmic image;[26] the verbal sign is in no way a substitute for the mental image, but rather a vehicle toward it. In the film, on the other hand, signifier and signified are identical (the sign for a table *is* a table); hence the ease with which the filmic image becomes a substitute for the spectator's constantly fluctuating mental image.

With the idea that the spectator is visually furnished with the stuff, at once catalyst and substitute, of his perceptions, it would seem that we return to the popular notion of spectator passivity. This is not the case, however: the succession of filmic images controls only one part of the spectator's creating process, that part which is perceptual and, since it changes from moment to moment, linear: the syntagmatic part. Each filmic image—and now *just as* in language and literature—has, in addition, a potentially dynamic relation with every other image. For the spectator to carry out the task of construction, even at the most basic level, he must link, across time and within what is now his own reservoir of mental images, one image to another image that is not spatiotemporally adjacent. This second part of the spectator's creating process, which corresponds to the *reflexive* mental function, may be called paradigmatic. It calls on the spectator's memory to juxtapose with the presently perceived image other images that are in absentia (i.e., already mental images of the memory), in order to form a cognitive axis noncongruent with the syntagmatic axis.[27]

26. Cf. Metz's "five radical differences" between the filmic image and the verbal sign: "Problèmes de dénotation dans le film de fiction," *Essais*, p. 118.
27. Barthes, "Eléments de sémiologie," in *Le Degré zéro de l'écriture* (Paris, 1964), pp. 131-32. Cf. Saussure, *Cours de linguistique générale* (Paris, 1915, 1972), pp. 170-75.
Note that "syntagmatic" and "paradigmatic" are simply the linguistic

For example, it is a most common device of the cinema to present a moving train syntagmatically as follows: the rapidly turning wheels of the locomotive, a seated passenger looking out the window, the engineer at his throttle, and a close-up of tracks quickly disappearing into the foreground of the frame. This sequence is a most summary one; another might include these same shots dispersed throughout a long interlude between several passengers or between the engineer and the coal-stoker. In either case, however, the spectator establishes, by clustering together disparate images out of any number of shots, a paradigmatic ensemble of a moving train. Eisenstein refers to this primary distinction between syntagmatic and paradigmatic when he compares "the process of perceiving a work of art" to "the process of remembering": "there are two very essential stages: the first is the *assembling* of the image, while the second consists in the *result* of this assembly and its significance for the memory."[28]

In summary, the movie spectator *is supplied*, syntagmatically, with a filmic image, a substitute for his own mental image, though the spectator *supplies*, paradigmatically, a mental construct that associates images along various axes. The spectator is like a dreamer or a voyeur in that self-consciousness is reduced to a minimum and he easily projects some part of his mind, be it conscious or unconscious, onto the objects referred to by the filmic image. But unlike the dreamer, the spectator is not simply the passive observer: he retains the needed power to surmount the passing flux of images by applying his reflexive mind to their organization.[29] The movie spectator is

---

(and for the moment more analytically useful) terms for two mental activities (Saussure, p. 170): perception and reflection. These two mental functions, constantly at play in the cinematic experience, should not be confused with the "pre-reflexive" part of consciousness, or self-consciousness, which, as seen above, fades at the moment of the subject's perception, is absorbed in that perception.

28. *The Film Sense*, pp. 16–17; Eisenstein's emphasis.

29. Cf. Morin, pp. 127–32. Morin is, in general, the best source for an extensive bibliography on the relation of cinema to dreams and the unconscious. Recent contributions to this field of inquiry, which add a substantially new perspective on the question, include Thierry Kuntzel, "Le Travail du film," *Communications* 23 (1974) and "A Note Upon the Filmic Apparatus," *Quarterly Review of Film Studies* 1, no. 3 (Aug. 1976), and J.-L. Baudry, "The Apparatus," *Camera Obscura* 1 (Fall 1976).

also like a thinker, *if* we assume that the stuff of thought is images.[30] Bergson examined at some length the fundamental similarity between the thought process and the cinematic process.[31] Each successive mental image of the cognitive process is fixed, just as each successive filmic image is a photogram with fixed spatial relations, arrested for a split-second before the projecting lens; yet the thinker's impression is one of continuity of the thought, just as the spectator's is of continuity of the perception. But again, the movie spectator is ultimately unlike the thinker for the simple reason that, syntagmatically, he is provided with the otherwise self-generating mental image of thought.

30. This is by no means an easy assumption to make. Cf. Valéry's musings on the "source" of his thoughts and J. Derrida's commentary on these notebook entries in "Qual quelle," *Marges* (Paris, 1972), pp. 340–45.

Cf. also Sartre: "between image and thought there is not an opposition but simply the relation of a species to the genre that subsumes it. Thought takes on image-form when it wishes to be intuitive, when it wishes to establish its affirmations on the *vision* of an object before it, in order to *see* it, or even better, in order to *possess* it." *L 'Imaginaire* (Paris, 1940), p. 158; Sartre's emphasis.

31. "Le Mécanisme cinématographique de la pensée et l'illusion mécanistique . . .," in *L 'Evolution créatrice* (Paris, 1957; orig. 1907). It is important to note that Bergson uses the cinematic metaphor to show the *constraints* fostered by mechanistic epistemology.

4 From Film Technique to Novel Technique: Language and Narrative

At the end of chapter 1, I discussed how, during the impressionist era, the novel underwent important remodeling. It was, even at that time, a genre overburdened with conventions. Writers like James and Conrad, taking their cue from the earlier French "realist" tradition of Flaubert and Maupassant, sensed a need for the novel's total reorientation. Perhaps influenced by the prevailing doctrines of scientific causality, they posited a new relation between creating subject and created object. By means of a method that may have owed something to the impressionist painters, the emphasis was on showing the object rather than telling about it, on seeing it and making it seen. Since they insisted that their version of reality was more true to *lived* experience, to the interpenetration of present events with past memories, it was natural that they became interested in multiperspectivism: in the radical switching of point of view—even though the most fragmented vision at this period was still usually surmounted by a surface and a structure of cohesion (e.g., *Heart of Darkness, The Ambassadors*). Finally, their impatience with the stock responses established by conventional nineteenth-century fiction led them to emphasize the reader's participation in the elaboration of conceptual images.

It should be clear by this time that the earmarks of this new turn-of-the-century novel dovetail completely with those of the new film sensibility. The advent of the movies served to reinforce the anti-nineteenth-century bias of the radical novelists. Thriving in the midst of a new machine culture and the general change of heart associated with the *contre-décadence*, the movies necessarily took a proscientific, documentary attitude toward the object. All was visual, hence all was shown: rendered, not told. There were, of course, especially from about 1910, explicative titles; but these tended, except in the most blatantly literary cases, to establish a context for the action and to provide certain crucial links that the spectator was not yet accustomed to making.[1] In all cases, from the first Lumière clips forward, signifier and signified were simultaneously present and indivisible: the "fictional" world was immediate, just like the real world.

During this period of growing relativism in all fields, the movies demonstrated most graphically the effects of changing point of view. An object had to be presented from more than one viewpoint in order to suggest its total contour and, in certain cases, its direction of movement. The distance and angle of vision between the object and the camera further attentuated the establishment of anything resembling a fixed or authoritative point of view. So long as the simultaneity of multiple viewpoints was impossible (and cubism was accomplishing this in other arts), an object or action had to be rendered in discontinuous fragments that only in sequence and hence through time could be fully apprehended.

Apprehension, consequently, required from the outset, the active participation of the movie spectator (cf. above, chap. 3, sec. D). On the purely denotative level of understanding, a mass of convenances had to be accepted by the movie-goer before the shots that flashed before his eyes could make sense or assume the outline of a story. Logical leaps for economy's sake (ellipsis), allusion to events off the screen, outside the frame of reference (e.g., the passage of a train without a shot of the train in Chaplin's *A Woman of Paris*, 1923), dissection of the established space through the use of close-ups—all these effects and more demanded a rather sudden accommodation

1. Early films, as I suggested in the Introduction, also took on certain traits of the traditional novel, especially in the realms of morality and sentimentalism. The most obvious carry-overs from literature, such as a title reading "Meanwhile . . . ," demonstrate, on the one hand, a slightly delayed action in the cinema's becoming fully aware of its own potentials and, on the other hand, the contemporary difficulty of separating narrative from its specifically literary ties.

on the part of spectator, like the perceptual adjustments required of untutored medieval readers who were at first unable to connect the units of writing. The spectator's task was not simply to see what was being shown to him more vividly than ever before, but also to see what was being revealed purely by implication.

The spectator's acquired ability to perceive and retain a total spatial entity by means of the image of a part only, like the rhetorical process known as synecdoche, has been interpreted by some as the foundation for all the other aspects of this visual apprenticeship and one that explains the movie spectator's unique position vis-à-vis the art object.[2]

Common to all these new perspectives by which the movies nourished certain iconoclastic tendencies of the modern novelist was the technique of montage. In a great deal of writing on montage, what is emphasized is the disjunctive, nonsequential nature of the two or more shots joined together. Eisenstein himself stresses the gap between two assembled shots and the conflict that their juxtaposition ought to engender. These descriptions are all perfectly accurate; but they neglect the inevitable continuity imposed on the film at the time of its projection and viewing. When two shots, mutually illogical, unconnected, or even contradictory, are brought together in the film, the automatic and relentless flow of images forces at least the appearance of sequence. There is no such thing as a non sequitur in the movies.

Even in films that seek to challenge our expectations about continuity, like Buñuel's *Chien andalou*, we sense the power of the film's relentless flow. The sole difference is the opaqueness of interrelationship that results in such a film. In the sequence in which the major male figure reveals the insect-infested wound on his palm to the female protagonist, the montage sequence is carried along not in the least by the laws of cause and effect but rather by a vaguely connoted notion of sexual impropriety, perhaps a metaphorical externalization of the man's thoughts. The woman's consternation at seeing the wound is transformed into outright scandal when the

2. Cf. Robert Scholes's notion of "narrativity," more or less similar to what I have been referring to as spectator participation, in "Narration and Narrativity in Film," *Quarterly Review of Film Studies* 1, no. 3 (Aug. 1976):283–96.

man wipes the palm across his mouth, which becomes healed shut and encircled by hair. Beside herself, the woman looks under her arm to discover the hair gone from her armpit.

Of even greater consequence in such an experimental film is the imagistic matching that carries over from other sequences, like the prickly sea urchin, which suggests that whatever tentativeness is involved in making the connections here will be graphically resolved or reinforced at another point. In other terms, such films rely almost exclusively on erratically formed paradigmatic axes which, far more than the syntagmatic or linear axis, hold the work together.

Thus, the spectator may bring any degree of cognitive or psychological resistance to a film, and yet the image track will constantly seem to be asserting that all follows, as demonstrated by the Kuleshov experiment, discussed below. This primary antinomy of film experience, which can only be called discontinuous continuity, explains the ease of switching cinematic point of view, the virtual disappearance of the need for author or narrator, and the consequential shifting to the spectator of the burden of forging the connective links.

Before moving on to the specific means by which cinema was to serve as object of inspirational predilection for the novel, it would be useful to reclarify the pertinence of the choices made amid the tremendously diverse cultural phenomena of this period. I have entitled this whole section "Convergence" because my major purpose is to detail, at both the historical and theoretical levels, the palpitating openness, formally, of nearly all the arts during this heyday of relativism which characterizes the late nineteenth and early twentieth centuries. Forms and genres within specific arts converge, and arts converge with one another as well. How can one do justice to this period, it may be asked however, without analyzing the *Sacre du printemps*, Schoenberg's twelve-tone row, the stage sets of Meyerhold and Piscator, and paintings by Picasso, Braque, Léger? Why should one privilege, in other words, the relation between cinema and literature when the "convergence" alluded to is by no means restricted to these two fields of artistic activity?

In comparison with other artistic cross-fertilizations of the modern period, such as the yoking of verbal text and plastic configuration by the surrealists and Klee or the use of film clips by Brecht, the convergence of cinema and novel is at once more pervasive and more typical. More typical because, in fact, the actual mixtures of arts have been rareties, seemingly doomed, no matter how daring, to the history of artistic curiosities. Even cinema, as I have argued elsewhere, will not permit of straight literary emulation, for fear of betraying its own specificity.[3] The more common, and yet far more difficult to define, phenomenon is the formal mimickry and outright borrowing whereby one art will suddenly leap into the mode of another or demonstrate an apparently incongruous yearning for the qualities of that other art. The convergence focused on here is also more pervasive because it deals with the two most popular arts of the last three hundred years. As will become clear, the capacities for language and narrative evident, albeit in very different ways, in novel and cinema, provide the conditions for speaking of this special convergence as exemplary. Furthermore, it is hoped that the very typicality and pervasiveness of this convergence, far from throwing other such phenomena unduly into shadow, will serve as model for the abundant research that still needs to be done in the general field of cross-art affinities.

The idea that through discontinuity a more dynamic continuity can be achieved is perhaps the cornerstone of twentieth-century art. We see it in the paintings of the cubists and futurists, in the music of Debussy and Stravinsky, in the poetry of the imagists, of Eliot, of Apollinaire, and in all forms of surrealist art. It is also at the very root of the "classic" modern novel.[4] "The discontinuity

3. "Eisenstein's Subversive Adaptation," in *The Classic American Novel and the Movies*, ed. Peary and Shatzkin (New York, 1977), esp. pp. 255-56.
4. By "classic" modern novel, I mean, historically, the novel of the 1910s and 1920s in Europe and America. The form of this novel, as is generally agreed today, although posited on an aesthetic of radical experimentation, can be spoken of as fully evolved. As a result, we can sketch the technical parameters of the classic modern, very much in the manner that Barthes sketches those of the classic nineteenth-century novel or Metz those of the classic Hollywood film, by restricting the field of reference to a set number of conventions, codes, or fields of activity. The contention here and in the next section will be that the technical capacities of the classic modern novel take on sharpest definition when considered against the backdrop of cinematic innovation.

of the plot and the scenic development, the sudden emersion of the thoughts and moods, the relativity and the inconsistency of the time standards, are what remind us in the works of Proust and Joyce, Dos Passos, and Virginia Woolf of the cuttings, dissolves and interpolations of the film, and it is simply film magic when Proust brings two incidents, which may lie thirty years apart, as closely together as if there were only two hours between them."[5] Joseph Frank notes the same sort of discontinuous continuity in describing the "spatial form" of the modern novel.[6] In order for the reader to put together the elements of narration and character portrayal, often presented discontinuously (i.e., by breaking up the traditional chronological flow of time), he must establish a continuity in his own mind, reflexively. Hence the notion of "reflexive reference," whereby the discrete threads and levels of narration are brought together by the reader in an instant of time, as if they were fleshed out before him, spatially composed.

In fact, the growing modern need to *posit* continuity over the increasing discontinuity and fragmentation of experience might be seen to transcend literature and art altogether (without, however, receiving any better formulations from other sources). Hans Meyerhoff has pointed out the persistence with which philosophers, from Kant and his "transcendental unity of apperception," to Bergson who took over Leibniz's definition of the self as "unity within multiplicity," to Whitehead and other modern "rationalists," have wished to establish a unity of selfhood by assuming the interpenetration of time and self.[7]

The montage sense, which can be very generally defined as continuity out of discontinuity, forms a conceptual basis to many of these developments in modern thought and artistic creation. The most innovative and ultimately influential techniques of the movies all proceed from the montage principle, especially insofar as the physical process of montage exploits the fundamental interdependence of space and time (cf. above, chap. 3, sec. A). The very event that gave rise to the first forms of montage resulted from an acci-

5. Arnold Hauser, *The Social History of Art*, 4:244.
6. "Spatial Form in Modern Literature," *Sewanee Review* 53 (1945):230 ff.
7. *Time in Literature* (Berkeley, 1955), pp. 35-37.

dental tampering with cinematic time. Before Méliès's discovery at
the Place de l'Opéra in 1896, the cinematograph (which was precisely for this reason not yet the motion-picture camera, as Edgar
Morin explains) consistently recorded external events in terms of
chronological time, continuously, like a stage play, without gap or
incision.[8] The famous accident occurred when Méliès's camera
jammed for a minute and then continued running as before. The
rushes showed images of people, carriages, and horses that were
suddenly, at the point of mechanical failure, transformed into
other images because of the lag in time. This incident led, in the
short run, to all of Méliès's disappearing tricks on the screen and, in
the long run, to much wider application of the stop-camera technique, which automatically created a discrepancy between chronological and referential time. No narrative progression was possible
so long as the camera lens was trained on one set of people and
objects and the celluloid kept rolling without a halt.[9] (Hence, the
"single-event," essentially documentary quality of early film-strips:
a train coming into a station, an acrobat act, the coronation of a
queen.) Once the camera was intentionally stopped, chronological
time no longer corresponded exactly to referential time, once
absence and allusion entered into combination with the transcription
of presence, then was narration possible. Thus, film negates its
regulatory chronological time so as to present a diegetic sequence
in time.

From this negation of time, a function of the stop-camera technique, proceed the many tamperings with diegetic time that were
to prove so inspiring to artists of other media. Fast- and slow-
motion, reverse motion (as in Lumière's *Charcuterie mécanique*)
dramatically demonstrated the crucial dependence of filmic time on
the spatiality of its hardware, the way in which filmic time can be
"reduced to the level of a dimension analogous to space."[10] The

8. Méliès, excerpt from *Les Vues cinématographiques* (1907), in M. L'Herbier, ed., *L'Intelligence du cinématographe* (Paris, 1946), p. 186. Morin
discusses the event in *Le Cinéma ou l'homme imaginaire*, pp. 48-49.
9. Cf. André Malraux, "Esquisse d'une psychologie du cinéma," in L'Herbier; orig. in *Verve*, 1941.
10. J. Epstein, quoted in Morin, p. 54, where Lumière's *Charcuterie* is also
mentioned.

most significant of these means of undoing chronological time was
Eisenstein's "expansion of time" in the *Battleship Potemkin* (1925).
A sailor on kitchen patrol comes upon a plate marked "Give us this
day our daily bread" and throws it against the table in a rage. This
single action is of paramount importance to the film's general development, because it marks the beginning of a defiant resoluteness
in all the sailors that leads to mutiny and ultimately to the 1905
revolution. By filming it many times from different angles and then
editing so that the fragments of each one of the angles overlap
one another by a number of frames according to the unitary time of
the action, Eisenstein presents an impression of a split-second
act that lasts for many seconds on the screen. He shows the same
action from many different points of view without either stopping
or wholly repeating the action. This technique thus reveals, formally, a profound kinship with earliest attempts to chart motion:
the external action is left intact and the recording is at once syn-
chronized (i.e., movement for movement: cf. Marey) and serialized
(cf. Muybridge). Insofar as the spectator has the feeling of being
not simply in front of the sailor but all around him at once, expansion of time represents the closest cinematic approximation of
cubism. It exploits the spatiality of the filmic medium to distort
its temporality.

Spatial distortion, like the negation of temporal linearity, can be
considered a residual effect of montage. The compression of time
is an inevitable side-effect of any edited jump through space; and,
in the same manner, as a result of this seeming ubiquity of the
movie camera, two places, miles or even continents apart, can be
yoked together and space suddenly shrinks. Other specific techniques of spatial disorientation, such as shortening or lengthening
the standard 25 cm. lens length and tampering with "normal"
depth of field, serve further to throw off conventional point of
view and perspective.

The one technique that seems to incorporate many of those
mentioned above has been variously called parallel editing, cross-
cutting, and (by Metz) "syntagme alterné." These terms refer to
the juxtaposition of two or more spatially noncontiguous sequences
by alternating segments cut from each one. The most celebrated

example of parallel editing is Griffith's *Intolerance* (1916). Here, we move in discontinuous fashion from one of four time-spaces to another: decadent Babylon, the Passion of Christ, persecution of the Huguenots in sixteenth-century France, and the modern-day drama of struggling strikers and an innocent man sentenced to death. Each parallel story acts as a giant metaphor, or analogy, to the other, the major paradigmatic thrust being, of course, to demonstrate the universality of intolerance and prejudice. Under ordinary circumstances, cinema cannot, any more than literature, present simultaneously two noncontiguous, noncoterminous events. Parallel editing, however, is the technique that most nearly achieves this effect.

If the negation of chronological time was necessary for the advent of montage and the most primitive sequence of events, then we might say that parallel editing and the accompanying idea of going back in diegetic time were necessary for the advent of a full-scale cinematic narrative. Most dissimilar from literature in this respect, where narrativity was for ages considered in mainly linear lerms, the cinema seems to have arrived at narrativity *through* the concept of simultaneity. This observation follows from our definition of the movies' fundamental mode of existence: i.e., simultaneity led to truly cinematic (as opposed to theatrical) mise-en-scène because it translates the interdependence of space and time into a unified, seemingly continuous dimension.[11] The method of simultaneity, then, rather than the cinema itself, is the artistic expression of the "space-time continuum."

The intrinsic nature and specific techniques of the cinema: standardization of mimetic objects, temporal distortion, shifting point of view, and discontinuous continuity, were applicable and ultimately transferrable to the novel in very concrete ways (as will be seen in the next section). The assertion of such an exchange

11. See A. Einstein, "On the Electrodynamics of Moving Bodies," in *The Principle of Relativity*, trans. W. Perrett and G. B. Jeffery (London, 1923), pp. 40-43. Einstein's definition of the "'time' of an event," for which he posits two synchronous clocks, one at the place of the event and one at another place, depends on the concept of simultaneity, or the codetermination of time and space; this concept, however, has "*absolute* signification" only with reference to a single "stationary system."

of artistic potentials, however, requires further investigation into the systems of relationships theoretically held in common by novel and film.

The fundamental difference between novel and film, which superficially makes them seem worlds apart, is that between written word and visual image. The first way of bridging this apparently limitless gap is by considering both word and image as signs aimed at communicating something. In this sense, word and image are each part of a larger system of signification—part of a *language*.

That the novel puts human phonological language to use is no outlandish assertion. But when it comes to the cinema, the problem is not so simple. Eisenstein, as early as 1929, tried to effect a rapprochement between the two "languages" by considering their mutual "concreteness."[12] To demonstrate the similarity, he used the Japanese ideogram as the example of written language and as median link between linguistic construction and montage. In this system of word-pictures, it is indeed possible to discern a certain concreteness by which graphically depicted figures yield intangible actions or concepts. Thus, the combination of two graphic representations "of the simplest series is to be regarded not as their sum, but as their product, i.e., as a value of another dimension, another degree." Eisenstein provides examples: the picture for water plus the picture for eye means "to weep"; dog + mouth = "to bark." By its similarity to montage, the juxtaposition process in the ideogram is "exactly what we do in cinema, combining shots that are *depictive*, single in meaning, neutral in content—into *intellectual* contexts and series."[13]

Such a rapprochement works out only on the basis of a highly *imagistic* language such as the hieroglyphic system of ideograms. If we consider the modern occidental languages in which the novels to be considered are written, we find the parallel doesn't hold up.

12. "A Dialectic Approach to Film Form" (1929), *Film Form*, trans. Jay Leyda (New York, 1957), p. 60. Theatre should not be considered ruled out of such a discussion. In fact, Eisenstein traces his own developing awareness of the functioning of montage as part of film language to performances in Moscow of the Kabuki theatre. See "The Unexpected," in *Film Form*.

13. "The Cinematic Principle and the Ideogram" (1929), *Film Form*, pp. 29-30; Eisenstein's emphasis.

This is primarily because phonological language possesses a "double articulation": a limited number of abstract signs, discrete units (phonemes) that are meaningless in themselves, which, in combination, go to make up a vast number of words or meaningful units (morphemes). Signifier and signified are, by definition, separate and distinct in written language, literary or otherwise. However, they are, as we have seen, simultaneous in the cinema: hence "single articulation."[14] In other words, while the sign *table* elicits different mental images for different readers, the filmic image of a table results in the same mental image for every spectator.

The fact remains, however, that in each case a mental image is created. Both novel and cinema *refer* to, or at least *evoke*, some global configuration that is summoned up by the receiver of their messages. The cinema composes bits and pieces of the outside world that function very differently in that world, in much the same way the novel composes words that function as utilitarian means of communication outside the work of art. In other words, the image comes into the film bearing the mark of the outside world, just as the word comes into the novel bearing the mark of verbal language and etymological history.[15] Unlike music and architecture, novel and cinema are consistently referential; they are "by nature condemned to *connotation*, since denotation always comes *before* their artistic enterprise."[16]

And it is precisely because novel and cinema, considered now primarily as artistic expressions, are rich in connotations that the

14. On the problem of articulation, in this linguistic sense, see Christian Metz, *Essais sur la signification au cinéma* (chap. 3, n.4), pp. 67-68, n. 2, and 117-19. Umberto Eco maintains that the cinema has not simply a double but a triple articulation: "Sémiologie des messages visuels," *Communications* 15 (1970):41-49.

15. Cf. David Lodge: "the writer's medium differs from the media of most other arts—pigment, stone, musical notes, etc.—in that it is never virgin: words come to the writer already violated by other men, impressed with meanings derived from the world of common experience." *Language of Fiction* (New York, 1966), p. 47.

16. Metz, *Essais*, 1:80; his emphasis. Metz goes on to sharpen this basic comparison: "literature is an art of heterogeneous connotation (expressive connotation on top of non-expressive denotation), whereas cinema is an art of homogeneous connotation (expressive connotation on top of expressive denotation)" (p. 82).

difference of motivation in their signs is minimized. Even though the written sign *table* requires an extra mental step toward "visualization," as compared to the filmic image of a table, the signs for *school desk, operating table,* or *banquet table*—whether written or visual signs—are each capable of triggering vastly different connotations for a given reader or viewer. This connotative process is really no more controllable in one art than the other. While the filmic image may seem to specify its image content with greater control and insistence, the immediate context of a given literary image similarly molds and determines the spectrum of possible connotations. Though the filmic image is *there* before the eyes, it soon disappears and eventually, blended with personal associations and connotations, occupies the same domain as the literary image: the memory. Thus, the syntagmatic process of perception may be more immediate in the cinema, but the paradigmatic process of mental linkage and recollection is the same for both cinema and novel.

Written language and cinematic language, then, though in certain respects diverging and operating at cross-purposes, run a close parallel on the level of artistic expression. On this level we must distinguish the novel from the ideological tract or essay, for example, and the fiction film from the documentary or propaganda film. According to this distinction, written language and cinematic language do not aim at communicating utilitarian messages or at precipitating a dialogue in the bilateral manner of ordinary conversation. They rather express or represent their messages in a communication void, without signals as to how these messages will be received.

There is still a stumbling block to this rapprochement of novel and cinema on the basis of their language properties—a stumbling block that arises, again, from the fact that literary language is founded on a specific, idiosyncratic *langue*, while film constitutes a "langage sans langue."[17] The *langue* furnishes literary language with syntactic rules that, to a greater or lesser extent depending on period and author, condition its formation. The film is subject to

17. Ibid., p. 70. The film, for example, "is always like a book, never like a conversation" (p. 86).

no such inherent rules of composition. We might work around this objection by simply saying, as above, that the film organizes bits of the world just as the novel organizes bits of a particular *langue*. But obviously, the organization is far more predetermined in the novel than in the film. Metz, working on the basis of a rough similarity between the shot and the written phrase, meets the objection by proposing a "grande syntagmatique":[18] all cinematic shots, according to this theory, can be classified into eight different syntagmas, just as literary language can be broken down, for example, into narrative, descriptive, singulative, or iterative phrases.

Still, the organization of syntagmas seems much freer in the cinema (and it is precisely this freedom of composition, real or apparent, that was to inspire the novelist). Two experiments will demonstrate this. The first is Kuleshov's experiment of juxtaposing alternately with the passive face of an actor, various images, such as a steaming bowl of soup, a revolver, a half-naked woman, in order to demonstrate that, in each case, the montage creates a meaning (hunger, fear, desire) without further cinematic explanation. The second is the surrealist word-game, called "Le Cadavre Exquis," in which a group of people pass around a folded piece of paper, each writing a different word on the successive fold without conscious reference to the preceding words, and ending up with a bizarre, patchwork sentence. In the surrealist game, however, each participant is assigned a part of speech in the sequence of normal sentence order: noun, verb, object. In other words, literary sentences can be ready-made or communally made only when the syntactic rules are followed. Cinematic sequences depend on no such convention.

But once we have made this distinction, we come to the more profound significance of these experiments and the more important unity that lies behind novel and cinema. If cinema lacks the precise syntax of literary language, it nonetheless shares with phonological language in general an essential temporal succession. Over and above the specific problem of cataloguing syntagmatic possibilities, novel and cinema are similar in their sequentialization of

18. "Problèmes de dénotation . . . ," ibid., pp. 125–46; orig. in much abbreviated form (with only six syntagmas) as "La Grande Syntagmatique du film narratif," in *Communications* 8 (1966).

discrete units. The randomness common to the Kuleshov and surrealist experiments points to the fundamental and seemingly inevitable *narrativity* of cinematic and literary language. In each case
a little story is told, or at least begun: "This man is hungry"; "Le
cadavre exquis boira du vin nouveau."

Indeed, narrativity is the most solid median link between novel
and cinema, the most pervasive tendency of both verbal and visual
languages. In both novel and cinema, groups of signs, be they literary
or visual signs, are apprehended consecutively through time; and this
consecutiveness gives rise to an unfolding structure, the diegetic
whole, that is never fully *present* in any one group yet always
implied in each such group.

Thus, while the expressive material of the novel—the sequence
of verbal phrases that make up the narrative—is decidedly different
from that of the cinema, the reverse is the case when it comes to
the diegesis. The cinematic narrative is constructed out of an immediate space and time that are shown in dynamic interaction
through the movement of the mimetic objects and the movement of
the camera amidst and around them. The sequential passage of the
film is governed by the electrically timed projecting mechanism.
The narrative of the (traditional) novel forsakes space altogether
—just as do most literary forms. It is governed, rather, by the temporality of phonological language. Yet if novel and cinema are both
possessed of narrativity, then they both produce a diegesis, or, put in
the simplest terms, they both tell a story. It is in the nature of
narrative to produce a succession of diegetic images (by no means
synchronic with the succession of the narrative itself) in the mind of
the viewer or reader. To apprehend a story, the perceiver must
construe for himself spatial images that succeed one another in time.
Thus, though in the cinema the telling is accomplished essentially in
spatial terms and in the novel in temporal terms, the story in both
cinema and novel unfolds along imaginary coordinates of space and
time supplied by the spectator or reader.

It is in terms of this interior space and time that imaginary events
are recalled as having happened and fictional characters never cease
to exist. And it is, no doubt, on the basis of this similarity of diegetic production that the perennial temptation to adapt novels to the
cinema arises.

Owing to the historically predominant visual element in cinema, *narrative space* determines the progression of the diegesis to a far greater extent than in the conventional novel, where such a category could only refer to the typographical layout of words and paragraphs. Yet the "spatiality" of the modern novel (cf. note 6) may, in this sense, owe more to the cinematic precedence than to any other single phenomenon.

A specific example of the cinema's dependence on spatial elaboration for its narrative strategies may be seen in Jean Epstein's *Fall of the House of Usher* (1926). This experimental film maintains a fairly coherent diegetic development in spite of its many film tricks, employing narrative space both to propel its story as well as to digress from it. Following the Poe story in its main lines only, Epstein begins the film by inserting a whole sequence entirely absent from Poe's original: Roderick's visitor at the inn. One of the striking elements in Poe is the exclusion of all persons other than the major characters, Roderick, Madeline, the visitor, and the doctor. It might therefore seem, at first glance, that Epstein introduces the local gentry at the inn in order to prepare us, through their horrified reactions to the word *Usher*, for the grim story about to unfold. Or else, to set a thoroughly familiar, secure image at the inn as contrast to the awesomely unfamiliar, *unheimlich* events to follow.

But, while these effects are surely there in the opening sequence, Epstein's major concern seems, rather, to elaborate a certain spatial principle which, both in its form and in its implications about the uncanny relations among things, will inform the succeeding in a far more fundamental way. To begin with, our first views of the visitor at close range are disturbingly fragmented. After the first establishing shot of him walking across the moor, the second shot presents him from the shoulders down, stopping to put his bags down for a moment. The fifth presents only his hands being rubbed together, as though from the cold. Let us note, before even commenting on this dramatic truncation of the first human figure we see, that the visitor's arrival at the inn is in itself insufficiently explained. It remains unclear how he has gotten to the desolate spot where we discover him. His initial existence is simply a given. Even after we glance over his shoulder at the letter from Roderick, we are allowed to distinguish, as motivation for his trip here, only the

From Jean Epstein's *La Chute de la maison Usher.*
Courtesy of the Museum of Modern Art Film Archives.

words *Madeline* and *malade*. In a sense, this is all we shall need to know for what follows, but Roderick's urging of him to pay a visit, clearly stated in Poe, is left out, or rather, not discernible.

Once the visitor arrives at the inn, we are presented with a place that defies clear spatial orientation. The entire sequence is composed almost exclusively of medium shots or close-ups. There is not a single establishing shot either outside or inside the inn. One can deduce roughly three diegetic spaces: the area near the door where the visitor converses with the innkeeper, the table where two old men are playing dominos, and the other table against a wall where a third man is stretched out. The first space is related to the other two by eye-line matches between the innkeeper and his various clients. This is enough to tell us at least that they are all part of the same interior. But otherwise all three form so many *floating spaces*, counteracting the conventional notions of closeness and interrelated- ness associated with an inn. The extreme of this impression is given when the innkeeper's wife or helper, who has previously appeared near the door seeming to offer tea to the visitor, backs down a hall- way, suggested by a narrow funnel of light, and disappears. In this sole long shot of the entire sequence, the woman is literally swallowed up by the narrow space.

The space of the inn, then, far from bringing these minor charac- ters together in an atmosphere of the familiar, separates and alienates them, cutting them off from one another in a manner analogous to the truncation of the visitor in the opening shots. As the visitor leaves in the carriage, the same woman watches furtively from two windows of the inn. The windows are close to the ground, yet all we see is her face, first on the right, then on the left, and finally in ex- treme close-up. We are left with an impression of the inn as a place that swallows up its occupants in its floating spaces and traps them there like patients in an asylum, sensing the horror of Usher before it happens.

This motif of entrapment, entombment, then, is very clearly pertinent to the story of Madeline. Her inability to be close to Roderick in any way other than that of the model's physical proxim- ity to the painter, results, it would seem, in her otherwise inexplicable death and premature entombment. The preliminary depiction of a claustrophobic, voracious space links up with later scenes surround-

From Jean Epstein's *La Chute de la maison Usher.*
Courtesy of the Museum of Modern Art Film Archives.

From Jean Epstein's *La Chute de la maison Usher*.
Courtesy of the Museum of Modern Art Film Archives.

ing Madeline's burial: the descent into the crypt, the nailing of the coffin, the shots of the pendulum inside the clock. And Madeline's eventual return from the tomb causes, metaphorically, the physical destruction of the House of Usher.

The important point here is that Epstein's film employs narrative space in a way that leads us away from strict diegetic development. Yet in so doing, the spatial digressions act as a powerful metaphorical emblem of the very diegetic development we will witness.

Diegetic time in both novel and cinema is always based on an illusion of temporality. In the cinema, however, congruence with anything like normal chronological rendering is ruled out from the start, since, as we have seen (above, pp. 84-85), diegetic action must be "negated"—that is, cut, deleted, or reversed before the film can begin to tell a story. In the cinema, in other words, temporal distortion is more palpable, more fundamental to the medium, and as such sets a powerful precedence for the experimental novel.

The ease with which the cinema can baffle the spectator expecting an immediately consumable temporal organization is perhaps nowhere clearer than in *Last Year at Marienbad* (1961). In Resnais's and Robbe-Grillet's film about persuasion and recollection, we are presented with no clear-cut rules for combining the sequences, which at first glance seem to have nothing in common save the abstractly denoted characters, X, A, and M—like so many algebra problems awaiting solution. Conventional continuity cues do not come to the aid of the viewer: A's dress changes without any predictable consistency—even within what appears to be a single sequence; pan shots, which by their nature usually signify a "real" homogeneous space, embrace logical impossibilities, such as the pan that begins with X disappearing from the left and ends with X reappearing mysteriously on the right;[19] and X's voice, which seems to be narrating a discrete,

19. *Last Year at Marienbad* (New York, 1962), pp. 52–53.

The illustrations on pages 99–102 from the film *L'Année dernière à Marienbad* are reproduced by courtesy of Macmillan Audio Brandon Films.

unified event in the past, entertains no stable relation to the image, as when it describes A shutting the door as we witness her leaving it ajar (pp. 124–25).

Robbe-Grillet has, in conversation, admitted to the psychological interpretation the film seems to invite yet, in print, insists that it would be wrong to posit any prior or future existence for X and A.

> The universe in which the entire film occurs is, characteristically, that of a perpetual present which makes all recourse to memory impossible. This is a world without a past, a world which is self-sufficient at every moment and which obliterates itself as it proceeds. This man, this woman begin existing only when they appear on the screen the first time; before that they are nothing; and, once the projection is over, they are again nothing. Their existence lasts only as long as the film lasts.[20]

Hence, we are left with the task of disentangling the temporal relations within the narrative as presented. And nothing is more characteristic of such a task than the experience of discovering a seemingly continuous thread of diegetic action, which is then rendered inconsistent with later images, or else downright contradicted. For, as

20. *For a New Novel*, trans. Richard Howard (New York, 1965), p. 152.

anyone knows who is familiar with Robbe-Grillet's art, innumerable traps lie in wait for the unsuspecting viewer. First of all, repetition, which traditionally functions to anchor the fictive universe through insistence and reduplication, has here precisely the opposite function. Events return at moments that seem least likely, thus destroying our mental construction of them when they first occurred: the breaking of A's shoe out in the garden, for example, or X in the shooting gallery. Cause-and-effect, motivation, recall—the very stuff of traditional fiction—have no place here. Each moment, as Robbe-Grillet's description suggests, is a new beginning, which destroys itself, leaving the field (both the diegetic field and the viewer's perceptual field) wide open for the ensuing moment.

This principle of nonprogression within a generally achronological framework is most evident in the structural loop that playfully ties together the beginning and end. After the dreamy opening series of pans that lead us into the small theatre for the production of *Rosmersholm*, we settle down almost comfortably into the play within the film. The final moment of the performance is preceded by a single artificial sound effect, the tinkling of a bell, upon which the actress delivers her final lines, "Maintenant, je suis à vous." Needless to say, this motif of the woman who finally gives in to the man is tightly bound up with the drama between X and A that is to follow.

The play, one might say, is a dramatic representation of the crux of what little plot we can discern—before the fact. In the final sequence of the film, at which point, from all we have gathered, A does seem prepared to give in to X (though it remains unclear whether this is happening now or being told to A by X as having already happened last year), we hear the same tinkling of the bell. Eager for such clear-cut diegetic cues, we are compelled to place this moment in time alongside the opening moments of the film. But in that case, when did all the intervening "events" of the narrative take place? And furthermore, since the camera showed us both X and A as spectators in the little theatre, how can they be simultaneously preparing to leave the hotel? In view of such questions, the only possible conclusion to draw is that, first, the intervening "events" have no durational substance, remain in an uncomfortable no-man's-land between already and just about—in other words, in the constantly obliterated present, which is the celluloid itself; and second, X and A can and must have the ability to occupy two different places at once. They are physically here and mentally there. As one speaks to the other, he or she is in the process of insinuating one version of a past (which we never see, of course, in toto) into the other's imagination. It is perhaps this dual process of persuasion, along with Resnais's refusal to differentiate between experiencing presence and hypothesized

imagining, that begins to explain the incessant time-shift that virtually defines the film's articulation.

What might be tentatively asserted, then, is that the film is a rendering of a generalized, half-conscious, half-unconscious state of affairs. X can only lend a seemingly logical coherence to the conscious half—and since nearly all is filmed with the same degree of visual verisimilitude, the same degree of presence, it is impossible to label any one shot as definitively conscious or unconscious. Perhaps even those scenes where the phsyical being-there of X or A seems most strongly marked, are actually fantasies of one or the other. In any love affair, in any love act, there is a shared unconscious that can never be accounted for. *Last Year at Marienbad* attempts to suggest that shared unconscious, that plurality of imaginaries.

It might seem implausible to cite *Marienbad* as an illustration of filmic narrative, when in fact it is mainly notable for its rule-breaking narration. Yet it would be wrong to construe from the foregoing an argument for the *necessarily* narrative character of film. Narrative has simply been the historically dominant form the film has taken, for important cultural and technical reasons. *Marienbad* marks the point at which cinema was able to cast aside all but the vestiges of traditional narrative structure in order to create a fiction by radically new means (repetition, temporal inconsistency, "impossible" spaces). In this sense, this film corresponds roughly in the history of the movies to the radical novels of Joyce, Woolf, and Proust in the 1920s, since, like the writers, Resnais has rejected the prevailing codes of representation in preference for as yet unclassifiable techniques that were nonetheless to be systematically exploited by the New Wave.

A rich and vast field of research opens up once we consider this seminal period of mutual artistic awareness occupied in the 1950s and 1960s by the *nouveau roman* and the *nouvelle vague*. The New Novel's emphasis on the visual, on the descriptive, and on the present unfolding of action brings to mind irresistibly a cinematic sensibility. The New Wave, in turn, directs its attention to isolated objects in a way immediately reminiscent of the New Novel. More fundamentally, both of these new forms turn their backs on conventional means of storytelling and opt for various kinds of set pieces, collage composition, and repetition. Godard and Robbe-Grillet, for example, so different in terms of subject matter, compose according to similar structural principles. If we juxtaposed *Jealousy* and *Weekend*, we could note a similar habit of yoking two pieces of narrative together on the basis of an auditory correspondence rather than on the basis of cause-and-effect or spatial contiguity. *La Maison de rendez-vous* could be compared to *2 ou 3 Choses que je sais d'elle* on the basis of how in each work the stereotypes of mass media and bourgeois consumer culture are aped only to distort them, to prevent them from facilitating the slick functioning of society's discourse and the false consciousness it propagates. The aesthetics of the New Novel, then, I would emphasize, opens another whole area of potential investigation, the first steps of which have been suggested by Jean Ricardou.[21]

Dynamic narrative space and an infinite potential for temporal distortion, then, are the two basic characteristics of filmic narration that will serve as a powerful influence on the postcinematic novelists. In the next chapters I shall examine how the literary sign undergoes some important changes in the hands of twentieth-century

21. *Problèmes du nouveau roman* (Paris, 1967), *Pour une théorie du nouveau roman* (Paris, 1971).

experimenters. Assuming that, at a certain level of abstraction, the language properties of both media are comparable, and that, regardless of the sign by which it is communicated, narrative units can be classified across media,[22] I shall describe one of the most powerful galvanizations of artistic affinities in the twentieth century.

22. Cf. Claude Bremond, "Le Message narratif," *Communications* 4 (1964): 31-32.

PART II / EXCHANGE

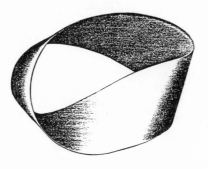

Introduction: Cinematic Form in the Novel

Although the specificity of cinematic narrative was implicit, if not entirely palpable, from the first days of montage, it took film makers some time to forsake the dramaturgical, scenographic approach of the theatre, where image is always predominant over sequentialization of images. Even Méliès, to whom has been attributed the discovery of the montage principle, was never able to give up the proscenium of the magic show and an ordering of materials based around the idea of the *tableau vivant*. The great lesson to be learned in the formative years of the cinema was that narrative need not—should not—be exclusively associated with literature, that the cinema has its own techniques of effecting narrative, not least of which is montage: "for the image, an element in the *reproduction* of the real, is substituted montage, a factor in the *production* of sense out of this real."[1]

The period from 1895 to 1903 witnessed the first attempts to get at the imaginative potential stored up in the cinematic vision of things, and the following period, from 1903 (Porter's *Great Train Robbery*) to 1914 (Griffith's *Birth of a Nation*) witnessed the development of special means of handling the cinema's inherent capacities of spatial and temporal dynamization, so as to realize a specifically cinematic narration. It was at this time, with the

1. Marie-Claire Ropars-Wuilleumier, *De la littérature au cinéma* (Paris, 1970), p. 65; her emphasis. On the vicissitudes of the theatrical approach, see pp. 48-53.

narrative principle gradually detached from a necessarily literary base, that there was created a fertile culture—in the biological sense—for the exchange of ideas of movement and sequence between cinema and novel. It remains now to gauge the impact of movie sensibility on novel technique, to suggest the ways in which specific novelists—even before the time of Dos Passos's self-conscious borrowings, before the Hollywood novelists and the New Novel—registered this tidal wave of new aesthetic perception and artistic construction.

Here it will be a question of fundamental isomorphic structures, not a study of influences. In other words, the view is toward literary artists who observe, absorb, react to, and handle the external reality of a given period in ways strikingly similar to their fellow film artists. Whether or not one can go so far in certain cases as to posit an influence is actually irrelevant: the object is rather, in the framework of a specifically comparative study, to use the peculiar vantage point of the rapidly developing cinematic language as a means of isolating similar innovations in the novel. Cinema is perhaps the finest chart against which to set this sort of technical innovation because, seemingly out of nowhere, it becomes in a few years the epitome of twentieth-century experimentation in the dynamic handling of space and time, the radical shifting of point of view, and the reconstituted patterning (montage) of fragmented narration.

Thus, Part II offers a new perspective on the novel of 1900 to 1925—in particular on Gertrude Stein's *Three Lives*, Jules Romains's *Mort de quelqu'un,* Marcel Proust's *A la recherche du temps perdu,* James Joyce's *Ulysses,* and Virginia Woolf's *To the Lighthouse*. The remaining chapters aim at a redefinition of what everyone agrees to be the innovative aspects of the early twentieth-century novel, but from the admittedly strict point of view of film form. In the cases of writers like Proust and Joyce, this intentional bias is bound to result in a one-sided or otherwise incomplete description of the works in question; but in any case, there is no attempt to "explain away" or to minimize the importance of other ingenious techniques and effects that, inevitably, cannot be discussed here. Nor should the present study be considered a reduction of the new novel to a flat, preconceived notion of film form. Rather, it hopes, by taking a global viewpoint, to suggest one way of situating the "classic" modern novel in the cultural and aesthetic movement of the times.

5 Objects, Inside and Out

Within, within, the cut and slender joint along, with sudden
equals and no more than three, two in the center make two
one side.
    If the elbow is long and it is filled so then the best example
is all together.
    The kind of show is made by squeezing.
                                    Gertrude Stein, Tender Buttons

In a famous sequence from *Potemkin*, a statue of a lion is presented
rapidly in three positions, from reclining to poised for a leap, thus
giving the impression of movement, or more specifically, of arousal.
In a sequence from *Last Year at Marienbad*, X and A are seen wandering through the hotel among people who stand stock still, though
they seem to have just been dancing or engaged in conversation or
a game. Cinema has often exploited this special ability to animate
objects and petrify human beings, suggesting that both subject
and object simply occupy different (and variable) positions along
a continuum of artificially produced representation. Until the
modern period, narrative literature has consistently maintained
a strict distinction between subject and object. But among certain
postcinema experimenters, in so-called stream of consciousness
writing, this situation changes.

In the cinema the status of subject and object is reversed in two ways. In one sense, there is an initial leveling between these two categories—a leveling inherent in the cinematic medium from the very first film-strips of the Lumière Brothers. In contrast to what happens in the theatre, human beings are shot and recorded onto the cinematic material in the same manner as objects. Before being filmed, self and object exist in two distinct realms; once part of the filmic image, they share the same artificial, ambiguous existence. The image of a sailing ship has just as much existential immediacy as the image of its captain.

So, in this first sense, the undifferentiating cinematic medium "reduces" people to the state of objects. But in another sense, objects are raised to the level of conscious beings. The persistent "present tense" of the cinematic image causes us to experience the *durée* of inanimate objects (e.g., in a series of close-ups) more vividly than we could in life. In contrast to the theatre, where props "are not true things of the universe,"[1] film creates a world in which objects, like human beings, seem endowed with some innate dynamism.[2] This cinematic principle, most clearly evidenced in certain Chaplin films such as *Modern Times*, in Buster Keaton's *The General*, and in *Potemkin*, is carried to its logical extreme in animated films, where flowers sing and houses smile.

If we can speak, then, of a precise reversal in mode of existence between self and object as they appear on the screen, can we speak generally of a similar reversal in the new literature of consciousness? At least one film theoretician has attempted to answer this question by drawing up a complete, one-to-one correspondence between the potential of the film medium to present "the whole course of thought" and the "inner monologues" of *Ulysses*.[3]

Lucien Goldmann places such a subject-object reversal into a Marxist framework by regarding it as essential to the process of

1. Gilbert Cohen-Séat, *Problèmes du cinéma et de l'information visuelle* (Paris, 1961), p. 66.
2. Thus Vachel Lindsay spoke of objects taking on personality in the movies (*The Art of the Moving Picture* [New York, 1915], pp. 53–54; cf. pp. 25, 116–17, and 133), and Béla Balázs referred to the "soul" of objects (*Theory of the Film*, trans. E. Bone [London, 1952], pp. 28, 47, and 91–96).
3. Sergei Eisenstein, "A Course in Treatment" (1932), in *Film Form*, trans. Jay Leyda (New York, 1957), p. 104.

"reification" that characterizes economic as well as novelistic change in the twentieth century. Reification is here considered to be the general process that typifies the economic transformation from liberal capitalism, where the individual still plays a considerable role in economic and social life, to monopoly capitalism, where the individual is virtually swallowed up by the giant trusts' financial machinery and ceases to have an active role as regards economic and social determination.

The cinema, we have seen, was intimately involved with the development of the machine and the formation of what has been called a "technocracy," and its formative years corresponded precisely to the decade during which, according to Goldmann, this economic transformation takes place (1900-10). As such, the cinema was perhaps not simply the first significant machine art, but the first aesthetic expression of reification, by which originally human interest and activity are transformed into purely material interest and, just like objects, are recognized merely for their exchange value or price.[4]

The actual reversal of self and object in the movies has only an approximate, though nonetheless important, parallel in the new novel's *leveling* of self and object. In the new literature that in the 1920s begins exploring human consciousness, or the private thoughts of characters, by revealing that process more or less directly to the reader, the new elements cut across the old boundaries between plot and character. The character's act of consciousness, in other words, such as Stephen Dedalus's repetition to himself in *Ulysses* of "Agenbite of Inwit" when he recalls his mother's death, must be considered as a constituent of both plot and character. It is not absurd, therefore, to speak of self and object assuming greater or less importance according to the self's preoccupation with him or herself or with the object, that is, with the process of cognition or with the object of that process.

In *To the Lighthouse*, Mrs. Ramsay's reflections often lead toward a leveling of herself and some object external to herself—ultimately to an absorption of that object by her consciousness. In the follow-

4. Lucien Goldmann, *Pour une sociologie du roman* (Paris, 1964), pp. 288-98.

ing passage, one external action, her accomplishment of "something dexterous with her knitting needles," loses its textual hegemony to the flow of her thoughts, which in turn becomes captivated by the external light of the Lighthouse.

> . . . and there rose to her lips always some exclamation of triumph over life when things came together in this peace, this rest, this eternity; and pausing there she looked out to meet that stroke of the Lighthouse, the long steady stroke, the last of the three, which was her stroke, for watching them in this mood always at this hour one could not help attaching oneself to one thing especially of the things one saw; and this thing, the long steady stroke, was her stroke. Often she found herself sitting and looking, sitting and looking, with her work in her hands until she became the thing she looked at—that light for example.[5]

It is important to note that Mrs. Ramsay's reflective process is entirely described by the narrator, that we never get her very "thoughts" unmediated by the narrative voice, and that the whole identification of self and object takes place only insofar as the narrator asserts it. In *Ulysses*, on the other hand, while it is rarely a question of mutual absorption between self and object, we do get the unmediated thoughts of characters in such a way that they are scarcely distinguishable, formally or dramatically, from the external actions. While Bloom, for example, converses with M'Coy near the beginning of the "Lotus Eaters" episode, he watches a woman across the street who is preparing to climb into a carriage:

> Mr. Bloom gazed across the road at the outsider drawn up before the door of the Grosvenor. The porter hoisted the valise up on the well. She stood still, waiting, while the man, husband, brother, like her, searched his pockets for change. Stylish kind of coat with that roll collar, warm for a day like this, looks like blanketcloth. Careless stand of her with her hands in those patch

---

5. Virginia Woolf, *To the Lighthouse* (Harmondsworth: Penguin, 1964; orig. 1927), pt. 1, chap. 11, p. 73. All references will be to this edition, with page numbers, preceded by part and chapter, given in parentheses.

pockets. Like that haughty creature at the polo match.[6]

The sentence "She stood still . . ." begins as a narrative description of the woman, the external object. In the midst of it, however, we find ourselves momentarily in Bloom's consciousness. Here, "internal actions" of consciousness and the external actions outside of consciousness are juxtaposed and interlaced, without either one's losing, of course, its identity. Each is given weight and importance in such a way that self and object seem somehow made of the same stuff—as in the movies.

The more tangible problem that the new novel's leveling process leads to is, as we shall see in chapter 8, the particular disposition of the newly leveled elements—object perceived externally, object perceived from within, self perceived externally, self perceived from within—in other words, to what extent montage composition prevails in the new literature, to what extent "the montage form, as structure, is a reconstruction of the laws of the thought process."[7]

There is a preponderance of inanimate objects in the modern novel. They preponderate not so much in their number as in the peculiar force with which they are experienced, both by the characters and by the reader himself. These objects are categorically different from those that thicken the texture of _Robinson Crusoe_, and even somewhat different from those more recent objects—from which they may nonetheless directly descend—like Binet's lathe in _Madame Bovary_ and the implacable furniture in _The Spoils of Poynton_. Before 1900, objects were almost always shown in direct interaction with characters.[8] They were props whose significance was always dependent upon their manipulation by human possessors and whose temporary dominance, like the _maison Vauquer_ in _Père Goriot_, was designed primarily to give thrust to a purely human significance. In the modern novel, objects stand in relation to their predecessors somewhat in the same manner as the dynamized film object stands in relation to the dead, deracinated theatrical prop.

6. James Joyce, _Ulysses_ (New York: Random House, 1961; orig. 1922), p. 73. Page references will be to this edition.

7. Eisenstein, _Film Form_ (chap. 4, n. 12 above), p. 106.

8. Cf. Alain Robbe-Grillet, _For a New Novel_, trans. Richard Howard (New York, 1965), pp. 145–47.

We experience now, as in a close-up, the "life" of an object, how it evolves even when divorced from human contact or in spite of such contact. In *Ulysses*, for example, the Elijah throwaway is first seen when thrust into Bloom's hands, then spotted, crumpled up, through an intermittent series of "close-ups," as it makes its way down the Liffey.

In the manner of *The General* or *Potemkin*, objects can even become principal "characters" in the unfolding events of the novel. In *Ulysses*, Dublin and its multifarious objects stand within and behind each episode, a fundamental key, an essential link in the often disconnected chain of events. In the middle section of *To the Lighthouse*, entitled "Time Passes," we witness, in a far more dynamic and concrete manner than ever before attempted, the evolution of an object: the Ramsay summer house and the things it contains. And Gertrude Stein's prose experiments, forgoing the narrative element altogether by the time of *Tender Buttons*, reach an important culmination when objects become the sole apparently palpable designators in the text.

The new focus on objects has as its somewhat inevitable counter-part a radical change regarding characterization "in depth." Among the various tendencies to be eliminated by the modern novelist was the nineteenth-century "psychological realism," by which, in reaction to the neoclassic notion of a permanent, quasi-universal human nature, people were seen as evolving, reacting with nuance to each situation they encountered. The narrator's discourse entered freely into commerce with the unfolding action, halting diegetic flow in order to comment, elaborate, or even draw lessons. For most of the new novelists, on the other hand, narrative discourse was not to make such bald interventions. The narrator might *know* every-thing, but he was under no obligation to *tell* everything. And in most cases, he did not appear to know everything either (which leads to the split, greatly exploited in modern fiction, between narrator and author). For this new form of narration was as much linked to a particular view of consciousness as were the earlier forms.

Consciousness was not constantly evolving, or carefully integrat-ing each new experience, as the nineteenth-century novelist would have us believe. Experiments by William James (and by his short-term disciple, Gertrude Stein) showed that the mind returns to, repeats, gets stuck on certain stimuli much too frequently to justify this view of permanent development. Yet certainly consciousness was not a permanent, unchangeable entity formed all at once, as the neoclassics held. Rather, it was a constantly changing entity which could never be known in its entirety, formed erratically and disjunctively by its own habits of memory and fantasy as much as by the ordinary inductive processes of everyday life. Thus, characters are portrayed more and more objectively, the victims of their own thoughts, actions, and words rendered immediately to the reader. Furthermore, according to the leveling process of self and object, typified most concretely by the cinema (where there is, similarly, no immediately apparent narrator), there was a growing temptation to treat characters with the same dispassionate air that was beginning to circulate with greater frequency among objects.[9]

An excellent example of this modern approach can be found in Virginia Woolf's short story, "Kew Gardens" (1921). Here, four groups of human beings pass before a fixed and totally anonymous narrator, speaking or more often mumbling to themselves, and then wander off. There is no attempt whatever to interpret the random words and gestures of these "characters," though it is noted, for example, that, in the case of the first couple, "the man was about six inches in front of the woman." Down on the ground in the middle of the oval-shaped flower-bed, which seems to be, by various indications, the physical location of the narrative viewpoint, a snail moves

9. The leaps and jolts of consciousness were probably first explored extensively by the romantics. The poets, however, unlike the nineteenth-century novelists, according to René Girard, were unable "to come together with the *Other*" (*Mensonge romantique et verité romanesque* [Paris, 1961], p. 151). Their introspective investigations remained, in other words, wholly circumscribed within the self.

Modern psychology since Freud has a special pertinence in a discussion of methods of character portrayal in the twentieth century. The influence of Freud's analyses of fetishism and the more general process of object-cathexis has been immeasurable on the modern writer's insistence on gauging psychic situations in terms of objects—or at least on the critic's ability to account for this insistence. Furthermore, post-Freudian studies on the nonintegrated subject and the prevalence of multiple selves have enriched our critical vocabulary to the point of making possible for the first time an in-depth examination of the literature of consciousness. See an interesting summary of these developments in Hélène Cixous, "The Character of Character," *New Literary History* 5, no. 2 (Winter 1974).

slowly and painstakingly along. Only the snail (admittedly not an inanimate object, but the closest biological equivalent) has in this story "a definite goal." Innumerable objects lie in the path of this goal, and the snail, repeatedly faced with decisions, is obliged to use a trial-and-error method. For our present purposes, the snail can be seen as a parodic figure of the conventional protagonist of earlier fiction. The reversal here is complete: the human beings make apparently random appearances in their "irregular and aimless movement," while the snail carries on with determination, "taking stock" of each obstacle and adversary that crosses its path.

A similar displacement of focus can be seen in a story by the Uruguayan Horacio Quiroga, "La Insolación" (1908), where the death of a North American *ranchero* is perceived wholly by reference to his dogs' actions, observations, and conversations with one another. Raymond Roussel in *Locus Solus* (1914) concentrates all his descriptive efforts on, first, the mysterious and complicated functioning of various objects (hybrid machines, toys, and assorted gadgets) and, secondly, the equally complex causes that lie behind this functioning. For Roussel, the human element is only relevant insofar as it instigates the odd constructions (e.g., Canterel) or insofar as it comes to play an active part in the operation of a machine (e.g., Faustine or the inscrutable *reître*)—and in this latter case what is most noteworthy is, again, the perfect leveling of the human and nonhuman. Gertrude Stein often posits her characters, without previous or ulterior elaboration, in terms of a single piece of setting or decor. Thus, in the short prose piece, "A Saint in Seven" (1926), the theatrical-like "list of personages" includes "A saint with a lily," "A girl with a rooster in front of her and a bush of strange flowers at her side and a small tree behind her," and "A woman with a sheep in front of her and a small tree behind her." Proust's Marcel, in a similar, though structurally far more subtle manner, associates characters with the particular landscape or setting in which he first saw them or heard of them,[10] for instance, Albertine and her group of girl friends set against the Balbec seascape.

In Stein's experiments, little distinction is ever made between the landscape and the human inhabitants of that landscape. With her the

10. Cf. Genette, *Figures III* (Paris, 1972), p. 50.

dislocation of a certain traditional psychological focus seems to reach an extreme. Only much later in the century do we get a reversion to traditional psychology by means now of a total devotion to the object, as in Robbe-Grillet's *La Jalousie*, where the "jealousy" of the narrator is virtually signified by, among other things, the description of a slip of blue writing paper sticking out of a shirt pocket.

The leveling of self and object is, we have seen, built into the cinematic medium itself. For example, a woman's grief over a departed lover cannot be dynamically expressed without reference to the shut door by which the lover has just left. Grief, that is, proceeds as much from the image of the door as from the image of the grief-stricken woman. But no such built-in quality exists for the novel. As a result, certain formal devices are used to achieve a similar dislocation in the emotive force of character portrayal.

"Funnily enough," wrote Gertrude Stein, "the cinema has offered a solution of this thing. By a continuously moving picture of any one there is no memory of any other thing and there is that thing existing, it is in a way if you like one portrait of anything not a number of them." Referring to the problems she had to overcome in writing her *Portraits* (1912)—the problems, that is, of etching out an existence in space by means of a primarily temporal medium—she goes on, "I was doing what the cinema was doing, I was making a continuous succession of the statement of what that person was until I had not many things but one thing."[11] By this method of repetition, she also created the monolithic characters of *The Making of Americans* (1906–08) and *Three Lives* (1909). In direct opposition to her nineteenth-century forebears, Stein portrays life as an instantaneous whole: "a whole human being felt at one and the same

11. *Lectures in America* (New York, 1935), pp. 176–77. The accuracy of Stein's description of the psychological process involved in viewing a film seems questionable (especially "there is no memory of any other thing"), but the point here is that, while her medium lacked the inherent, material self/object identification of the cinema, Stein chose an entirely different aspect of cinematic *effect* to imitate and thus achieved roughly the same goal.

Stein's actual experience of going to the movies has not been recorded. However, it is interesting to note, in this regard, that Joyce wanted at rather an early date to open a chain of movie houses in Dublin.

time."[12] Each statement of character bears a close resemblance to previous and subsequent statements, and the total impression is the result of an incremental piling up.

> Now Jeff knew very well what it was to love Melanctha. Now Jeff Campbell knew he was really understanding. Now Jeff knew what it was to be good to Melanctha. Now Jeff was good to her always.[13]

Just as these cumulative portraits attempt to capture the whole at every moment they treat the part, so the oddly memorable characters that almost come to life are the result of many bland, general adjectives applied to a particular being: "Rose Johnson was a real black, tall, well built, sullen, stupid, childlike, good looking negress" (p. 85). In *The Making of Americans*, Stein had already established a sort of metalinguistic paradigm whereby "repeating" equals personality, since people are what they are essentially by means of their repeating: "There is then always repeating in all living. There is then in each one always repeating in their whole being, the whole nature in them."[14]

Thus, in *Three Lives*, immutable, invariably repeating characters, like the quotient of an uneven division problem, stand out amidst the simple, integral, monotonous events. There is a sense of one life or another caught sight of in midstream, followed for an undetermined length of time, and then suddenly ended. Instead of leading up to a climax, each life is present all at once. Hence, the effect of stasis, lack of development, and continuous being.

Incremental repetition is Stein's fundamental device for establishing character. The frame is an important, though secondary, compositional device used not only to establish character but also to break down even further the conventional relationships between plot and character, event and psychology.[15]

12. Ibid., p. 145.
13. *Three Lives* (New York: Random House, 1909, 1936), p. 204. Page references will be to this edition.
14. Excerpted in Carl Van Vechtan, ed., *Selected Writings of Gertrude Stein* (New York, 1945), p. 270.
15. Frame composition is not exclusively a modern narrative technique. V. Shklovsky considers it to be a technique fundamental to all narrative, especi-

Each of the three "lives" is structured in the same way. The first few pages open onto a series of facts and circumstances in a dominant present period. Then there is a reversion to a remote point in the past. From here there is an apparently chronological working back up to the present of the first pages, which as is now clear, constitutes a sort of climax period. A few pages devoted to the final events that succeed this dominant period follow, including generally the death of the central character. "Melanctha," the longest and most moving of the three portraits, begins (p. 95) with Melanctha Herbert doing "everything that any woman could" to help her friend, Rose Johnson, bring her baby into the world. After block-type descriptions of Melanctha and Rose, there is an account of how the two women met at church (p. 87) and then a much greater leap back through time to describe Melanctha's childhood and background (pp. 89 ff.). From here follow over a hundred pages describing Melanctha's unhappy, inconclusive relationships with Jane Harden and Jeff Campbell. Then we reach (i.e., learn of again) Melanctha's meeting with Rose Johnson at church (p. 199). The final thirty-some pages redevelop this relationship, describe the reactions of Jane and Jeff, and sketch Melanctha's abortive relation with Jem Richards, leading up to her getting "awful blue" and finally dying of consumption. The frame here consists of Rose and Melanctha's beginning friendship, reinforced and elaborated by specific repeated details: their meeting (pp. 87 and 199); the question of why the sensitive Melanctha would lower herself to become associated with the ordinary Rose (pp. 86 and 200); Rose's difficult lying-in and Melanctha's selfless aid (pp. 85 and 225); and Melanctha's serious "blue" periods during which she wonders if it would not be easier to kill herself (pp. 87 and 226, 235).

---

ally insofar as it helps to "integrate more and more the material external to the body of the novel"; "La Construction de la nouvelle et du roman" (1925) in T. Todorov, ed., *Théorie de la littérature* (Paris, 1965), p. 196; see esp. pp. 189-92.

However, Shklovsky is concerned here mainly with different *levels* of narration, for example, the frame structure that results, in the *Decameron* or the picaresque novel, when a character introduces a secondary narrative. The earmark of the modern framing used by Stein and Woolf is the literal repetition of referential phrases on the same level of narration, thus forcing the diegetic time to double back on itself.

The same frame device and the same flashback structure of time are used in smaller units of "Melanctha" as well. The first appearance of Melanctha's father occurs during the time when Melanctha has been seeing a certain John. "One day James Herbert came to where his wife and daughter lived, and he was furious. 'Where's that Melanctha girl of yours . . .' "(p. 91). Then follows a description of James Herbert and an account of his occasional drinking bouts with John in the past, which culminated in a razor fight over John's seeing Melanctha. After the razor fight, we read, "The next day he came to where his wife and daughter lived and he was furious. 'Where's that Melanctha, of yours?. .' "(p. 94).

In the third part of *Three Lives*, "The Gentle Lena," even individual paragraphs are composed as a frame. Lena's employer, Mrs. Haydon, is searching among the German immigrants of Bridgepoint for a good husband for Lena. She chooses Herman Kreder, whose indifference toward marriage is indicated in exactly the same manner, with exactly the same words, as that of Lena.

> Herman Kreder did not care much to get married. He was a gentle soul and a little fearful. He had a sullen temper, too. He was obedient to his father and his mother. He always did his work well. He often went out on Saturday nights and on Sundays, with other men. He liked it with them but he never became really joyous. He liked to be with men and he hated to have women with them. He was obedient to his mother, but he did not care much to get married. [. . .]
>
> Lena did not care much to get married. She liked her life very well where she was working. She did not think much about Herman Kreder. She thought he was a good man and she always found him very quiet. Neither of them ever spoke much to the other. Lena did not care much just then about getting married. [pp. 251-52]

The frame device is similarly used by Virginia Woolf in *To the Lighthouse*, a novel whose overall structure is "framed" by the project of going to the lighthouse. A famous passage describes Mrs. Ramsay, as she knits, from radically different points of view (I,5). The viewpoint which seems to represent some omniscient narrative voice (though it might include Mr. Ramsay, who later blurts out that "he did not like to see her look so sad:" I,12; p. 79) and which, as Erich Auerbach has pointed out,[16] has only the vaguest spatial and temporal relation to the external action of Mrs. Ramsay knitting, is indicated thus:

> Never did anybody look so sad. Bitter and black, half-way down, in the darkness, in the shaft which ran from the sunlight to the depths, perhaps a tear formed, a tear fell, the waters swayed this way and that, received it, and were at rest. Never did anybody look so sad. [p. 34]

The frame functions, in the case of a single paragraph, as a specific variant of the simple technique of repetition. If narration implies temporal progression, and description the suspension of temporality, then the frame acts to emphasize formally that the time of description is at a standstill. Lena and Herman's attitude toward marriage and Mrs. Ramsay's sadness are thus set off from the diegetic development. When Stein uses the device over more extensive portions of text, the repeated narrative elements function literally to *frame* the intervening diegetic development. The precise repetition engenders in the reader the paradoxical feeling of having witnessed a certain series of events and yet now of being thrust back to the borderlines of the fictional world, right back where he started from. The frame lifts events out of the diegetic flow and turns aspects of character into billboards that stand out from even an entirely static description.

Stein herself has pointed out this peculiar quality of "Melanctha," where "there was a constant recurring and beginning." Throughout this period she was using repetition and the frame, because, as she says,

> Beginning again and again is a natural thing even when there is a series.
>
> Beginning again and again and again explaining composition and time is a natural thing.[17]

16. *Mimesis*, trans. W. Trask (Garden City, N.Y., 1957), p. 476.
17. "Composition as Explanation" in *Selected Writings* (see n. 14 above), p. 516.

It was a "natural thing" during this period because, among other reasons, the cinema had demonstrated more profoundly than ever before the physicality, the malleability of referential, or diegetic, time (cf. above, pp. 66–67). Since the cinema projects a series of permanently present moments against the screen, events can be condensed or drawn out, excised or returned to, with a concreteness and dynamism capable of exerting a significant impact on the predominantly linear manner of traditional narrative. What is more important, events can be interchanged without regard to their strict chronological relation to one another. In the same way, by repeating James Herbert's furious visit to Melanctha's mother, Stein breaks the chronological flow of the diegesis, suggesting that the plot is no longer there merely to provide a stage for the development of her characters, that it has a decidedly and demonstrably artificial quality by which key actions may come back to frame a certain chronological sequence, and that the very notion of chronology has little meaning apart from the relative placement it suggests, nearer the beginning or the ending of the composition. "It is understood by this time that everything is the same except composition and time, composition and the time of composition and the time in the composition."[18] The narrated sequence of events ("the time *of* the composition") is fixed once and for all by the writer, while the time to which these events allude ("the time *in* the composition"), diegetic time, need follow no external guideline so strict as standard chronology.

18. Ibid. I take Stein's distinction between what is *of* the composition and what is *in* the composition to be more or less comparable to the distinction I have stressed between narrative and diegesis. Since this distinction will be crucial in the chapters that follow, I reiterate that, following Genette's *récit/ histoire* dichotomy (*Figures III*, p. 72), by *narrative* I mean the concrete realm of the text or celluloid, the realm of the signifier where all elements are *in praesentia*; and by *diegesis* I mean the imaginary realm of the signified where all elements are, vis-à-vis the text or celluloid, *in absentia*.

6 Temporal Distortion

A sleeping man holds encircled around him the thread of hours, the order of years and worlds. He consults them instinctively as he awakes and reads there in a second the point on earth which he occupies, the time that has flowed by up to his awakening; but their rows can mix together, break.
                    Proust, Du côté de chez Swann

Repetition, we have seen, whether it is used to achieve a continuous, cumulative image of character or to create a sudden stasis or *reprise* of plot, raises fundamental problems with regard to conventional temporality. Once the aims of the new fiction become more complex, however, with the simultaneous representation of two different events and the intermingling of distinct moments of time, the novel's traditional sequential development is dealt a severe blow. Once time in the novel is conceived of as physical, malleable, and above all else artificial, as is the case with the cinema, the flow of time loses its relentlessly forward motion and the very notion of chronology begins to seem foreign.

A. *The Prolonged Present*

In those works of Gertrude Stein where it exists at all, the time sense in its traditional acceptance is set aside either with the frequent rude jolts of unexpected repetitions or else by the deft summaries of what is to happen before the fact. In each part of *Three Lives*, the essential données of the story are provided in the first several pages—an economic device learned, no doubt, from Flaubert's *Trois Contes*,[1] but whose effect is the virtual banishment of all suspense. The death of Melanctha's mother provides the best specific example of this sense of summary and conclusion before actualization. "During this year," Stein writes, " 'Mis' Herbert as her neighbors called her, Melanctha's pale yellow mother was very sick, and this year she died" (pp. 109-10). It is only much later (p. 133) that "Mis" Herbert actually dies. Rather than showing, dramatizing the sequence of events that precede the death, Stein draws that diegetically later event forward in her narrative. In so doing, she stresses the artificiality of fictional time, drops the traditional pretense whereby the narrator metes out the information, bit by bit, according to the chronological order of the story. There is basically no forward development: all exists at once at the time *of* composition and can therefore be alluded to indiscriminately before or after its temporal place *in* the composition. We begin to understand the dramatic rationale behind this procedure when we note that little of "Mis" Herbert's agony is referred to in comparison to the lengthy descriptions of the burgeoning friendship between Melanctha and her mother's doctor, Jeff Campbell. The mother's sickness, dramatically, serves as pretext for this relationship and, narratively, frames it.

This special time sense tends toward no time sense at all. Despite conventional references to the passage of time, as "during this year" in the sentence quoted above or, even more vaguely, "during these last years" and "in those days," one has instead the feeling that time is at a standstill. The prospect of establishing a time-scheme for "Melanctha" seems not only next to impossible but, unlike for Faulkner's works, not particularly enlightening. The moving quality of a narrative like "Melanctha" seems to be, precisely, in its lack of progression and its insistence on a static cluster of present moments.

1. Gertrude Stein, *The Autobiography of Alice B. Toklas* (New York: Random House, 1960; orig. 1933), p. 34.

There are several stylistic traits that significantly contribute to the establishment of this no-man's-land between past and present, what Gertrude Stein has herself called a "prolonged" or "continuous" present. The German critic Käte Hamburger has noted the signal use in fiction of "deictic" adverbs like *now* in combination with the past tense, which distinguishes fiction from history.[2] Stein employs this adverb, along with *always* and *never* not simply to distinguish her narrative from history but to lift it out of all strictly past existence.

Now there was no way Melanctha ever had had to bear things from him, worse than he now had it in him. Now Jeff was strong inside him. Now he knew he was understanding, now he knew he had a hot love in him, and he was good always to Melanctha Herbert who was the one had made him have it.

And so now Jeff Campbell could see Melanctha often, and he was patient, and always very friendly to her, and every day Jeff Campbell understood Melanctha Herbert better. And always Jeff saw Melanctha could not love him the way he needed she should do it. Melanctha Herbert had no way she ever really could remember. [pp. 204-05]

Roland Barthes has pointed out the signal use of the *passé simple* in the traditional (French) novel of the nineteenth century: "By means of the past tense, the verb implicitly makes up part of a causal chain, participates in a series of solidary and directed actions, functions as the algebraic sign of an intention; sustaining an equivocation between temporality and causality, it calls for an unfolding, that is, for an intelligence of the narrative."[3] Stein tends to couple the English preterite, as seen above, with iterative adverbs like *always* and *ever* and otherwise to prefer by far the imperfect, including the use of *would* in a past iterative sense, as in "And then, too, Melanctha would learn to know some of the serious foreign

2. Discussion of an article by Roy Pascal in David Lodge, *Language of Fiction* (New York, 1966), p. 39.
3. *Le Degré zéro de l'écriture* (Paris, 1953, 1964), p. 30.

sailors . . . " (p. 101). The English imperfect, of course, insists much more plainly on continuous action than the French because it includes the present participle, which, along with the gerund, is one of Stein's all-around favorite forms of the verb. Unlike the traditional narrative, then, Stein's trades singulative sequence for iterative repetition. "Always repeating is all of living, everything that is being is always repeating, more and more listening to repeating gives to me completed understanding."[4] It should nonetheless be said in passing that an important turning point in the conventional conception of the novel's temporality came well before the 1900s in *L'Education sentimentale*—as has been pointed out by Proust,[5] himself a careful master of that tense.

As in the cinema, then, where a continuous here and now is flashed before the spectator's eyes (cf. above, chap. 3, sec. A), Gertrude Stein creates her impression of what William James called an "ongoing present," even though the tense is, strictly speaking, past. In *The Making of Americans*, where the present tense is dominant even in scenes alluding to the past, there is even less of a sense that time is or has been passing. The same is true for her later prose pieces, such as "Portrait of Mabel Dodge at the Villa Curonia" (1912) and *Tender Buttons* (1914). Here, it is not even any longer a question of when and how events have taken place and in what relation to one another. Each element goes to make up not a diegetic action but rather a spatial, "still-life" configuration that seems to exist at the textual level only and thus to "escape" time altogether.

The attempt to capture the present moment, to extend it, to memorialize it, to reinforce it against the inroads of past and future, can be seen in other works, though perhaps never in the stubborn way that it exists in Gertrude Stein's. One of Joyce's central achievements in *Ulysses* is to have lifted a single day, with all its random occurrences and ephemeral events, outside of historical time, outside of the conventional chain of cause-and-effect. It is a work

4. *The Making of Americans,* excerpted in Carl Van Vechtan, ed., *Selected Writings of Gertrude Stein*, p. 276.

5. "A propos du 'style' de Flaubert," *Chroniques* (Paris, 1927), pp. 193-211.

"conceived as a moment in all time," according to Leon Edel,[6] who appropriately quotes part of Stephen's ruminations in the "Scylla and Charybdis" episode: "Hold to the now, the here, through which all future plunges to the past." Taking, as we must, Stephen's frequently sophistical reflections with a grain of salt, we can turn to Joyce, the accomplished craftsman, and see how he puts these ideas into compositional practice in, for example, the "Wandering Rocks." As Father Conmee sits in the tram car, he takes note of his fellow passengers, beginning with a woman seated across from him:

> Father Conmee perceived her perfume in the car. He perceived also that the awkward man at the other side of her was sitting on the edge of the seat.
> Father Conmee at the altarrails placed the host with difficulty in the mouth of the awkward old man who had the shaky head.
> [p. 222]

Father Conmee's "present" perception of the awkward man and the past scene of his offering the same man the host are juxtaposed without distinction as to relative time: the verbs are both simple preterites, "perceived" and "placed." The effect is an expansion of the present moment (i.e., three o'clock, June 16, 1904) to include all that is present in Father Conmee's mind, whether past or present. This same expansion or thickening of the present moment can be seen in the type of future fantasies Bloom is given to, where the simple past tense is similarly maintained, as in the bursting open of Patty Dignam's coffin: "Bom! Upset. A coffin bumped out on to the road . . . " (p. 98).

With Proust and Woolf, the attempt is less to *capture* the present moment or to expand its actuality as to recapture it, to give new, present sustenance to a past moment, and thereby to memorialize it. The effects of these novelists are, therefore, somewhat removed from the cinematic "presentness" identifiable in Stein. They are closely related to a specifically literary tradition stemming from the nineteenth century and related to romantic doctrine, whereby

6. *The Modern Psychological Novel* (New York, 1964), p. 76.

inspiration and creation are the fruits of tranquil introspection and recollection (cf. Wordsworth), whereby the most moving of artistic achievements comes in the successful rekindling of an image, experience, or feeling buried deep in the vaults of memory (cf. Hugo's "sacré souvenir").

Proust's work is, of course, best known for this process or reliving in the present half-forgotten moments of the past. As the special operation of the *mémoire involontaire* functions most importantly, however, in terms of the global structure of the *Recherche* rather than as a device for maintaining present actuality, we shall find it more pertinent to a discussion of specific temporal distortions (section B below). Marcel, it might be noted nonetheless, has throughout a rather peculiar attitude toward future events. His mental labor of anticipation is often so great that when the culminating present moment arrives, he realizes it has already been consumed by future longings, which are, of course, now part of the past, as with the first time he attends a performance by la Berma.[7] All that is left for him to do is to reconstruct his palpitating pleasure of the unkown as he originally experienced it in the past. One might go so far as to assert that, for Marcel, the present is so fugitive as to be completely absent, that it can never be experienced, only reexperienced.[8]

To the Lighthouse is full of exultations of the present moment, such as Mrs. Ramsay's meditation on the lighthouse beam with which she identifies herself (I,11; pp. 72 ff.), Lily Briscoe's epiphany of Mr. and Mrs. Ramsay as they watch the children play ball (I,13; pp. 84-85), or the lighting of the candles at dinner that engenders the feeling of a "common cause against that fluidity out there" (I,17; p. 112). Virginia Woolf's most ambitious attempt to expand the present comes in a fictional essay, "The Moment: Summer's Night."[9] In answer to the self-posed question, "What composed the present moment?" she furnishes a long list of sense impressions,

7. *A la recherche du temps perdu* (Paris: Bibliotèque de la Pléiade, 1954), 1:440–50. References will be to this edition, with volume and page number given in parentheses.
8. Cf. Georges Poulet, *Studies in Human Time*, trans. E. Coleman (Baltimore, 1956), p. 291.
9. *Collected Essays* (London, 1966), 2:293-97.

physical sensations, a certain "knot of consciousness" divided up among four different people, the fantasies that issue therefrom, overheard words, and glimpsed scenes inside a nearby cottage. Yet, as in Proust, this moment becomes "horrible" and is willfully "smashed"; in *To the Lighthouse* such willfulness is not even necessary, since, again as in Proust, the most joyous moments give way all too naturally to the next moments, so that once Mrs. Ramsay, at the end of her dinner, waits "a moment longer," the very room that has contained her experience "changed, it shaped itself differently; it had become, she knew, giving one last look at it over her shoulder, already the past" (I,17; p. 128).

Lily's attempts, on the other hand, to summon up various recollected scenes with Mrs. Ramsay at the center, do result in a denser, richer present. Here, not quite in the manner of Joyce, who juxtaposes past and present without comment, nor yet in the manner of Proust, whose past is like a secret and unexpected benefactor of the present, Woolf interweaves the present scene of Lily painting with past scenes of Lily, Mrs. Ramsay, and Charles Tansley on the beach, Lily's reflective process being the connective thread throughout (III,3; pp. 181-82). The beach scene preoccupies Lily to such an extent that finally it meshes itself entirely with her actions:

> And she began to lay on a red, a grey, and she began to model her way into the hollow there. At the same time, she seemed to be sitting beside Mrs. Ramsay on the beach,
>
> "Is it a boat? Is it a cask?" Mrs. Ramsay said. And she began hunting round for her spectacles. And she sat, having found them, silent, looking out to sea. And Lily, painting steadily, felt as if a door had opened, and one went in and stood gazing silently about in a high cathedral-like place, very dark, very solemn. Shouts came from a world far away. Steamers vanished in stalks of smoke on the horizon. Charles threw stones and sent them skipping.
>
> Mrs. Ramsay sat silent. [pp. 194-95]

The remembered past has been resurrected to thicken the present, to reverberate suggestively against the present's sham solidity. In the last four sentences, it is uncertain which portion of pastness is being referred to—Lily's painting or the beach. We know, of course, that Lily is alone with Augustus Carmichael as she paints. Yet, while the last two sentences must certainly refer to the beach scene, the two preceding them could fit into the framework of either scene. This confusion reaches its climax when Mrs. Ramsay seems actually to materialize before Lily from the stuff of her thoughts: "Mrs. Ramsay sat there quite simply, in the chair, flicked her needles to and fro, knitted her reddish-brown stocking, cast her shadow on the step. There she sat" (III,11; p. 230).

B. *Achronological Narration*

The establishment of a multifaceted, fully textured, though not necessarily expanded, present time is important in light of specific maneuvers that negate all traditional notion of past, present, and future. In the above example of Lily's bringing back the scene of Mrs. Ramsay on the beach, the juxtaposition is unusually vivid because the present moment and the past moment are each so minutely mapped out. They are both in the same simple past tense, and neither one seems subordinate to the other. As in the cinema, where one here-and-now image yields to another here-and-now image that may, however, take place at a remote point of time—that is, where sequential contiguity on the celluloid does not necessarily signify temporal contiguity in the diegesis, so in Lily's scene the remote past (which has already been carefully described in previous passages) succeeds directly the "present" past without the traditional signs of temporal differentiation. It should be noted that this procedure differs markedly from a character's ordinary recollection of a past event, accompanied in most cases by precisely such temporal or reflective signs as "he remembered" or "she mused." *To the Lighthouse* is itself filled with these conventional modulations between present and past. The simple recollection of the past does not, however, result in the peculiarly cinematic juxtaposition unless both present moment and past moment are submitted to a hewing-down process of temporal (and tense) distinction and presented in direct narrative sequence.

The image of the line (as in "time-line," "line of development") is perhaps limited as a critical tool but nonetheless indicative of what the new novelists were working against in traditional fiction. The example of the movies may have been useful precisely for the divorce they inherently suggest between linear sequence (i.e., the uninterrupted forward movement of the celluloid) and straightforward temporal progression. Part I, chapter 13 of *To the Lighthouse* ends with Mrs. Ramsay's question, "Did Nancy go with them [Paul and Minta]?" Chapter 14 then follows a long parenthesis, which begins by explaining the circumstances that obliged Nancy to go indeed with Paul and Minta. Its temporal relation to Mrs. Ramsay's question is antecedent, as indicated by the tense, "Certainly, Nancy had gone with them," and, more precisely, by previous allusions to Paul and Minta's walk that stretch all the way back to I,10 (pp. 64, 66, 71, 78). In terms of absolute chronology, then, I,14 begins long before the time of the question that terminates I,13. This prior time is then elaborated in the simple past: Paul and Minta's walk with Nancy and Andrew, their separation on the beach and the rocks, Minta's losing of her grandmother's brooch, the fruitless search, and their return to the house.

Again, in terms of absolute chronology, I,14 extends far beyond the time of I,15, I,16 and the beginning of I,17. As Paul and the others approach the house, it is already dark and he is aware that they are late for dinner. The chronological progression, left off with Mrs. Ramsay's question, does not "catch up" to this point in diegetic time until the middle of I,17, when Minta and Paul enter along with the *boeuf en daube* (p. 113); I,15, in fact, carrying on the diachronic narration, simply provides Prue's answer to her mother's question: "Yes, . . . I think Nancy did go with them." Thus, I,14 is not simply a flashback. It is a real embroilment of the time-scheme. The linear sequence of chapters (13, 14, 15, 16, 17) does not reflect the nonlinear, synchronic development of the diegesis. The diegetic time of the novel might be sketched thus:

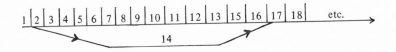

Achronological narrative techniques are not in themselves an innovation.[10] Sterne delighted in throwing the reader off the track by introducing substantial digressions that revert to a time prior to the present diegetic moment, and long before Sterne, Homer framed Odysseus's *récit* at the Phaeacian court as a digression back to an anterior time and provided the background to Odysseus's scar in a flashback that quite removes us from the foot-washing scene. However, in these earlier examples, the anachronistic material remains clearly cut off and delimited from the present diegesis. The achronological narrative sequence has a "common and externally coherent development"[11] (Odysseus's scar itself, Sterne's stated goal of an "ab ovo" narration or his Lockean conception of the "association of ideas"), whereas in Woolf's sequences the juxtaposition of the beach scene with Lily's painting is not justified by any such externally identifiable nexus (rather, if at all, by a thematic consonance, e.g., that of "vision"); nor is the separation of Mrs. Ramsay's question and its response by the beach promenade scene really justified, in length or in particularity, by any immediately identifiable common denominator. The passages from *To the Lighthouse* have the peculiarly modern quality of yoking together disjunct elements so that, though these elements retain all their heterogeneity, the narrative surface appears smooth and perfectly continuous.

An even better exemplar of this modern discontinuous continuity of time in narration is Marcel Proust. His world is one in which past and present, at the very moment of greatest dissimilarity and even antithesis, suddenly fuse together.

The joy experienced through the *mémoire involontaire*, however, takes on its most profound meaning mainly in contrast to the pain of external, moment-to-moment time. The key moment of Marcel's good-night kiss from his mother—a moment that Proust returns to over and over again—is, nonetheless, as originally experienced, inserted in this irreversible flow of chronological time.

But this good-night lasted so short a time, she [my mother] went back down so quickly, that the moment I heard her come

10. Cf. Genette, who shows that "l'anachronie" is one of the oldest traditional resources of narrative literature: *Figures III*, pp. 79–80.
11. Auerbach, *Mimesis*, trans. W. Trask (Garden City, N.Y., 1957), p. 476.

up, then the gentle sound, as she passed through the hallway with the double door, her blue muslin garden dress from which hung little braids of plaited straw, was for me a painful moment. It announced the moment that was to follow, when she would have left me, when she would have gone back down.[I,13]

Thus, the pleasure of the kiss is curtailed, from the very beginning, by Marcel's doggedly eschatological vision of the moments, like the braided knots of his mother's dress, that will inevitably follow. The horror of this implacable current on which he is borne along with the rest of humanity returns to Marcel with particular vividness when his father remarks that, being no longer a child, Marcel's tastes and attitudes are more or less fixed from now on. Marcel realizes all at once "that I was not situated outside Time, but subject to its laws, just as those characters in a novel who, for this reason, filled me with such unhappiness when I read their lives. . . . My father had all of a sudden made me appear to myself within Time . . ." (I,482–83). And even at the moment when he conceives the idea for a novel in which characters would not so develop, in which Time could be deployed in "a new, distinct material," Marcel again discovers, in the aging, decrepit figures of himself and others, "that destructive action of Time" (III,871,930).

At the time of Marcel's realization and definition of the *mémoire involontaire*, Proust employs the same cinematic device that we saw operative in *To the Lighthouse*: the subjugation of the linear development of the diegesis by the nonlinear, achronological juxtaposition of past and present. Until the *matinée* at the Guermantes mansion, Proust's presentations of Marcel have consistently been—with several important exceptions—entirely discontinuous. We have experienced, throughout the *Recherche*, not moments or sequences of true duration, but rather what Poulet calls "atoms of full time" which have no precise linear relation to one another.[12] "All these memories added on top of one another formed but one mass, yet not without one's being able to distinguish among them . . . if not fissures or true faults, at least those veins, those slashes of coloration that, in certain rocks, in certain marbles, reveal differences in origin, in age, in 'molding'" (I,186).

12. Poulet, *Studies*, p. 316.

The principles of organization, especially in the first sections of *Du côté de chez Swann*, are thus based on fidelity to Marcel's own memory rather than on any external logic of composition and action. In *Le Temps retrouvé*, however, we are repeatedly presented with two distinct images, one past and one present, juxtaposed with one another within the otherwise continuous narrative; taken together, these two images transcend the chronological flow of the immediately narrated circumstances, for Marcel experiences the physical sensations that act as common denominator "at once at the present moment and at a distant moment, to the point of making the past infringe on the present, of making me hesitate before saying which of the two I was at. . . ." He calls the experience "extratemporal," since it permits him "to live, enjoy the essence of things, that is, outside of time" (III, 871).

In examining specific examples of the *mémoire involontaire*, we must distinguish between those fusions of past and present that are simply the psychological residue of Marcel's (or Swann's) total life—part of which, naturally, takes place outside the narrative proper—and those that exist fully, in both past and present form, within the boundaries of the text. The famous episode of the madeleine (I,44 ff.), for example, exists for us, the readers, only in its present manifestation, when his mother suggests, one winter's day, that Marcel have some tea. The grown man's past experience of dipping the madeleine into his tante Léonie's tea as a child comes to life for us only through his recollection of it: it is already, as Marcel himself says, an "image" and not an event actualized within the text. The exclusive presentness of this experience is emphasized, in fact, by the unusual use of the present tense: "I take a second swallow. . ." (I, 45).

The same is true for Swann's reactions each time he hears the "petite phrase de Vinteuil." Marcel compares Swann's experiencing of something similar to the *mémoire involontaire*, "the sudden pain that the little phrase by Vinteuil had caused him by returning him to those very days, just as he had felt them before" (III, 869; cf. 877-78), to his own joyful sensations on that climactic morning at the Guermantes'. But Swann's first hearing of the phrase occurs a year before his memorable savoring of it at the Verdurins' (I, 208); all that we experience in the evolution of his *moment privilégié* is the original association of the phrase, "the national anthem of their love," with Odette (I,218). Thus, when the moment of extra-temporality arrives (and it is interesting to note that for Swann it is a bitter-sweet moment, revivifying as it does, "my worries" as well as "my loves of that period"), we learn of the mnemonic "density" that the phrase holds for Swann; but most of the details it brings back to him, "that foliage in array, painted, encircling her . . . an entire springtime that he could not enjoy in days gone by" (I,535-34), refer to events not recounted within the text.

The three "miracles" that occur in rapid succession, however, toward the end of *Le Temps retrouvé* are each linked to a previous episode in the text. The procedure is exactly the same for each one: first the present sensation, be it the unevenness of the cobblestones in the courtyard, the tinkling sound of a spoon against a saucer, or the feel of a stiff napkin; then, the sudden, mysterious substitution of another sensation, only this time a sensation that returns over many past years and juxtaposes itself with the original sensation; and finally, an intellectual realization of what this spatiotemporal juxta-position consists of. Here, the effect for the reader is materially very similar to the effect for Marcel. In the case of the starched napkin, for example,

I wiped my mouth with the napkin that he had given me; all at once, like the character out of the *Arabian Nights* who unwit-tingly performed precisely the rite that made materialize, visible to him alone, a docile genie *ready to transport him far away*, a new vision of *azure* passed before my eyes; but it was *pure* and *salty*, it swelled up into bluish breasts; the impression was so strong that *the moment I was reliving seemed to be the present moment*; . . . I felt as though the servant had just opened the window onto the beach and that everything was urging me to go down and take a walk along the pier at high tide; the napkin I had taken to wipe my mouth had precisely the same type of *stiffness* and *starchiness* as that with which I had had so much trouble drying myself in front of the window, the first day I arrived at Balbec, and now, in front of these bookshelves at the Guermantes hotel, it unfurled, spread out within its flaps and folds, the plumage of an ocean green and blue like a peacock's tail. [III,868-69; my emphasis]

Not only does Marcel have the impression of reliving in the present a previous, long-forgotten moment of the past, but the spatial contours of that ancient moment ("the azure, the window on the beach, a green and blue ocean") are also reincarnated. In the same way, the reader, in experiencing along with Marcel this elated moment of touching the napkin, also reexperiences the brilliant morning scene at Balbec, when Marcel "holding in my hand the *stiff, starched* towel, makes useless efforts to dry myself" (I,672). The reader may even, however unconsciously, recall Marcel's first evocation, much "earlier" in terms of the text, of his Balbec room "whose enameled walls contained, like the polished sides of a swimming pool where the water turns blue, a *pure, azure, salty* air" (I,383; my emphasis throughout). The words *stiffness* and *starchiness* in the first passage act as a sort of sensuous "objective correlative" both for Marcel and for the reader, releasing the spatiotemporally contiguous sensation of something "pure, azure, and salty."

The present moment is, therefore, no longer singular, solitary, or ephemeral; nor is the previous moment absent any longer or irrevocably lodged in the purely causal succession of past time. The two have been thrust together, doubling one another, to create a dynamic exchange of energies. In fact, without this unique mutual effect, the two moments would remain neutral, if not dull, experiences in ordinary places (the sunlit seashore, the Guermantes library—where, immediately before, Marcel has had dreary thoughts about his career as a writer). As in the cinema, the significance is in neither of the momentary images taken by itself, but in their abrupt "montage."

In Proust's work, then, where the narration takes nonetheless the form of a straightforward chronicle far more often than in the works, say, of Virginia Woolf or Gertrude Stein, moments are presented in an ultimately discontinuous manner: the continually forward-moving external time is secondary insofar as it can be transcended by the internal movements of the *mémoire involontaire*. Poulet has described how the long patches of oblivion in the *Recherche* serve ultimately to "negate" time.[13] But the reversibility of Proustian time, with its accompanying effects of ubiquity—effects that Marcel labels "superterrestrial," can be sensed from the very

13. Ibid., p. 317.

beginning of his work in the description of the magic lantern. Like Combray itself, or either one of the two *côtés*, the magic lantern becomes a landmark in Marcel's spiritual development. Given to him "to amuse me on those evenings when they found I seemed too unhappy" (I,9), it comes to represent all the phantasmagorical figures that haunt (and, to some degree, delight) Marcel in the early part of "Combray." Its images are, phenomenologically, the precise opposite of his mother's good-night kiss, which is one of the few "events" in this section clearly anchored in space and time. The magic lantern, on the contrary, emblem of Marcel's teetering, phantasmic mental state as he awaits the kiss, produces shadowy images of quasi-mythological figures without real extension or duration.[14] The dreams that Marcel describes in the opening pages are troubling because they, too, lack specific orientation in space and time. He compares this inability to establish precise coordinates to the impossibility of isolating the discrete movements of a running horse amidst "the successive positions that the kinetoscope affords us" (I,7)— an interesting comparison in view of the importance the running horse had for the history of cinematography. (The magic lantern itself represented a key development in this history insofar as it established, with its succession of slides, an image of movement, however primitive, resulting from serial fragmentation, i.e., the germ of the motion-picture principle.)

The first associations with Combray, then, after the opening reveries of sleeping, waking, and dreaming, are these images of the magic lantern, "impalpable iridescences, supernatural, multi-colored appearances, in which legends were depicted as on a vacillating, instantaneous stained glass window" (I,9). This ambiguous duration of the "instantaneous," coupled with an uncanny substantiality of the intangible, establishes a fairly obvious affinity between the magic lantern and the cinematic image. It suffices to add that the magic lantern, as metaphor for disorientation in space and time, overhangs everything associated with Combray, of which Marcel can recall only "that sort of luminous surface, cut apart in the middle by indistinct shadows. . . ." (I,43). Thus, for example, memories—simple, "voluntary memories, which Marcel later will refer to as *instantanés*,"

14. Cf. ibid., pp. 292–93.

or snapshots, because of their tenacious immobility in the past—
linked to certain streets and the church in Combray, become for
him "still more unreal than the projections of the magic lantern"
(I,48).

The most extreme example of the ultimately physical apperception of time is Marcel's depiction of the church interior. (Here the
interior of the church contrasts with the exterior, as seen above, in
much the same way as do Proust's internal vs. external times.) The
two magnificent tapestries representing the crowning of Esther,
traditionally associated with real personages in local history, along
with the sacred objects of the church, similarly originating with
quasi-legendary figures—"all that made [the church] for me something entirely different from the rest of the town: an edifice oc-
cupying, if one may say, a four-dimensional space—the fourth being
that of time. . ." (I,61). But the actual spatialization of time—no
more than a metaphor here—can only be seen by standing back and
taking a look at the global structure of the *Recherche*.

Taking one intermediary "step back," we can note the peculiarly
Proustian habit of organizing diegetic materials, regardless of their
respective chronological relationship, according to the spatial, or
geographical, layout of the place in question. (Hence, a subordination of diegetic time to diegetic space.) The best-known instance of
this are the two itineraries at Combray, *le côté de Guermantes* and
le côté de Méséglise, or *de chez Swann.* Genette has excellently
demonstrated that the narrative sequence of the events associated
with each itinerary "has no relation to the temporal order of the
events that make it up, or simply a relation of partial coincidence."[15]
The section devoted to the Méséglise walk (I,135-65) includes a
cluster of Marcel's memories and associations, such as the first
appearance of Gilberte, the death of tante Léonie, and the view of
Vinteuil's daughter's sadistic relation with her friend. Yet each
"event" is rigorously subordinated to the general, more or less
timeless, *propos* of describing the various paths and the attendant
weather. Hence, the sequence as read does not account for the
fact that Léonie's death occurs well *after* the sadism voyeuristically
witnessed at Montjouvain.

15. *Figures III*, p. 120.

What is more, this death which, from one point of view, acts as a definitive closure to a long series of fond reminiscences of Marcel's aunt, is relegated itself to a subordinate clause within another subordinate clause (though later slightly expatiated by a brief flashback), whose main clause concerns the Méséglise walk and, by implication, the rainy weather Marcel associates with it:

> But I then developed the habit in those days of going for a walk alone along the Méséglise way, in the autumn during which we had to come to Combray to settle the inheritance of my aunt Léonie, for she had finally died. . . . [I,153]

Something very similar occurs in the Guermantes portion (I,165-86). Here, the actual events are scarcer, all being subordinated to the flow of the Vivonne, which is the true "subject" of this section—if only grammatically: "Soon the course of the Vivonne becomes obstructed with water plants. . . . But further along the current slows down, it crosses an estate. . . . Upon leaving this part, the Vivonne starts to run again" (pp. 168-70). The two specific scenes, that of the duchesse de Guermantes and that of the Martinville steeples, have an ambiguous temporal relation; but, in any case, they too are clearly antecedent to tante Léonie's death. Thus, not only is external chronology ignored in preference for Marcel's haphazard internal associations, but, more precisely, narrative ordering is conditioned and, in a way, controlled by concrete spatial entities that compose the diegetic events.

If from here we look at *Du côté de chez Swann* in its entirety, we see that the noncongruity of narrative sequence and diegetic time is reflected in the larger structural units as well. While in the above case this noncongruence seemed to arise mainly from the subordination of diegetic time to diegetic space, here it is the result of large-scale dislocation of narrative sequence with respect to the diegetic events. The first section, "Combray," itself full of temporal delays and anticipations, centers around Marcel's early childhood, almost exclusively during summer vacations spent at his aunt's house. There is a regular shifting back and forth between the general present of composition ("for a long time I went to bed early. . . . I spent the better part of the night recalling our life of days gone by . . ." [I,3,9]) and the specific, though most often iterative, times of the past ("in Combray, every day beginning in the later afternoon. . . . We were all in the garden when the two hesitant rings of the bell sounded" [I,9,23]).[16]

But the focus is generally fixed on the memories of childhood and how these memories arrange themselves. The following section, "Un Amour de Swann," has no clear-cut temporal relation to "Combray" (though Swann appears in both): we know only that, contrary to its position in the narrative sequence, it takes place long before Marcel is even born. The third and final section, "Nom de pays: le nom," principally concerns Marcel's later childhood in Paris, though it, like "Combray," begins with a temporal wavering between Marcel's present memories of his room in Balbec and his past reveries, as a child in Paris, of what Balbec, Florence, and the other projected travel destinations might be like (I,383-93). (Once the Paris chronicle begins, it should be noted, with the contingencies of Marcel's health and his doctor's prescription of walks with Françoise along the Champs-Elysées, the narrative sequence is most often in concordance with the diegetic development throughout the rest of the work.[17]) The first volume of the *Recherche*, then, by juggling narrative sequence and diegetic time, provides a structural emblem of Proust's peculiarly spatial handling of the normal linearity of time, thus preparing, even without the madeleine episode, for the condensation of past and present time by means of the *mémoire involontaire*. It is no doubt this opening, with its continual shifting between a vague present consciousness at the time of Marcel's sleepless nights and the more precise, apparently chronological evocations of Combray, Balbec, and Paris, that leads Poulet to refer to Proust's work as a "march in reverse."[18] Of course, the *Recherche* is still an essentially forward-moving chronicle, but one that explodes the conventional notion of "chronicle" by mixing with it an unconventional conception of time, which, as perceived

16. See Genette's brilliant analysis of "Combray," in which he carefully describes this "vast coming-and-going movement": *Figures III*, pp. 85-89.
17. Cf. ibid., p. 87.
18. Poulet, pp. 296-97.

from within Marcel's consciousness, makes a peculiar impact on the narrative sequence.

C. *Simultaneity*

It is important to bear in mind that, as we noted in discussing the effects of parallel editing in the movies (cf. above, pp. 85-87), simultaneity embraces both time and space: temporal coincidence and spatial disjunction. In so doing, it poses many problems at once: the nature of "present" time in narrative, priority of point of view, and textual *découpage*—problems dealt with, or to be dealt with, at greater length under separate headings. Furthermore, it is not simply on the basis of parallel editing that a trend toward simultaneity seems to have been fostered in the novel. Cinema presents an image that is plastic, mobile, and perceivable at a glance. Consequently, a single shot can conglomerate two or more separate actions taking place at the same time. This generalized effect of simultaneity may be seen to earmark cinema as an essential precedent to colliding narratives and multiple presentations attempted in the novel, which is, strictly speaking, confined to a single focus, a single effect at a time.

As with achronological narrative sequence, simultaneity is not an entirely new technique with the postcinema novelists. It was used in the nineteenth century, most famously by Flaubert in the *comices agricoles* scene of *Madame Bovary*, and the whole epistolary tradition of the eighteenth-century novel assumes moments of simultaneity, though, by the very nature of that genre, they are not graphically presented in the text in the manner of Flaubert. It is only after 1900, however, that multiple events, presented simultaneously over an extended portion of text, assume the utmost narrative and dramatic importance—as in Jules Romains's *Mort de quelqu'un*. Romains, the least "classic" of the novelists studied thus far, is best known as the expounder of *unanisme*. This doctrine stresses the bond of fellowship that unites all humanity, despite outward differences of appearance and opinion. The main doctrinal point of Romains's novel is that Jacques Godard's death (to which the title refers) serves to bring together people who, though neighbors or acquaintances, never knew each other before and, even after his death, to signify the unspoken but deeply felt sense of brother-

hood that some of the strangers retain. My main point in referring to
unanisme is to suggest that, as a theme, it is unusually well adapted
for effects of simultaneity (just as Proust's *temps perdu* and then
retrouvé is the thematic impetus for his startling temporal disorien-
tations). In order to show, for example, the gradual centripetal
motion of everyone toward Godard's body on the night before the
funeral, Romains describes the different actions discontinuously
and intercalatively so that they may be conceived of as occurring
simultaneously.

The two central instances of simultaneity focus primarily on
Godard's father, who leaves his little provincial village to make a
long trip to Paris for the funeral. In each case, two other groups
of events intertwine themselves with this main line of action: Jacques
Godard's slowly decaying corpse and his spirit that, once cut loose
from his body, goes on feeling and reflecting; and the neighbors'
buying of a funeral wreath for the deceased.

In the first case,[19] the simultaneity begins abruptly (at the beginning of chapter 4), without any indication as to which of the
three motifs will be dominant.

> In Paris, in the room on the fourth floor, the flesh of the dead
> body fought against nothingness. After the last gasp of agony,
> it had at first experienced a sort of relief. But the death that
> had just engulfed the man now ate away the man's flesh bit
> by bit.
>
> On the second floor of the building, a woman had gone out,
> holding the noisy keys in her right hand, and had knocked on
> the next door: "I have an idea: what do you think of it? What
> if the tenants presented a wreath to the old man who died this
> morning, a little wreath bought from contributions?"
>
> Meanwhile, on the road, the father approached the town. It
> was evening. The light detached itself from things to return to
> the west with the sun; it was no longer so closely concentrated
> as during the day, when things were scarcely distinguishable

19. *Mort de quelqu'un* (Paris: Gallimard-Livre de Poche, 1923; orig. 1911),
pp. 51-55. References will be to this edition.

> from their light. It floated a short distance away, a veil that
> the breathing of things seemed to raise up.
>   The dead man tried to keep his mind on the house in Paris.
> [pp. 51-52]

This opening statement makes clear the spatial separation between
the three events: "In Paris, in the room": Godard's corpse; "On
the second floor": the wreath-offering event; and "on the road":
Godard's father in the provinces. The fact of simultaneity is, moreover, clearly indicated by means of a traditional word, *Meanwhile*.
Once the convention is established, however, the three disjunct
locales are cited serially, without further narrative insistence on
their coterminousness: it becomes a linear, diachronic rendering
of something that must be nonetheless conceived of nonlinearly,
synchronically.

> The little girls, charged with the dead man, listened to the
> sound of the ring plunge into the family whose soul was dug
> out like a funnel. The concierge on the front steps of the build-
> ing thought: "It's sad to lose a son at that age!"
>   On the edge of the glimmer that stretched out from the office,
> the old man looked at the ground, hesitating, like an ox who
> finds the grass bitter.
>   In the dead body, the soul of the muscles burst, a rocket about
> to go out. [p. 55]

It is important to note that the action of the neighbors' pitch-
ing in to buy a wreath is, simply on the level of information, a
repetition. In chapter 2 the reader has already learned about this
activity—the common outburst of sympathy, the wives who get
together and decide on the project, the two little girls who go from
door to door asking for contributions—though it is recounted rather
summarily and in the traditional, uninterrupted, chronological
manner (p. 31). The rest of chapter 2 is devoted to a general description of the girls' itinerary and a single vivid scene of three of
the wives going out to buy the wreath.

Thus, in terms of the generally straight chronological development
of the diegesis, the paragraphs of chapter 4 devoted to the wreath

and its *cotisation*, though coterminous with the other intercalated
events, are actually achronological in terms of the diegesis already
initiated in chapter 2. As it is only by the wreath-offering event
that we can identify the time of chapter 4 in relation to the rest
of the diegesis (though certain details of the old man's journey
roughly corroborate this), namely, early in the evening on the day
after Godard's death, it becomes clear that much of chapter 2 has
carried on into a time posterior to the action of chapter 3 (the
arrival of the telegram and the reaction of Godard's parents). As
in Virginia Woolf's work, of which *Mort de quelqu'un*, in certain
details of tone and fragmentation, is oddly reminiscent, two distinct
actions have overlapped for a time, and only later have they been
adjusted to each other in terms of the overall chronology. Most of
chapter 2, in other words, is simultaneous with chapter 3; but only
through the discontinuous simultaneity of chapter 4 do we understand their precise relation.

In fact, the wreath-offering event (one of the key scenes for the
unaniste philosophy) is cut up into three distinct parts: (1) the idea
of the gift and the little girls' door-to-door calls; (2) the three wives'
buying of the wreath; and (3) the women's return to the house.
Only the second part comes in the brief, vivid disconnected vignettes
of chapter 4: the original idea (p. 51, quoted above), one mother's
agreement with another to send their daughters around to the
neighbors (p. 52), the girls climbing the steps with a list in their
hands (p. 53), the concierge's sight of the girls and his consequential
reflection (p. 54), and finally, the girls' ringing of the bell (p. 55,
quoted above). And the third part comes only in chapter 5 amidst
the description of old Godard's ride to the train station. Thus,
even within this first instance of simultaneity, we recognize in the
wreath-offering event that makes up one part of it, a further distortion of chronological time by means of an achronological (2-1-3)
découpage.

The second case of simultaneity (pp. 78-89) extends over a greater
portion of text, and the passages devoted to one event or the other
are longer than the one-or-two-paragraph vignettes of chapter 2.
It takes up most of chapter 5 (minus three pages at the beginning
and end). Here the simultaneity of the Paris apartment house and

old Godard, who is now trying to sleep on the train to the city, becomes, formally, less pronounced because of the less frequent alternation between scenes. The sense of ubiquity, however, sharply augments, as a result of the dream catalogue of the fellow lodgers. The fact of temporal coincidence is not insisted upon, yet we gradually realize that the miniature *récits* formed by the "dream work" are a collective production that only makes sense when conceived simultaneously.

Nearly all the dreams, including that of the old man on the train, contain at least a passing image of Jacques Godard. In the final vignette of this section, the ubiquitous and simultaneous meanderings of the dead man are recounted all together. He is at once beside a locomotive with his father, with a woman holding a wreath, running beside a little girl out of breath. "In particular he oscillated widely from the third to the fourth floor; at times his glow penetrated several souls together; he was a single ring that went through and remained in them. The beings who had come together that morning, within the walls of the funeral parlor, experienced for a few minutes a sleep so similar and so animated that they overlapped one another" (p. 89).

Though Jules Romains stands as a prescient exemplar of the techniques of simultaneity in the twentieth century, later writers used them with even greater subtlety and complexity. One of the most often quoted passages of Virginia Woolf's works is the sky-writing sequence that culminates Mrs. Dalloway's walk through the streets of London.[20] The passage is notable for its discreet simultaneity, achieved through the repeated formations of uncertain letters traced in the sky by an airplane as it soars over the city. The nonlinear peregrinations of this plane, the diegetic focal point as Mrs. Dalloway walks home, seem to serve as an implicit model of discontinuous ubiquity for the narrative as a whole by providing a visual rallying-point to which random characters across the city simultaneously turn their eyes.

20. *Mrs. Dalloway* (New York: Harcourt, Brace and World, 1925), pp. 29–42. See Robert Humphrey's analysis of this passage: *Stream of Consciousness in the Modern Novel* (Berkeley, 1954, 1968), pp. 55–56.

Simultaneity is achieved in this same implicit way in the third part of *To the Lighthouse*. As Woolf reached the final stages of writing this novel, she was "casting about for an end."

> The problem is how to bring Lily and Mr. R. together and make a combination of interest at the end. . . . I had meant to end with R. climbing on to the rock. If so, what becomes of Lily and her picture? Should there be a final page about her and Carmichael looking at the picture and summing up R.'s character? In that case I lose the intensity of the moment. If this intervenes between R. and the lighthouse, there's too much chop and change, I think. Could I do it in a parenthesis? So that one had the sense of reading the two things at the same time?[21]

The solution she used to preserve "the intensity of the moment" was not simply, as we know now, the use of a parenthesis. The bulk of "The Lighthouse" (chapters 3–13) charts at once Mr. Ramsay's expedition with two of his children and Lily's concluding work on her picture. The method is simple alternation—the odd-numbered chapters depict Lily and Carmichael on the lawn, the even-numbered ones describe the small group in the boat as it crosses the bay—so that, just as in Romains's work, serial alternation of events presented linearly and sequentially in terms of reading time are to be conceived of as parallel and simultaneous. One has, in fact, "the sense of reading the two things at the same time."

It seems unnecessary to show in detail how the two events are articulated simultaneously. Let us simply note the subtle, indirect devices that Woolf uses to guarantee this effect. To begin with, Lily periodically turns to look out over the bay and watch, wonder about, or imagine the progress of the boat (pp. 184, 193, 207, 213, 236). Inversely, Mr. Ramsay and Cam periodically turn back to watch the dwindling of their island home (pp. 188-90, 193, 207, 231-32). In this way, the two events are not simply alternated but are carefully interwoven by a play of specific glances and thoughts.

21. *A Writer's Diary* (1953), excerpted in Morris Beja, ed., *Virginia Woolf: To the Lighthouse*, Casebook Series (London, 1970), p. 59; entry for 3 September 1926.

Furthermore, Woolf exploits the implications of simultaneity by emphasizing throughout this final portion of the book the relativity and interchangeability of space and time. "So much depends . . . upon distance," says Lily (p. 217). And, in fact, as Mr. Ramsay and his fellow sailors move farther away, Lily realizes that "Distance had an extraordinary power, they had been swallowed up in it, she felt, they were gone *for ever* . . ." (p. 213; my emphasis). As the space that separates them becomes greater and greater, it takes on a temporal quality—as if Lily were across the universe and not simply across the bay. In the same way, "the little house" and the surrounding property, distorted by the distance between them and the boat, lose their claim to the real, present world. Cam identifies the house for a moment, but then loses sight of it altogether. "She was thinking how all those paths and the lawn, thick and knotted with the lives they had lived there, were gone: were rubbed out, were *past*, were *unreal* . . . " (p. 189; my emphasis). So great is the temporal distortion due to spatial extension that Mr. Ramsay, who has just been teasing Cam about the need for being accurate in one's ability to mark the points of the compass, loses his past associations with the place as it gradually dwindles from view. "And seeing her gazing, with her vague, now rather frightened eyes fixed where no house was Mr. Ramsay forgot his dream; how he walked up and down between the urns on the terrace; how the arms were stretched out to him" (p. 190).

Simultaneity is also a central effect in *Ulysses*, where distinct actions must be juxtaposed with one another for dramatic or ironic purposes. It is most clearly evident, in increasing order of importance, in the "Nausicaa," "Sirens," and "Wandering Rocks" episodes. It should be noted, however, that Joyce's characteristic method in *Ulysses* tends rather to forgo simultaneity in scenes where it might be expected, particularly through the first nine episodes, since there the diegesis remains adamantly linear in development, emphasizing the moment-to-moment sequence of thought, word, sight, and gesture and their intimate configuration.

The function of simultaneity in the "Nausicaa" episode is to stress, first, the dramatic and erotic encounter taking place by proxy between Gerty MacDowell and Bloom and, secondly, the ironic similarity between the scene on the strand and the scene in the church during the men's temperance retreat. There are thus three distinct locales, Gerty with Cissy, Edy, and the children; Bloom seated on an adjacent rock (though in view of the girls, he is dramatically apart for the reader); and the church retreat—all of which come together decisively only at the end of the chapter. The first half of the episode repeatedly juxtaposes the scene of the girls and children with the church scene. Though the total effect is similar to that of *Mort de quelqu'un*, the technique is far more synthetic, the two events continually confounding themselves within a single sentence.

For example, immediately after Gerty imagines Cissy tripping over her high French heels—"That would have been a very charming exposé for a gentleman like that to witness"—we get:

> Queen of angels, queen of patriarchs, queen of prophets, of all saints, they prayed, queen of the most holy rosary and then Father Conroy handed the thurible of Canon O'Hanlon and he put in the incense and censed the Blessed Sacrament and Cissy Caffrey caught the two twins and she was itching to give them a ringing good clip on the ear but she didn't because she thought he might be watching but she never made a bigger mistake in all her life because Gerty could see without looking that he never took his eyes off her and then Canon O'Hanlon handed the thurible back to Father Conroy and knelt down looking up at the Blessed Sacrament and the choir began to sing *Tantum ergo* and she just swung her foot in and out in time as the music rose and fell to the *Tantumer gosa cramen tum*. [pp. 359-60]

The narrative switches back and forth between the two scenes three times within this single long sentence, with no more transition or sign of demarcation than the word *and*. All flows together, moreover, with the aid of the church music (which often serves the same function at the Ormond bar). The ironic parallel is emphasized by the signs of sexual inversion common to both scenes. On the strand, Cissy plays the authoritative mother to the mischievous little boys; in the church, the grown men congregate to adore the virgin mother, herself depicted in an authoritatively sovereign rather than maternal role ("queen of patriarchs, queen of prophets"). Beyond this is the more subtle, more sacrilegious, parallel between the thurible and the swinging of Gerty's foot. The metronomelike foot seems to chop up the Latin phrase into gobbledygook. The "he" referred to who "never took his eyes off her" turns out, of course, to be Bloom, so that the simultaneous rendering suggests a kinship between the kneeling Father Conroy who "looks up at the Blessed Sacrament" and the reclining Bloom who looks up Gerty's skirts. Just below, Bloom will be said to be "literally worshipping at her shrine" (p. 361).

Similar effects are achieved through the next pages by intermingling the two events within a single sentence, most memorably when baby Boardman spits up his recent meal at the precise moment when Canon O'Hanlon gives the benediction (p. 363). The final, codalike statement of the three events comes, contrary to what we noted in *Mort de quelqu'un*, only with the chiming of nine o'clock at the end of the episode. Joyce thus reserves for a moment when external, chronological time is being sounded loud and clear, the direct juxtaposition of the three events that are to be imagined taking place simultaneously.

A bat flew. Here. There. Here. Far in the grey a bell chimed. Mr. Bloom with open mouth, his left boot sanded sideways, leaned, breathed. Just for a few.

Cuckoo

Cuckoo

Cuckoo

The clock on the mantelpiece in the priest's house cooed where Canon O'Hanlon and Father Conroy and the reverend John Hughes S.J. were taking tea and sodabread and butter and fried muttonchops with catsup and talking about

Cuckoo

Cuckoo

Cuckoo

Because it was a little canary bird that came out of its little house to tell the time that Gerty MacDowell noticed the time she was there because she was as quick as anything about a thing like that, was Gerty MacDowell, and she noticed at once that

that foreign gentleman that was sitting on the rocks looking was

> *Cuckoo*
> *Cuckoo*
> *Cuckoo*   [p. 382]

The bat provides a bird's-eye preview of the sensation of ubiquity that follows: "Here. There. Here." The nine "coos" of the cuckoo are regularly punctuated by each of the three scenes. Besides simply signaling the hour, they provide an ironic commentary on the events: the *découpage* is such that the clergymen seem to be talking "cuckoo," or nonsense, and the "foreign gentleman" ends up being, through no fault of Gerty's, himself "cuckoo," or cuckolded. This last amounts practically to an "intertextual" irony (if we think of each episode as a separate text), since we know that during the afternoon Mr. Bloom has in fact been cuckolded—and all the more so if we think of the further parallel between this bell-ringing and Miss Douce's talented elastic garter (like Gerty's precious underthings) when she performs her *"Sonnezlacloche,"* which, by the way, becomes for Bloom ("Love's old sweet *sonnez la gold*") one of the many reminders of his being cheated on at that very moment (pp. 266, 274). The net effect here, then, is of the bell ringing not so much to tell the time as to unite spatially the three locales, to comment ironically on each of them, and to set up resonances with other "distant" events across the narrative space of the novel.

The effect of simultaneity in the "Sirens" episode is somewhat similar, except that here the diverse actions are thrust together most often by means of the rhythmic repetition of music, which characterizes the whole of this section. In other words, the time is not simply chronological time (we know it is somewhere between three and four o'clock) but the metrical time of a measure of music. The three actions that take place in tandem to the central one at the Ormond bar:

1. Bloom's arrival and departure;
2. Boylan's arrival, departure, and subsequent trip to Eccles Street;
3. the blind piano-tuner's arrival

are presented like rhythmic motifs "announced" first in repeating fragments before appearing in full amidst the central strains of the score.

The Bloom motif, for example, enters very near the beginning of the episode with: "A man. Bloowho went by Moulang's pipes . . ." (p. 258). Similar variations on Bloom's name continue to appear on the next three pages, so that Bloom's gradual and simultaneous approach to the Ormond is carefully planted, with a more or less regular periodicity, amidst the mirth and banter around the bar.

Shortly before Bloom actually arrives at the Ormond, a new motif is sounded: "Jingle" (p. 261). It reappears, amplified, on the following page: "Jingle jaunty jingle"; but it is only on page 263, when Lenehan is said to be waiting "for Boylan with impatience, for jingle jaunty blazes boy" and Bloom, buying writing paper, catches sight of "a gay hat riding on a jauntingcar," that we realize these words are a metonymic sign of Boylan's approach.

Boylan stays only a short while at the bar, and as he leaves, his motif begins again: "Jingle a tinkle jaunted" (p. 267). Throughout the rest of the episode, Boylan's passage to Eccles street will be periodically alluded to (pp. 269, 271, 277, 279, 281, 282), either by the same simple "jingles" or by more elaborate descriptions: "By Graham Lemon's pineapple rock, by Elvery's elephant jingle jogged" (p. 272). The "jingle" sign touches off, of course, a special association within Bloom (who "heard a jing, a little sound. He's off," p. 268), for it is nearing four o'clock, the hour of Boylan's rendezvous with Molly. Thereafter, besides the simple diegetic simultaneity of Boylan's approach to Eccles street, we have the ironic appearance of the Boylan motif amidst Bloom's thoughts: "Jingle jaunty. Too late. She longed to go. That's why. Woman. As easy stop the sea. Yes: all is lost" (p. 273). So intent is Bloom on following Boylan in his mind that there are actually two arrivals at Eccles street, the first imagined: "Jing. Stop. Knock. Last look at mirror always before she answers the door. The hall. There? How do you do?" (p. 274), the second apparently the actual arrival of Boylan: "Jog jig jogged stopped. Dandy tan shoe of dandy Boylan socks skyblue clocks came light to earth" (p. 282).

Just before Boylan's arrival at an entirely different point in Dublin, a final new motif enters as Miss Douce puts a shell to her ear.

She held it to her own and through the sifted light pale gold in contrast glided. To hear.

Tap.

Bloom through the bardoor saw a shell held at their ears. He heard more faintly that that they heard . . . a silent roar. [p. 281]

The "tap" will eventually be identified as that of a blind stripling's cane. This personage has, in turn, been previously identified, through Miss Douce's commentary (p. 263), as the piano-tuner. The momentarily incomprehensible sign appears in a context that is, with regard to what we later find out, sharply ironic. Bloom imagines he *hears* as he merely *watches* the adjacent scene, and what Miss Douce actually hears in the shell is nothing, "a silent roar." From his very first, paradoxically aphonic and purely metonymic appearance ("tap"),[22] the piano-tuner reverses the paradigms of the scene: he sees nothing but hears sharply. He is the precise opposite of Bloom, the proto-Ulysses of the "Sirens" as elsewhere, who watches all but can hear only in bits and pieces. The blind boy hears all, and with precision— so long as he has his molylike tuningfork, the object of his present mission, but he risks not the "whiffs of a mermaid" painted on a poster in Daly's window (p. 289).

Thus, the "Sirens" episode, with its refusal to provide a comprehensive summary view or anything resembling an "establishment shot," splinters its auditory signs, metonyms of various personages, across the text, reminding us aurally of other events, invisible for the moment, that are taking place in tandem to the centrally focalized event. The most apt analogy in this case, and one that underscores Joyce's linguistic genius, is the sound fiction film of the New Wave period. Resnais, for example adapts the montage principle to the sound track and, introducing audial cues that cannot be immediately identified in the image, excels even Eisenstein in dramatically presenting a diegetic whole which is built up piecemeal by auditory as well as visual fragments. The "prologue" of *Hiroshima mon amour* and the opening sequence of *Muriel* are excellent examples of this complex process.

22. Note that the "tap" motif is not included in the list of abbreviated themes at the head of the chapter. It's as if the piano-tuner were off in the wings during the overture.

The "Wandering Rocks" episode is a tour de force of simultaneity from start to finish. Each discrete sequence of actions takes place at the same time (approximately three o'clock), and carefully inlaid fragments of preceding or subsequent actions that intersect here and there remind us that each time there seems to be some diegetic advancement, we are actually back at the same temporal starting point—even though located at a different point in space. This tenth episode, moreover, stands out in structural relief from the nine preceding episodes, which are notably linear in their development.

The logic of this vast development of simultaneous action is that each of the nineteen sections contains at least one repeated fragment of an action from another section. Hence, the following formula applies to the whole episode: if x is coterminous with y, and y is coterminous with z, then x is coterminous with z. A whole complicated network of cross-references is thus established, having as its prime visual objective an indirect evocation of the city of Dublin.

In section 2, for example, Corny Kelleher, chewing a blade of hay, looks out the door: "Father John Conmee stepped into the Dolly-mount tram on Newcomen bridge" (p. 225). This information, with practically the same words, has been carefully established in the first section (pp. 221–22), just after "Father Conmee passed H. J. O'Neill's funeral establishment where Corny Kelleher jotted figures in the daybook while he chewed a blade of hay. A constable on his beat saluted Father Conmee and Father Conmee saluted the constable." Speaking to Constable 57C, "Corny Kelleher sped a silent jet of hay-juice arching from his mouth while a generous white arm from a window in Eccles street flung forth a coin" (p. 225). In section 3, which describes the itinerary of a begging one-legged sailor, this white arm reappears and makes the same gesture: "The blind of the window was drawn aside. A card *Unfurnished Apartments* slipped from the sash and fell. A plump bare generous arm shone, was seen, held forth from a white petticoatbodice and taut shift-straps. A woman's hand flung forth a coin over the area railings" (pp. 225–26). According to the above formula, we ascertain that Father Conmee's tram ride from Newcomen bridge is coterminous with the woman's (Molly Bloom's, we find out from yet another repetition on p. 234) offering to the sailor.

The final figure of the viceregal cavalcade, like the H.E.L.Y.'S.

sandwich men on a smaller scale, serves to tie together many of the more obscure passing references that crop up during the preceding eighteen sections. It is like the mysterious motorcar in *Mrs. Dalloway* (which is said to have been modeled on Joyce's cavalcade). It produces few instances of simultaneity, at least of the "double-take" variety characteristic of what precedes, but rather provides one single, continuous thread that extends over a large part of Dublin and to which previously random passersby are now attached. (The cavalcade has itself appeared "earlier": pp. 233, 239, 241, 248).

In fact, the essential structure of the "Wandering Rocks" is this contrast between isolated, disconnected elements (people or groups of people) sticking out precisely like so many rocky points above unknown waters, and several connecting lines that, like the wake of a boat, suggest heretofore unsuspected rapprochements, temporally and spatially. It would therefore be wrong to think that the whole point of this episode is the simple pleasure of simultaneity. Rather, each section offers a certain number of spatial coordinates on a graph whose x- and y-axes are themselves entirely unknown. When one of the connecting lines (capable of *connecting* precisely because composed of more than one set of spatial coordinates) is then superimposed over this graph, it suddenly becomes clear how the scattered points fall into place, how some have actually been duplicates or in some way congruent with one another all the while.

The two principal connecting lines occur at the beginning and the end of the episode: Father Conmee's walk and the viceregal cavalcade. It is not surprising that the connectors, or the containers, as we shall see, are representatives first of the Church, then of the State. Joyce's dim view of these two institutions is well known and reflected throughout his writing prior to *Ulysses*. More important is the thematic relation thus suggested between the "Wandering Rocks" and the very first episode, "Telemachus," which is full of references to and symbols of Church and State. The thematic kinship is all the more relevant in that the two episodes are in a sort of structural equilibrium in the book, "Telemachus" being the first of the first nine chapters, "Wandering Rocks" the first of the second nine. Thus, the two figures or movements that structurally *close in* this episode are the same Church and State that thematically *close in* on all of Joyce's Dubliners. What appears inescapably in this episode, then, is the structural play between continuity and anarchic randomness, the latter being just barely contained by the two continuous structures (of society) and, even at that, constantly on the point of breaking loose or spilling over.

Father Conmee's walk and the viceregal cavalcade, moreover, are the only two events that have any considerable amount of duration and extension, and the details of this extension are noted in each case with great particularity. Likewise, they correspond with more of the small points that appear in the intervening sections than any other one of these sections. Finally, they are the only two events that are posited as actually taking place simultaneously.

Though neither refers directly to the other, the approximate simultaneity of these two major movements can be established in the manner cited above. Toward the beginning of the cavalcade, "Mr. Thomas Kernan beyond the river greeted [the viceroy] vainly from afar" (p. 252). We know of Mr. Kernan's disappointment from a previous passage: "Mr. Kernan hurried forward, blowing pursily. His Excellency! Too bad! Just missed that by a hair" (p. 241). Shortly before this (though temporal precision is, as we know, related to a long string of contingencies), "a crumpled throwaway, rocked on the ferry-wash, Elijah is coming" (p. 240), floats by. This same throwaway has recently ridden "lightly down the Liffey, under Loopline bridge, shooting the rapids" (p. 227). It is mentioned just after Katey and Boody Dedalus come home, disappointed that Maggy was unable to pawn some books. And it is just in the midst of their conversation that we read, "Father Conmee walked through Clongowes fields, his thinsocked ankles tickled by stubble" (p. 226), information established near the end of Father Conmee's walk (p. 224).

According to this analysis, it may be most accurate to say that the cavalcade starts up just as Father Conmee leaves off. Thus, the lapse of time necessitated by the separate appearance of the Elijah throwaway, which connects the two intermediary scenes of Kernan and the Dedalus sisters, would be about equal to, on the one hand, Father Conmee's reading of his offices (p. 224) which concludes his section, and, on the other hand, the initial passage of the cavalcade from the Phoenix Park gate to Bloody bridge, where Kernan catches sight of it.

In the "Wandering Rocks," then, we are not simply presented, in the manner of most of the previous examples of simultaneity, with two or three events whose parallel unfolding is signified by regular intercalation. Instead, there are two continuous actions, taking place simultaneously, which overlap and intersect with other actions at key points. The final effect is of one intense, rather brief movement whose totality is only glimpsed twice (thus immediately raising the problem of point of view) and whose *actants* are continually changing. And this total movement, experienced only in its parts and named only in the attendant streets and squares, is Dublin. It is perhaps the finest example of a city described without a single generalization made on its behalf and without a single character standing out as "representative."

7 Point of View

One wanted fifty pairs of eyes of see with. . . .

Virginia Woolf, To the Lighthouse

Like many of the techniques discussed thus far, the novelist's concern with point of view, by no means an unexplored realm by the early twentieth century, must first be considered in terms of its development within the novel itself. If we take point of view to be, in its widest meaning, the narrative vehicle by which the story is told, then important variations can be found in many traditional forms of fiction: for example, the found manuscript in *Don Quixote*, the secondary narrative (*métarécit*, or narrative within narrative) in *Manon Lescaut*, and the discursive alternations of the epistolary novel. If, on the other hand, we take point of view to refer to the specific angle and distance established between the diegetic matter and the narrative vehicle, we can agree with Robbe-Grillet that Balzac was rarely concerned with the problem and that the modern novelist has, consciously or unconsciously, staked a trail that leads to perspectival techniques strikingly similar to the continual shifting of angle and distance in the camera set-ups of cinematic narration, or montage. "The perpetually omniscient, omnipresent novelist is thus challenged. It is no longer God who describes the world but man, *a* man."[1] But this preoccupation with relativity,

1. "Notes sur la localisation et les déplacements du point de vue dans la description romanesque," *Cinéma et Roman*, special number, *La Revue des Lettres Modernes* 36-38 (Summer 1958):257-58.

In *Figures III*, Genette tries to clarify once and for all the necessary yet often neglected distinction between narrative vehicle and narrative perspec-

the insistence that we are perceiving from one privileged point of view a reality potentially visible or recountable in an unlimited variety of ways, goes back at least to the period of impressionism that we examined in chapter 2. James and Conrad each represent important turning-points in their adapting of the conventional prob- lematics of narrative vehicularity to the modern concern for relative placement (cf. above, pp. 35–37). James combines omniscient and first-person narration, stock-in-trade viewpoints in the eighteenth- and nineteenth-century novel, in his "central reflector." He thus forges an essentially subjective medium seen at once from within and without, and whose relative detachment from the diegetic material depends on James's careful mise-en-scène. Conrad picks up the technique of displaced authority for the narrative, which was of prime use in early novels and which distinguishes his works from James's, where the ultimate authority still lies outside the story and the act of narrating it. He then, like James, creates from this intermediary vessel of information (e.g., Marlow) a participating nar- rator who approaches or withdraws from the diegetic object accord- ing to his epistemological vantage point (e.g., direct experience, rumored accounts, etc.) and his narrative position with regard to the second- or third-hand story he tells.

In fact, important point-of-view techniques that we might nor- mally associate with the postcinema novelists often have an impres- sionist precedent.

A soft tap at the winow-pane, as though something had hit it, followed by a gentle abundant fall as of grains of sand that might have been dropped from a window overhead, then the fall becom- ing extended, regular, adopting a rhythm, becoming fluid, sono- rous, musical, immeasurable, universal: it was the rain. [I,101–02]

tive (or "focalisation") by considering the first as a system of "voix" and the second as a system of "modes"; see esp. pp. 203–06.

Norman Friedman's discernment of eight possible points of view is also based, though somewhat unevenly, on this fundamental distinction: "Point of View in Fiction: The Development of a Critical Concept," *PMLA* 70 (Dec. 1955):1160–84; esp. valuable for its historical account of the concept of point of view.

See also F. Van Rossum-Guyon, "Point de vue ou perspective narrative," *Poétique* 4 (1970):476–97; this author concludes that "there exists today no unified, definitive theory of narrative perspective" (p. 477).

Proust's playful delaying of the cause of these auditory sensations is an attempt to recreate the original experience of hearing the rain. As such, it is an example of "a form of narration participating in the life of the characters, contemplating the events with their eyes. . . . Impressionistic," Spitzer goes on to explain, "that is, seen from the angle of the character (or of the reader)—Proustian description often comes across in this way."[2] This inversion of ordinary cause-and-effect relationships, one of the fundamental processes of impressionism (cf. above, chap. 1), if it opts, as Spitzer says, for the point of view of the participating observer, also places temporarily in abeyance the exact position of that observer. In the description of the rain, the reader is taken away from the immediate location (tante Léonie's bedroom) to follow the external signs as they succeed one another.

By presenting things, as Proust himself says, "in the order of our perceptions, instead of explaining them first by their cause" (I,653) and thus excising the narrative authority that usually establishes the perceptual logic, the problem of relativity of viewpoint is automatically broached. In something of the same way, the methods of "indirection" or "reader participation" developed by the Anglo-American novel at the end of the nineteenth century, and Degas's use of unusual or random points of view in framing, all stand behind the modern concern with relativity of observation. The movies thus served to "clinch" the problem, to dramatize more dynamically than ever before that "any observer is endowed with a particular point of view, any being is in a situation" and that "every proposition relating to a character is variable according to the angle from which it is made and the distance at which one has been placed to make it."[3]

A. Perspective Mobility

Perhaps the first, most compelling aesthetic pleasure of the movies, even before film-makers learned to stop the camera and thereby to

2. Leo Spitzer, "Le Style de Proust," in *Etudes de Style*, trans. A. Coulon (Paris, 1970), p. 461.
3. Claude-Edmonde Magny, *L'Age du roman américain* (Paris, 1948), p. 112.

narrate a story, was the spectator's sensation of moving along with the camera placed on a mobile support, such as a locomotive. Objects not in motion themselves, such as people standing along a train platform, grew or diminished in size or were displaced from one side of the frame to the other by the sole means of the camera's movement. This aesthetic experience, based on a constant variable of distance, will serve, as it is seized upon by Proust in much the same way, as a sort of emblem of the basic problem of shifting point of view.

Marcel's experience of seeing the Martinville and Vieuxvicq steeples from a moving coach makes an indelible mark on the text, since it gives rise to the first piece of writing *within* the text attributed to Marcel himself. Hence, for Proust, the set piece of description (that will later be "published"), is from the outset a play on narrative vehicularity: the author must write not simply what his narrator, Marcel, would be thinking and feeling but also what he would write. As the found manuscript (e.g., that of Cid Hamete in *Don Quixote*), which though at one remove from the act of narration, is aimed at establishing the "real" source of the action, so the fictional writing of Marcel, though at one remove in the opposite direction (because part of the diegesis), has a paradoxically true ring to it: we "know" the writer and "see" him writing.

The main point, however, is that what lies "behind this clarity . . . this obscure pleasure" (I,180), which prompts Marcel, "filled with a sort of drunkenness," to get his impression down on paper, is his own locomotion and the corresponding *apparent* locomotion of the steeples. In other words, within the general problem of narrative vehicularity, Proust poses the specific problem of narrative distance and perspective. Although the "special pleasure" is never named— neither in Proust's nor in Marcel's text, Marcel feels that by writing it, by not allowing the sensuous pleasure to pass vaguely into his crowded memory, he is "perfectly disburdened of those steeples and of that which they concealed behind them . . ." (I,182). The experi- ence is thus cast in the classic Proustian double form: first the material sensations as they are experienced *sur le vif*, then (as with the *mémoire involontaire*) the recovering of the sensations by a dif- ferent, indirect means—here, *voluntarily*, through the act of writing.

From the very beginning, Marcel realizes that "the movement of

our carriage and the sharp curves of the road *seemed* to make" the
two Martinville steeples change place and that the third one, though
"separated from them by a hill and a valley and situated on a higher
plateau in the distance, *seemed* nonetheless right next to them" (my
emphasis). Yet what is rationalized as mere seeming autonomy in
the main text becomes a fait accompli in Marcel's own written
description (I,181–82), in which the steeples are extensively personi-
fied. After seeing the first two, Marcel notes that, "moving over to
place itself in front of them with a bold turn-about, one lagging
steeple, the Vieuxvicq one, had come together with them." Later,
this one "strayed, moved off. . . ." The steeples take on the very
traits of human perception, as when, "left alone on the horizon
watching us speed away," they "moved their sunlit tips as a sign of
good-bye," just before being able to "perceive us for one more
instant. . . ." Thus, Marcel's own locomotion causes an elusive
fluidity of vantage point, which results in a reversal of subject and
object qualities, just as we noticed in other texts of this period that
do not necessarily exploit the mobile point of view (cf. above, chap.
5). As in the cinema, where distance, angle, and mobility of the
camera are the three outstanding factors that condition the image, so
here the distance that separates Marcel from the steeples distorts the
"actual" distance between the steeples; the angle of the roads with
regard to the valley below flattens the terrain in a way that makes
the Vieuxvicq steeple "level" with the others; and, finally, Marcel's
constantly shifting point of view vis-à-vis the steeples confers upon
them an autonomous movement all their own.

B. *Widening the Diaphragm*

The most pervasive technique in the movies, the one that lies at
the heart of the montage process, is the cut: one set of objects shot
from a specific angle and distance disappears and gives way to the
same or another set of objects shot from a different angle and distance. It is really on the basis of this simple procedure that the
movies have had such a tremendous impact on the twentieth-century
concern with disjunction and relativity. But the facility with which
the edited film passes from one set-up, one locale, to another,
cannot be specifically approximated in the language of the novel

without serious losses of coherence and continuity. Point of view in literature is a much more pervasive thing than the specific, measurable distance and angle of each discrete "take" in the cinema. Early twentieth-century novelists, rather, engage in a process of *assouplissement* of the traditional, solitary, generally omniscient point of view: by complementing the narrative point of view with that of one of the characters, by imagining supplementary points of observation that extend an inevitable singleness of point of view (in first-person narration), and by presenting the same person or object, at disconnected points of the text, from radically different perspectives.

The complementing of (third-person) narrative viewpoint is, in itself, not a particularly new technique. One need only think of the extensive use in the nineteenth century of *style indirect libre* (Flaubert and James, in particular), where the subjective attitude of a character is filtered through the narrator and transformed into a third-person enunciation; or even earlier, the general technique of adopting a character's viewpoint (i.e., "point de vue" in the former French acceptation), as in Stendhal's treatment of his heroes. The modern novelist, however, without ever entirely forsaking these methods,[4] expands the narrative viewpoint in a more "cinematic" way by allowing the character's point of view to command a portion of text without any direct narrative mediation. In this manner, scenes are constructed from a double vantage point: the point of view of the relatively detached narrator (the nonparticipating observer) juxtaposed with that of the protagonist (the participating observer). In the first chapters of *Ulysses*, for example, it is no longer the simple doubleness of character seen and character seeing (e.g., Emma Bovary's contemplation of suicide), but a dialectic complementarity between character at once seen and seeing and the nearly simultaneous narration of what is being seen. In other words, the character's viewpoint is crucial not simply insofar as it reveals the subjectivity of that character but also insofar as it provides a comple-

4. Cf. Humphrey, who gives evidence of the prevalence of *style indirect libre*—what he calls "indirect interior monologue"—in Woolf and others: *Stream of Consciousness in the Modern Novel* (Berkeley, 1954, 1968), chap. 2. Georges Blin elaborates the technique of adopting character point of view in *Stendhal et les problèmes du roman* (Paris, 1954).

mentary attitude toward the object observed by both character and narrator.

Thus, as Stephen watches the milkwoman measure out the milk in "Telemachus," his own, partly imagined, perception of her is, without transition, juxtaposed with the narrator's description.

> He watched her pour into the measure and thence into the jug rich white milk, not hers. Old shrunken paps. She poured again a measureful and a tilly. Old and secret she had entered from a morning world, maybe a messenger. She praised the goodness of the milk, pouring it out. Crouching by a patient cow at daybreak in the lush field, a witch on her toadstool, her wrinkled fingers quick at the squirting dugs. They lowed about her whom they knew, dewsilky cattle. Silk of the kine and poor old woman, names given her in old times. A wandering crone, lowly form of an immortal serving her conqueror and her gay betrayer, their common cuckquean, a messenger from the secret morning. [pp. 13-14]

The first sentence is an ordinary description by the narrator, up to the last two words: "not hers," which, along with "Old shrunken paps," indicates Stephen's subjective point of view. It is reminiscent of a sentence we examined before (p. 113) where Bloom's perusal of an unidentified woman interrupts the narrative voice: "She stood still, waiting, while the man, husband, brother, like her. . . ." But whereas there we noted that the internal and external, the subjective and objective viewpoints remained firmly separated, here the two blend, or are overlaid on top of each other. The point here is not so much Stephen's particular reaction to the milkwoman as his private interpretation of her, which adds a new dimension to the total description.

Thus, his own point of view is not clearly demarcated from the narrator's. While the third sentence is plainly the narrator's, the fourth introduces the pluperfect tense—suggesting the hypotactic structure of reflection—as well as the phrases "old and secret" and "morning world," which suggest Stephen's interpolation. Its final words, "maybe a messenger," are the keynote of Stephen's interpretation of the old woman and trigger the following description of her, after the narrator's sentence "She praised . . ." at a different point in space and time. The last four sentences present what might be a narrative description of the milkwoman milking her cows earlier that morning, except that the continual interpretative remarks, such as "a witch on her toadstool," indicate that Stephen's point of view is dominant: it is Stephen imagining the old woman's early-morning tasks and giving to them his characteristic heroic/mock-heroic cast. Only the second of these sentences has conjugated verbs, "lowed" and "knew"; otherwise, this final description is made up entirely of disconnected epithets, in apposition, for the old woman, which gradually depart from the narrative point of view, "pouring it out. Crouching by a patient cow," as Stephen interprets her for himself: "a messenger from the secret morning."

Proust, too, seeks in "Un Amour de Swann" a complement to Marcel's dominant point of view. What Proust does specifically, though, to expand Marcel's solitary viewpoint—that is, at the syntagmatic textual level, is to posit alternative viewpoints, real or imagined, by which the object viewed takes on a certain roundness or totality. Such is the case, as we have seen, with Marcel's description of the Martinville and Vieuxvicq steeples as his carriage ride dynamizes their spatial relations. Such, also, is the case with Marcel's vision of the sunrise on the train to Balbec (I,654–55), where again the constant mobility of the point of observation contributes significantly to the total effect. The zig-zag course of the train makes it impossible for Marcel to observe the sunrise as a whole from where he is seated. His perception of the first morning light, "of scalloped clouds whose soft down was of a fixed, dead rose color, which will never again change" (note the paradoxically eternal quality of the future verb added to a phrase in the past tense), gives way suddenly to "a nocturnal village with moonlight blue roofs." And, just as suddenly, the morning scene returns, "but red this time," in the *opposite* window from where he is seated: "so that I spent my time running from one window to the other in order to bring back together, to line up again the intermittent and opposing fragments of my lovely scarlet and versatile morning and to have a total view, a continuous picture of it."

This description is really just an extreme case of what happens throughout the *Recherche*. No object, thought, or person can be grasped directly in its totality, but must rather be apprehended successively, from various fragmented viewpoints. It would thus be wrong to think of Marcel as the all-seeing narrator recast in a first-person form—or even as the individual, normally myopic observer who, by the standard conventions of first-person fiction, takes in at a flash all the pertinent information in a given sequence of events. The massive change of point of view in "Un Amour de Swann" serves to emphasize, in this respect, that Marcel's recounting of Swann's love affair with Odette is based on partial (in both senses of the word) accounts of these events by Swann himself. Marcel is, rather, a thoroughly human, mildly obsessive-compulsive observer who, like Montaigne, can only be sure of one "vue oblique" at a time of any given event or object.

Besides the expansion of point of view provided by real mechanical means (carriage, train), Proust endows Marcel with imaginary viewpoints that further extend his vision at moments of reverie. These key moments occur intermittently throughout "Combray," the last, from an expanding point of view, acting as prelude to the fixed double perspective of "Un Amour de Swann:"

> But no sooner had the daylight—and no longer the reflection of a last ember off a copper curtain rod that I had taken for it—traced in the darkness, as though with chalk, its first white, rectifying ray, than the window with its curtains quit the doorframe where I had erroneously situated it, while, so as to make room for it, the desk which my memory had clumsily placed there speedily hurried off, pushing in front of it the fireplace and putting to one side the wall adjoining the hallway; a small court reigned in the place where, just an instant before, the washstand had sat, and the room that I had rebuilt in the darkness went off to join the rooms barely seen in the whirlwind of waking, placed in perspective by the pale sign traced above the curtains by the finger of dawn. [I,187]

The first, deceptive light of the morning causes Marcel to "perceive" the room according to a false orientation prescribed by memory. The actual ray of daylight is "rectifying." Rather than restoring order, as one might expect from such a qualification, it causes the window and the furniture to be thrown about, scattered, until they finally fix themselves in "other" locations. The disposition of this nonetheless stable interior perceived by a stationary Marcel is thus evoked not by means of a single, steady point of view but rather in contrast to another hypothetical view forged in part by memory, and the vanishing point lies nowhere among the objects themselves but rather in some netherworld between waking and sleeping.

The hypothesized or imaginary viewpoint operates in the opening pages of "Combray" as well.

> I wondered what time it could be; I heard the whistling of trains that, more or less far away, like the song of a bird in a forest, taking up the distances, described for me the expanse of the deserted countryside when the traveler hurries toward the next stop; and the little road he follows will be engraved in his memory by the excitement he owes to new places, to unaccustomed acts, to the recent chat and to the good-byes exchanged under the unfamiliar light which follow him still in the silence of the night, with the impending sweetness of return. [I,3-4]

Marcel's own point of view—here wholly within his imagination to begin with—is first displaced and thus expanded by an external, auditory sensation, the whistling of trains, that even has the power of delineating an unseen portion of space ("the expanse of the deserted countryside").[5] In the third clause, the first-person subject changes to "he," "the traveler," a purely hypothetical personage, assimilable though he may be as an alter ego to Marcel. It is, then, this anonymous traveler and his "own" recent experiences ("unaccustomed acts," "recent chat," "good-byes") that extend Marcel's momentarily confined point of view, catapult it by means of a simple sound into new spaces and unheard-of circumstances.

The catapulting of point of view is effected, too, at long range and at great intervals, by means of a succession of "takes" of the same object or character. The town of Combray, for example, we know mainly, through the first part of the opening section (I,3-48), from

---

5. Cf. in "Penelope" the way a train whistle suddenly brings Molly Bloom's mind back to the here-and-now (*Ulysses*, pp. 754 and 762)—exactly the opposite effect from this passage, in which the train whistle launches Marcel on an imaginary flight through space.

the inside out—that is, through Marcel's memories relating to his tante Léonie's house and the crucial events that take place therein. The second part begins with a long-distance view of Combray as Marcel and his family arrive on the train: "Combray, at a distance, within a range of thirty miles, seen from the railroad when we would arrive the last week before Easter, was nothing more than a church summarizing the town, representing it, speaking of it and for it to far-away places . . ." (I,48). Later on, this maximum perspective on Combray will be broken down into two main focal points, the famous "côté de chez Swann" and "côté de Guermantes." As we have seen, these two parts of the Combray environs act as geographical rallying points for any number of remembered characters or events, each rigidly associated with one *côté* or the other and thus viewed through its peculiar *optique*.

For, as Marcel explains at some length, the two *côtés* are not merely spatial or sentimental landmarks: they afford two essential points of view on Combray, "the ideal of the view of the plain, and the ideal of the river landscape"; and ultimately they become the very media of Marcel's perceiving consciousness, the two entities on which he confers "that cohesion, that unity which belong only to creations of our mind" and between which he places "the distance that there is between the two parts of my brain where I thought of them, one of those distances in the mind that do more than draw apart, which separate and place *onto another plane*" (I,134–35; my emphasis).

Far more than objects, it is individual characters who are subjected to this process of an episodically unfolding point of view. Odette is seen in a series of fleeting snapshots—first as the mysterious outcast from Marcel's family's closed society, then as the equally mysterious "dame en rose" at his uncle Adolphe's, then as the unidentified beauty of one of Elstir's portraits—before emerging as chief *habituée* of the Verdurin circle. Nor is it really inappropriate to speak in photographic terms, since Marcel does so himself in describing the difficulty of grasping Albertine's character, of being aware of it all at once at any one time. "That which we take in the presence of the loved one is only a negative; we develop it later, once we're at home, when we have found again at our disposition that internal darkroom whose entry is 'condemned' so long as we're seeing people" (I,872).

This initial "take" is entirely deceptive, as in the case of Albertine, who, the second time Marcel sees her, has "a glowing temple that was not very pretty to see, and no longer the singular look that I had always thought back on till then. But this was but a second view and there were others, no doubt, through which I would have to pass successively" (I,874). What is more, there is an inevitable imprint, in these successive "takes," of the photographer himself. Thus, if Gilberte and Albertine seem to bear an uncanny resemblance to each other at certain points, it is because "These women are a product of our temperament, reversed image or projection, a 'negative' of our sensibility" (I,894). Albertine is not one, but many, and each depends not only upon the Albertine being projected that day but also upon Marcel's particular point of view and temperament at the moment of registering the impression (I,947).

Virginia Woolf's Mrs. Ramsey is presented in somewhat the same way. As in Proust, direct perception becomes imperceptibly mixed with memory and projection in the depiction of the whole Mrs. Ramsay. In the famous passage following "Never did anybody look so sad" (I,5; pp. 34–36), analyzed by Auerbach, we have no less than three separate views of Mrs. Ramsay presented in tandem. First there is the anonymous, detached, poetically reflective view of "Never did anybody look so sad." It is a truly *oblique* view in that it ascribes to Mrs. Ramsay an attitude through negative comparison and exclusion and adds a purely metaphorical description that has, a priori, nothing whatsoever to do with Mrs. Ramsay. It is an interpretive leap even to assert that this paragraph is connected with Mrs. Ramsay by virtue of anything other than textual contiguity. There follows the point of view of "people": the rumors and popular attitudes toward Mrs. Ramsay's beauty. This view is more concrete than the first, though it is characterized—"falsely perhaps"—by the questioning mode and the uncertainty of vapid hypotheses. The third and most specific point of view is that of Mr. Bankes in the following two parenthetically enclosed paragraphs. Mr. Bankes pays Mrs. Ramsay an extravagant compliment over the telephone: "'Nature has but little clay . . . like that of which she moulded you,'" and then adds to himself, "'But she's no more aware of her beauty than a child.'" This point of view, then, though concrete and assignable to one individual, is congruent with the other two in its inability to pinpoint Mrs.

Ramsay's special quality, to *portray* her with anything but comparisons and negations ("He did not know. He did not know."). The narrator then brings us back to the diegetic point from which we departed and furnishes her own oblique view of the variousness of Mrs. Ramsay, "Her head outlined absurdly by the gilt frame, the green shawl which she had tossed over the edge of the frame, and the authenticated masterpiece of Michael Angelo. . . ."

The "absurdity" of such a framing of Mrs. Ramsay, notable for its flattening of ordinary perspective, is precisely that she cannot be depicted all of a piece the way a portrait artist renders a model. "Fifty pair of eyes were not enough to get round that one woman with," Lily thinks much later (III,11; p. 224), and in the course of *To the Lighthouse* we do seem to get upwards to fifty different points of view on Mrs. Ramsay. Through the first section, each of the main characters, Mr. Ramsay, Tansley, Lily, Prue, has his or her separate awareness of Mrs. Ramsay. In the second section, we have the detached laconism of Mrs. Ramsay's "having died rather suddenly the night before" (III,3; p. 147) in those excluding, minimalizing brackets, plus the "survival" of Mrs. Ramsay in the "they said's" as filtered through Mrs. McNab, who conjures up to herself some precisely remembered scenes of her late employer (II,8; p. 155). And in the final section, Mrs. Ramsay is mulled over again and again in the memories of Lily, Mr. Ramsay, and the children.

But at this point, as with the examples of Proust's Odette and Albertine, we begin talking about something else, namely the disjunctive manner of depicting character in the modern novel. After all, the task of expanding and revitalizing the solitary point of view by complementing it, adding hypothetical reflectors to it, and fanning out a succession of "takes" of the same object, is part and parcel of the movement away from the gradual evolutionary depiction of character and toward the fragmented, discontinuous process that marks the modern novel in more than one way.

C. *Multiperspectivism*

Though changes in distance, angle, and set-up cannot take place in the novel with the facility and automatism of the cinema because of fundamental differences in the production and articulation of their signs, experiments with such changes do nonetheless become more and more frequent in the postcinema novel. While in traditional forms of narration, a change in point of view (or scene or locale) required the drawing of a curtain, an intrusive explanation, or at least a break in the text, the film's narration is essentially transitionless. This is partly because each filmic image "bears the mark of the point of view from which it was taken."[6] In other words, cinematic narration, while it depends on a general process of "authorial" selection for its net effect, is not intrinsically burdened with the problem of the physical or psychological space that separates the narrative observer from what is observed. Distance and angle are built into the image, whereas in any discursive, literary art, such as the novel, they are subtle and constantly varying factors that are determined at another level, so to speak, of production.

Nevertheless, as with simultaneity, the novelist will find a means of overcoming this inherent difficulty. The narrator in the modern novel feels less and less obliged to justify each change of distance, angle, or location with an explicative phrase or with a spatial or temporal transition. Instead, two or more separate narrative vantage points meet head on, causing a complex multiperspectivism and thus giving a peculiarly vivid impression of contour and depth to imaginary spaces.

The most notable example of multiperspectivism[7] comes during Lily's final evocation of Mrs. Ramsay, immediately following the "fifty pair of eyes" passage.[8]

What did the hedge mean to her, what did the garden mean to her, what did it mean to her when a wave broke? (Lily looked up, as she had seen Mrs. Ramsay look up; she too heard a wave

6. Magny, *L'Age du roman américain*, p. 103.

7. This term could equally be applied to certain parts of Proust's work, but not on the same close, primarily diegetic level that I am interested in here. All the scenes involving voyeurism on Marcel's part partake of a basically triple perspective: Marcel the character viewing, Marcel the writer reminiscing, and some ambiguous, omniscient power reporting affective details of the scene that Marcel as simple witness would never be able to know (cf. Genette, *Figures III*, pp. 221-24). These diverse viewpoints are simultaneous at the level of enunciation, one implicit in the other—a sort of superimposition; the cases of radical switches from one narrative viewpoint to another are relatively rare.

8. Cf. Edward Murray's analysis of rapid changes in distance, angle, and

falling on the beach.) And then what stirred and trembled in her mind when the children cried, 'How's that? How's that?' cricketing? She would stop knitting for a second. She would look intent. Then she would lapse again, and suddenly Mr. Ramsay stopped dead in his pacing in front of her, and some curious shock passed through her and seemed to rock her in profound agitation on its breast when stopping there he stood over, and looked down at her. Lily could see him.

He stretched out his hand and raised her from her chair. It seemed somehow as if he had done it before; as if he had once bent in the same way and raised her from a boat which, lying a few inches off some island, had required that the ladies should thus be helped on shore by the gentlemen. An old-fashioned scene that was, which required, very nearly, crinolines and peg-top trousers. Letting herself be helped by him, Mrs. Ramsay had thought (Lily supposed) the time has come now; Yes, she would say it now. Yes, she would marry him. And she stepped slowly, quietly on shore. Probably she said one word only, letting her hand rest still in his. I will marry you, she might have said, with her hand in his; but no more. Time after time the same thrill had passed between them—obviously it had, Lily thought, smoothing a way for her ants. [III,11; pp. 225–26]

What begins as Lily's recollection of past iterative scenes ("She would stop knitting. . . . She would look intent."), becomes a single, definitive scene ("Mr. Ramsay stopped . . ."), yet still mediated by Lily's point of view and thus seen from the outside ("Lily could see him."). Then the memory of a singulative real scene (we have "seen" it ourselves in the first part of the novel) turns into an imaginary scene that Lily conjures up of Mr. Ramsay mutely proposing to Mrs. Ramsay. Lily now mimics the narrator, in a sense, by penetrating herself into Mrs. Ramsay's (conjectured) thoughts, so that the central sentence assumes a triple perspective: "Letting herself be helped by him, Mrs. Ramsay had thought (Lily supposed) the time has come now. . . ." The narrator presents Lily's supposition of Mrs. Ramsay's thought.

_____
location by cross-cutting in *Jacob's Room: The Cinematic Imagination* (New York, 1972), pp. 149–50.

Throughout this passage the three distinct viewpoints are juxtaposed. The narrator's position vis-à-vis Lily, in what Auerbach would call the "frame incident," is established by external and internal descriptive phrases: "Lily looked up . . ." "Lily could see him," "Lily thought, smoothing a way for her ants." At the same time, Lily's thoughts themselves are established without any textual intervention by the narrator (i.e., in *style indirect libre*): "What did the hedge mean to her . . . ?" "It seemed somehow as if . . . ," "An old-fashioned scene that was. . . ." And finally, Mrs. Ramsay's own actions and hypothetical actions and thoughts are established independently of either the narrator or Lily: "She would look intent," "she stepped slowly . . . ," "Yes, she would marry him." In the same way, three separate scenes or locations are, as elsewhere in these final chapters of the novel, spliced together and shuttled between:

1. Lily hovering over the ants;
2. Mrs. Ramsay knitting and Mr. Ramsay pacing before the summer home;
3. Mr. and Mrs. Ramsay in an "old-fashioned scene" in a boat by an island.

This passage, then, is an extreme example of the central device used throughout "The Lighthouse," that of cross-cutting—"parallel editing" between two separate scenes—or spatial montage.

Joyce's heteroclite narration of *Ulysses* affords some of the best examples of colliding viewpoints and dynamic shifts in perspective. Like Proust in Marcel's description of the steeples, Joyce manipulates point of view in both senses: nearly every episode (particularly in the latter half of the work) can be considered as rendered by means of a different narrative vehicle, or persona; and within certain episodes the narration splits or shifts in such a way that distance, angle, and mode are in perpetual motion. This second kind of manipulation, in which changing focal distance becomes a function of the nature of the narrative vehicle, will be of prime interest to us in a study of the "Cyclops."

I pause for a moment to examine the various personae of *Ulysses*, even though their isolated effect is not, strictly speaking, pertinent to this study of cinematic form. Considering the first three and second three chapters as narrative units, one "in responsion" to the other, we see that the more or less invariable, most exclusively anonymous narrative persona is dominant here—the voice which will superintend some succeeding episodes and which I shall label "Narrator." The "Telemachiad" uses Stephen as intermittent focal point just as the first three Bloom episodes use Bloom, but the Narrator, allowing for the expansions by means of these alternate focal points, remains otherwise in control. This same Narrator is dominant in the "Lestrygonians," "Scylla and Charybdis," "Wandering Rocks," and "Sirens," but reappears only intermittently thereafter and in successively diminished proportions: in the second half of "Nausicaa" and then in the italicized and parenthetically enclosed stage directions of "Circe," where the Narrator appears perhaps in his raw essence, "within or behind or beyond," according to Stephen Dedalus's famous formulation in *A Portrait*. From then on, the Narrator gives way to one persona or another, this withdrawal culminating in "Penelope," where the Narrator is totally absent, "returning" only as a phantomlike distillation in the few external events that break in on Molly's monologue.

One of the most dynamic aspects of *Ulysses* is its gradual "dumping" of the single, dominant Narrator. It should be noted, furthermore, that in no case can the Narrator be assimilated to the traditional omniscient narrator: the Narrator is always in clear, close contact with the scene and characters (or at most, hovering slightly above, as in the "Sirens" and the end of "Nausicaa"), while characters' feelings and thoughts, when present at all, are consistently represented without the Narrator's mediation (direct interior monologue). At the same time, this "dumping" of the Narrator—a dynamic movement within the specific narrative of *Ulysses*—is only tangentially pertinent to the proclaimed "disappearance of the author," as traced through the development of the novel from Flaubert on.

The persona technique as such is more interesting from a broadly cinematic perspective when a varying narrative vehicle is woven into the diegetic action in such a way that it becomes at the same time the global narrator's focal point, as in Dos Passos's and Faulkner's works.[9] The alternating focalization of Stephen and Bloom through-out the first eleven episodes, which had an obvious impact on these later novelists, has been considered at various points above and will be returned to in detail in the last chapter. Suffice it to say for the moment that, in this portion of *Ulysses*, point of view is in constant shift by virtue of inserted fragments of unmediated consciousness, but that, in terms of distance and angle, the Narrator is, on the whole, consistently at close range and steady.

The "Cyclops" episode offers perhaps the most interesting exam-ples of shifts in angle and distance, as the result of its split narrative vehicle. Point of view switches from an actively participating obser-ver—and hence at "eye-to-eye" angle with relative proximity—to a digressive, relatively distant observer, without any textual demarca-tion save the indention of a new paragraph. As will be clear in what follows, the changes in relative "angle" and "distance" are not so much measurable quantities (as they appear to be, for example, in the "Wandering Rocks") as functions of tone, diction, and the nature of the diegetic information communicated[10]—which are, after all, the more usual literary correlatives for the angle and distance of cinematic practice.

The digressive narration, interspersed through the sequentially coherent first-person account, is always excessively additive in terms

9. In *U.S.A.* and *The Sound and the Fury*, for example, individual charac-ters, who take part in the action throughout, alternate as narrative focal point (in whichever section of text bears their name in *U.S.A.*) for events that might occur from different points of view elsewhere. It should be added that the shifting of specific narrative focalization within a discrete portion of text, as in the examples to be studied from *Ulysses*, functions in an even more dynamic, if more obvious, manner through Dos Passos's cut-up technique in the mini-biographies and "Newsreels."

10. Cf. Genette: the two modes of "regulating narrative information" are "distance"—whether more or less information is conveyed more or less direc-tly—and "perspective"—the specific focalized object (character, group) through which this information is conveyed (*Figures III*, pp. 183–84).

We might note in passing the persistent recourse to visual and spatial meta-phors to describe literary effects. It should be borne in mind that the use of such terms does not necessarily imply a visual or spatial effect in the text: hence we speak of the "distance" produced by certain types of irony. Critics have gone so far in some instances as to adopt cinematic metaphors, such as Norman Friedman's "camera" point of view (see n. 1 above), which actually has no more to do with camera technique than does Dos Passos's "Camera-Eye."

of information and usually extraneous in terms of diegetic pertinence (if we assume that the principal narrative is that of the participating observer). It generally takes up a passing detail of the main
narrative as the point of departure for a long excursus characterized
not only by spatial and temporal coordinates at great variance with
the scene at Barney Kiernan's pub, but also by an exalted tone and
a stilted diction. The exaltation takes many forms (religious, bardic,
ceremonial), as does the stilted language (mock-heroic, pseudo-
epic, highly codified languages, such as legal cant). And this by no
means accounts for certain of the most peculiar excursuses, such as
black Lizzy, the hen (p. 315), and the love catalogue (p. 333). The
"Cyclops" episode thus occupies a special place in relation to the
preceding chapters of *Ulysses*, since it is the first in which the diegetically immediate scene is at times entirely subordinated to extra-
diegetic material—an effect heightened by the fact that the nonparticipating observer retains none of the Narrator's presence, which
serves to contain Stephen's mental meanderings even in "Proteus"
and Bloom's throughout. This is particularly ironic in that the pub
scene is charged, even more than previous scenes, with dramatic
tension.

The excursuses can very generally be broken down, according to
their relation to the diegesis, into two groups: those that are sequential (in that they include a character and/or action of the
diegesis) and those that are tangential (in that they elaborate an
extraneous or imaginary scene—a separate diegesis—on the basis of
a mere verbal suggestion of the main narrative). The essential relation often seems to be that of a commentator making additions
or emendations to a primary text (cf. below, p. 189, n. 7). The shifts
in point of view that interest us here occur at the points of transition
(or rather, collision) from the main narrative to a sequential excursus
and back again to the main narrative.

Ah! Ow! Don't be talking! I was blue mouldy for the want
of that pint. Declare to God I could hear it hit the pit of my
stomach with a click.

And lo, as they quaffed their cup of joy, a godlike messenger
came swiftly in, radiant as the eye of heaven, a comely youth,
and behind him there passed an elder of noble gait and coun-

tenance, bearing the sacred scrolls of law, and with him his lady
wife, a dame of peerless lineage, fairest of her race.

Little Alf Bergan popped in round the door and hid behind
Barney's snug, squeezed up with the laughing. . . . I didn't know
what was up and Alf kept making signs out of the door. And
begob what was it only that bloody old pantaloon Denis Breen
in his bath slippers with two bloody big books tucked under
his oxter and the wife hotfoot after him. [pp. 298-99]

The appearance on the scene of three new characters is first rendered
in the stilted language of the digressive narrator and then by the
colloquial main narrator. The first account has the effect of removing us from the scene by adding superfluous, mock-epic epithets
("radiant as the eye of heaven" "fairest of her race"). The characters
themselves remain anonymous, and the ceremonial tone increases
the sense of experiential distance. With the return of the main
narrator, who, as a raconteur, also has methods of distancing his
enunciation by appealing to the implicit "you" ("Don't be talking!
I was mouldy . . ."), we are back amidst the close conviviality of
the pub: the "godlike messenger" becomes Alf Bergan pointing
mockingly at the "elder of noble gait" and his "lady wife . . . of
peerless lineage," Denis and Mrs. Breen. Each detail, down to the
"two big bloody books," has been transformed ("sacred scrolls of
law") by the distant narrator. The overall change in point of view,
then, proceeds from the variable of participation/nonparticipation,
the difference of specificity of information, and the gigantic cleavage
in level of language.

The same transforming, distancing effect is achieved throughout
the episode. When Bob Doran, for example, commiserates with
Bloom over Dignam's death (pp. 313-14), the belabored, parenthetical dialogue, rendered in "direct" discourse by the secondary
narrator, takes us away from the scene of "shaking Bloom's hand
doing the tragic" that it only very indirectly refers to. The effect
is most decidedly transformational when "Herr Professor Luitpold
Blumenduft" offers "medical evidence" in the discussion on hanging
(pp. 304-05); when Martin Cunningham and friends, "Our trav-
ellers" arrive at the pub, a "rustic hostelry," and hurl Elizabethan

commands at the innkeeper (pp. 336-37); or when, most spectacular of all, Bloom is saved from the citizen's wrath in Martin Cunningham's carriage and ascends into heaven, amidst biblical locutions, as "ben Bloom Elijah" (p. 345). One of Joyce's main points here seems to be that all such stilted dictions—courtroom jargon, archaic English, the Bible—have the effect of masking the diegetic material and, for better or worse, turning it into something very different from what "happens" (which is impossible to know)—something as aesthetically prejudicial as the main narrator's account is ideologically prejudicial.

It might be noted, finally, that point of view is not always entirely stable within the excursus. In the midst of a confused discussion about Paddy Dignam's death, the excursive narrator transforms the scene into a seance that successfully summons up Dignam's shade. The point of view remains moderately detached and clinical throughout most of this imaginary interlude, clashing with the mundane, domestic requests of Dignam, and then suddenly takes on "heroic" distance at the end before returning us to the pub scene.

> Before departing he requested that it should be told to his dear son Patsy that the other boot which he had been looking for was at present under the commode in the return room and that the pair should be sent to Cullen's to be soled only as the heels were still good. He stated that this had greatly perturbed his peace of mind in the other region and earnestly requested that his desire should be made known.
>
> Assurances were given that the matter would be attended to and it was intimated that this had given satisfaction.
>
> He is gone from mortal haunts: O'Dignam, sun of our morning. Fleet was his foot on the bracken: Patrick of the beamy brow. Wail, Banba, with your wind: and wail, O ocean, with your whirlwind.
>
> —There he is again, says the citizen, staring out.
>
> —Who? says I.
>
> —Bloom, says he. He's on point duty up and down there for the last ten minutes. [p. 302]

The narrator's detachment gathers from the first to the second paragraph by a change from the active to the passive voice: "Assurances were given . . . would be attended to . . . it was intimated. . . ." The agents, in other words, of the first paragrph, are already absent in the second. With the third paragraph, the tense changes from past to present, the grammatical mode moves toward the imperative, the diction changes from careful, imperative description to a "high-style" vocabulary and epic epithets, and the tone changes from detached matter-of-factness to heroic exaltation. The vision of the narrator, as a result, seems to have removed itself once again from the already imaginary scene of the seance. The homey astrology changes to mythological invocation, and Paddy becomes another of the Irish antiheroes, "Patrick O'Dignam," that abound in the excursuses.

A further ironic note is sounded with the final switch back to the first-person account. The citizen's "There he is again" as he stares out of the pub, could at first refer to Dignam's shade; in fact, as we find out immediately, it refers to Bloom. But this confusion, due to the shift in point of view and the vague pronoun *he*, is interesting because it further relates Dignam to Bloom—who himself has earlier fallen prey to fantasies on Dignam's account and who later will remember his dead son as the dead Dignam remembers his living son—and prepares for Bloom's own mock apotheosis at the end of the episode.

Transitionlessness marks Joyce's shifts in point of view in the "Cyclops" just as it marks his switches in the earlier chapters from within a character's consciousness to without and vice versa, or from a narrow third-person narration to an expanded dual-vantage-point narration. The colloquial raconteur from Barney Kiernan's would provide a narrative far more of a piece than that of any previous episode, if it were not regularly interrupted by the excursive narrator. The repeated change in point of view gives rise, on the contrary, to a sense of extreme discontinuity. As in the cinema, shifting point of view goes hand in hand with discontinuity: a marked change in the angle of viewing an object or an event requires a cut in the narrative signifying material, be it printed text or celluloid.

It is interesting to note that, according to the conventions of cinematic practice, a change of camera distance with regard to the same object *must* be accompanied by a change of angle; otherwise, the resulting juxtaposition (called a "jump-cut")—as if one end of a telescope had been suddenly placed in front of the camera—tends to make the spectator excessively aware of the recording apparatus and produces a generally unpleasant visual effect. In the same way, motion in one direction within the frame must be followed by *contrary* motion when the moving object is not the same from one shot to the next; otherwise, the first motion appears to be absurdly continuing in a new form. Needless to say, each of these "rules" can be seen to have been broken for experimental and/or comic purposes in surrealist and American underground films.

It is thus evident that the decomposition of a scene or action into discrete, discontinuous parts that are visually in mutual conflict or at least dynamically juxtaposed, is not simply the cinema's prerequisite for narration but a modus operandi fundamental to its proper articulation of scenic space and against which other procedures are measured and compared. Were we to use a similar standard to measure Joyce's experimentation with radical shifts in perspective, it would be clear that *Ulysses* does not really culminate a long development in the history of literary narrative, as is so often claimed. Rather, it opens up a huge new area of novelistic experimentation by refusing to restrict the perceptual field through the use of a single narrator or persona. It is as though, in "Cyclops," the ideological stakes were too high, the drama of intersubjective perception too vast, to limit the rendition to a single, steady narrator. The perceptual field is distorted, blown apart, and mended unevenly, in an attempt to get a 360° look at the distorted ideological views set in motion.

8 Discontinuity

> *Angry tulips with you darling manflower punish your cactus
> if you don't please poor forgetmenot how I long violets to
> dear roses when we soon anemone meet all naughty night-
> stalk wife Martha's perfume.*
>
> James Joyce, Ulysses

James Ramsay, trying to reconcile his past prejudices about his
father with his present experience at the end of *To the Lighthouse,*
seeks "an image to cool and detach and round off his feeling in a
concrete shape. Suppose then that as a child sitting helpless in a
perambulator, or on someone's knee, he had seen a wagon crush
ignorantly and innocently, someone's foot? Suppose he had seen
the foot first, in the grass, smooth, and whole; then the wheel; and
the same foot, purple, crushed" (III,8; p. 210). The seeking of an
image to give "concrete shape" to feeling became, for leading innovators at the beginning of this century such as Pound, Eliot,
and the Imagists, a sort of ideal of poetic composition. For the
novelists of the same generation, the vorticist image—that dynamic
yet instantaneous "intellectual and emotional complex"—was, in
itself, not enough to transfigure their more fundamentally time-
allied art. Questions of sequence, transition, and point of view were
posed with much greater immediacy for them.

Virginia Woolf's narrator, focusing through the character of James,
makes a series of *suppositions* that end up putting the potentially
static image into motion. "Suppose" is a locution that politely

(and pseudo-scientifically) gives a command simultaneously to the character himself and to the reader. In its wavering between a direct imperative and a hortative subjective (like "let there be"), it is a conveniently concise signal of *style indirect libre*: it leaves unresolved the ambiguous question of who is presenting (or producing, or articulating) the images that follow. These images, "seen" hypothetically by James as a child and more immediately by the reader, are then juxtaposed in a fundamentally cinematic manner— first the foot, then the wheel, then the foot—but changed.[1] The reader imagines, or "supposes," what the film spectator would see: three distinct images, presented in sequence without transition or subordination, which imply a diegetic progression: something like "the wheel has crushed the foot." So, in the manner of Virginia Woolf, let us suppose that this imagined sequence, shared by James and the reader, stands for the montagelike process that became, like the poets' "objective correlative," an ideal modus operandi for the postcinema novelists.[2]

Montage in film is based on a principle of discontinuity. The discrete portions of an action or event are cut up into separate shots and then spliced together, so that the totality of a scene (except in long-distance "establishment" shots) is never visually present all at once but is only implied by this or that part. But if

1. This sequence recalls, for example, Kuleshov's early, influential experiments that demonstrate the intrinsic narrativity of two disjunct images spliced together and hence the power of montage to create "new relations among objects, nature, characters, and the developments of the film" (Kuleshov quoted in Ropars-Wuilleumier, *De la littérature au cinéma* [Paris, 1970], p. 16); and, more precisely, it recalls classic examples of Eisenstein's "intellectual montage," such as the rising lion sequence in *October*.

2. Ideal because it suggests an ultimately nonverbal narrative mode that could scarcely be put into practice over an extended portion of text: that in which the emitter of the image has not simply dissolved out of the picture (as in Hemingway or Dos Passos) but has simultaneously bequeathed a narrative thrust by which one image (or the signified of one syntagma) succeeds another and a diegetic configuration is formed without further grammatical subordination (still extant, for example, in Faulkner's Benjy and in Robbe-Grillet) or any other form of discursive intervention.

the narrative material is essentially discontinuous, the diegesis, or referential action, is nonetheless continuous: hence the term "discontinuous continuity" (cf. above, chap 4). The cinema's ability thus to narrate by successively *leaving out* had several important implications for other narrative arts.

A. *Paralipsis*

The art of storytelling has always made use, in varying degrees, of the discrepancy between narrative and diegesis. But the explicit excision from the narrative of pertinent diegetic material has been specifically identified as "ellipse," a technique used in Dos Passos's novels where "the most important is what is not said."[3] Magny points to a prescient example of ellipsis, the blank space—so much admired by Proust—in *L'Education sentimentale* followed by the terse phrases ("He traveled. He knew the melancholia of steamers . . .") that refer to a fifteen-year gap in Frédéric Moreau's life. It is roughly similar to the final question of the "Ithaca" episode in *Ulysses*: "Where?" followed in some editions by a huge dot, but in any case left unanswered: an example more precisely of "paralipsis."[4] The diegetic information is not stated in the narrative (ironically, since this episode is otherwise marked by exhaustive inclusiveness about what happens and never resorts to ellipsis or even abbreviated summary) but is implied, clearly, by everything that has gone before. We know *where* Bloom has traveled, and the recapitulative quality of the closing exchange, signaled in the answers by a change of tense ("He rests.") and by the hypnotic Sinbad

3. Claude-Edmonde Magny, *L'Age du roman américain* (Paris, 1948), p. 72.
4. Genette defines the *ellipse* as one of the four fundamental narrative "movements," that one in which "a null segment of narrative corresponds to some duration or other of story" (*Figures III*, p. 128), thus associating it with the temporal aspect of narration. Ellipsis in the broader sense, as Magny takes it, of elided information, comes under the name (as in rhetoric) or *paralipse*: "lateral omission" or "the omission of a certain important action or thought of the focal hero, which cannot be ignored by either the hero or the narrator, but which the narrator chooses to dissimulate to the reader" (pp. 211-12). In English, the term "ellipsis" is not necessarily confined to temporal discontinuity, but I have taken over the term "paralipsis," which I wish to apply in a rather specific manner.

catalogue, suggests that the burden of the final answer is thrown onto us. The huge dot, which does not *signify* anything, fills part of the blank space as a reminder that what has been excised here from the narrative is present elsewhere in the text and has a quite vast diegetic significance.

Paralipsis, taken globally as the omission or suppression of pertinent information, can be found in many novels: Genette cites examples from Stendhal, and Sterne would undoubtedly provide a rich terrain. It can most generally be associated with texts involving an epistemological problematic (from *The Turn of the Screw* to the detective novel): hence its growing importance in the postcinema period—if only as a function of the increased concern with relativity of point of view. In this discussion I wish to emphasize not so much the epistemological implications as the narrative effects of paralipsis, and therefore shall consider it more specifically as the virtual omission in the narrative of something that *nonetheless takes place* in the diegesis. In this way, we shall see that the technique is basically similar to the cinematic narrative, even if the aesthetic results are not always the same.

We have already noted that the narration of *Three Lives* is characterized by an amorphous present in which events never really happen but somehow come to be or are referred to as already having taken place, as with the death of Melanctha's mother. In "The Gentle Lena," the marriage between Lena and Herman Kreder is prepared for at some length: the frequentative relation between narrative and diegesis is more or less stable from "Three days before the wedding day" (p. 254), when Herman disappears, to his father's going to coax him to return, then the postponement of the marriage by a week, and finally the wedding day (p. 267). The marriage itself is then alluded to thus:

> Mrs. Haydon had everything all ready. Everybody was there just as they should be and very soon Herman Kreder and Lena Mainz were married.
>
> When everything was really over, they went back to the Kreder house together. They were all now to live together, Lena and Herman and the old father and the old mother. . . . [p. 267]

A miniscule narrative segment, "Herman Kreder and Lena Mainz were married," whose temporal relation to the whole is rendered imprecise by "very soon" and "When everything was really over," corresponds to a diegetic event that has been long prepared for and that will govern the rest of the story.

In later writings by Gertrude Stein, such as the various "portraits" and *Tender Buttons*, which are entirely dominated by the descriptive mode, it becomes less and less pertinent to speak of diegesis at all. The essential paradox in this phase of Stein's writing is that, with the near total lack of referentiality, the technique of repetition nonetheless prevails. That is, if the paralipses in the narrative begin to outnumber the instances of simple reference, the scant fragments of diegesis that remain are insisted upon with vigor. The brief "Storyette H.M.," from the period of the portraits (ca. 1912), provides a good example of this insistent narrative echoing through virtually empty diegetic spaces.

> One was married to some one. That one was going away to have a good time. The one that was married to that one did not like it very well that the one to whom that one was married then was going off alone to have a good time and was leaving that one to stay at home then. The one that was going came in all glowing. The one that was going had everything he was needing to have the good time he was wanting to be having then. He came in all glowing. The one he was leaving at home to take care of the family was not glowing, the one that was going was saying then, I am content, you are not content, I am content you are not content, I am content, you are not content, you are content, I am content.

Michel J. Hoffman, who quotes this piece in his study of Stein, suggests that the "interlocking repetition" here is essentially the result of a "cinematic technique," because "like the moving picture frames they resemble, each of the sentences repeats most of what has been stated in the previous sentence and adds a very small additional piece of information. And so, as in the moving pictures, we see the changing picture only after a number of frames flash

on the screen in sequence."[5] This observation, which makes a too
facile identification between the celluloid frame and the written
sentence, is nonetheless very helpful. It suggests a way in which
much of Gertrude Stein's later work, for all its turning away from
a figurative reality, may be regarded as ultimately cinematic in composition. The absence of traditional syntax and the resulting swirl
of disconnected images in *Tender Buttons*, for example, are analogous to the relatively free and uncodified syntax of cinematic
agencement: "Elephant beaten with candy and little pops and chews
all bolts and reckless rats, this is this."[6]

But the *effect* of Stein's excision, or at least reduction, of a
diegetic core is by no means the same as the effect of logical leaps in
cinematic narration. In Stein there is a deflation of whatever might
be dramatic, while the cinema deletes tiresome exposition and superfluous connectives in an effort to achieve greater dramatic intensity.
Jules Romains often uses the technique of paralipsis precisely to
achieve a greater immediacy or intensity of diegesis. When the
telegram arrives, for example, in the town near where Jacques
Godard's parents live, a little boy is asked to take it to their village.
The only evocation of the little boy actually delivering the telegram
is this:

> It was then that Jacques Godard arrived in the village for his
> second life. It began as words that a little boy mumbled in a
> kitchen, before a table on which two bowls steamed; it was
> stretched out into a loud cry; it became a lamentation, rolled
> upon itself as if to bite and kill itself. Then it left, went up the
> courtyard, and took off down the road. [p. 42]

The "words" are named but not given; the reaction of Godard's
parents is described only by the "loud cry" and "lamentation."
All is subordinated in the narrative to the vague, ever-present notion
of Godard's "second life." Thus, the climactic news-breaking scene,

5. *The Development of Abstractionism in the Writings of Gertrude Stein*
(Philadelphia, 1965), pp. 160, 163, and 165. "Storyette H.M." was originally
published in *Portraits and Prayers* (New York, 1934).
6. "A SOUND," "Objects," *Tender Buttons*, in *Selected Writings*, ed. Carl
Van Vechten (New York, 1945), p. 474.

whose narrative signifiers are limited to auditory manifestations
alone (words, cry, lamentation), is nowhere pointed out specifically
and can only be assumed from the context.

The same oblique relation between narrative and diegesis is evident at the moment the priest comes before the funeral party to
deliver a sermon over Godard's dead body.

> For a minute the priest was content to be at the altar and
> make the sacred gestures. "I was right to go into the seminary."
> He recalled former hesitations and recent regrets. "What other
> work could have given me such astonishing joy as that which I
> feel at this moment?"
>
> He loved the unknown dead man, loved him without giving
> him a face, but not with an impersonal love. He tried first to
> imagine him; he did not succeed. Was he an adolescent, an adult,
> an old man? He had not been told, and he did not find these
> things out.
>
> He could have chosen arbitrarily, given him an age, a height, a
> look. That would have been a game of wit that would have de-
> stroyed his emotion. He gave up, therefore, the attempt to evoke
> him; but the dead man was yet all the more present, like some-
> one standing next to you, in a room where it's getting dark,
> someone who grazes you and whose breath you feel on your
> eyelids. [pp. 120–21]

Rather than presenting the actual words of the sermon, the narrator
contents himself with describing the attitude of the priest toward
himself and toward the unknown dead man. Again, we must assume
from "He gave up, therefore, the attempt to evoke him" that in fact
the priest is delivering his sermon. Here, in particular, an ironic,
metalinguistic relation is set up whereby the priest's reluctance to
"evoke" the dead man echoes the narrator's reluctance to evoke the
priest's verbal performance, while the narrator's aim—here as in the
news-breaking scene and throughout most of the novel—is precisely
to evoke the dead Jacques Godard. The priest's diegetic reluctance
mimes the narrator's effective reluctance in such a way that the narrative and diegesis relate directly to one another only when the
narrator assumes the priest's traditional role ("but the dead man was
yet all the more present . . ."). It is as though the narrator, by

omitting from his narrative specific reference to fundamental units of action following the death (the news-breaking, the sermon) and forcing these units to be construed by themselves in the reader's mind, were better able or somehow specially authorized to refer with no uncertainty to the flights and peregrinations of Godard's soul (or phantom or shade—it's not quite clear), diegetic units that take place on a plane far different from that of the rest of the action. To make a full interpretation of *Mort de quelqu'un*, it would be necessary to study exactly how natural events and supernatural events correspond, or fail to correspond, to direct and indirect (or even paraliptic) narrative enunciations.

B. *Additive Fragments*

The narrative discontinuity created by paralipsis results, then, from leaving something out. This is, in a certain measure, to be expected in the relatively brief, concise narratives of Stein and Romains. In the longer works of Proust and Joyce, on the other hand, nothing is more characteristic than discontinuity created by the *addition* of fragmentary material into the narrative. In this case, the same discrepancy between narrative and diegesis is exploited, in that the relation of the supplementary element to the diegesis is often oblique, or even nonexistent. We have already seen that the intercalation of the extraneous, digressive narrator in the "Cyclops," for example, creates a singularly discontinuous narrative structure for a diegesis that is usually homogeneous and compact. The excursuses of this secondary narrator have only an oblique relation to what is happening at the pub: sometimes they make fanciful digressions on something the first-person narrator has just said or reported, other times they repeat the same action in a different mode, and only very rarely do they entertain a referential relation to the diegesis and thus promote it. As a general rule, when an excursus begins, the diegesis stops, or rather is held in suspension, the supreme example of this being the love catalogue: "Love loves to love love. Nurse loves the new chemist. Constable 14A loves Mary Kelly . . ." (p. 333).

The nonintegrated, apparently superfluous fragment appears nonetheless in Stein's and Romains's work in the mode of the parable.

The narrative refers to some simple event enacted by unspecified characters, yet which has no relation, save a universalizing or allegorical one, to the main diegesis. Stein's first long novel, for example, *The Making of Americans*, begins with such a parable:

Once an angry man dragged his father along the ground through his own orchard. "Stop!" cried the groaning old man at last, "Stop! I did not drag my father beyond this tree."

while in *Mort de quelqu'un* the supplementary fragment is inserted toward the end of the narrative (pp. 134-35). As in the final vignette of *U.S.A.*, the section entitled "Vag," there is only an oblique diegetic relation between the fragment of the young engineer and the adjacent narrative. This sort of fragment is the extreme case of discrepancy between narrative and diegetic ordering.

In the cinema, narrative discontinuity is inherent in the montage process, whether a fragment has been left out whose diegetic correlative must be silently construed, or a diegetically nonpertinent image has been added (such as the rocking-cradle motif in *Intolerance*). But in the novel, by virtue of the inherently diachronic and less differentiated medium of language, the supplementary fragment is often more plainly dissociated—for example, typographically—from the body of the text (which lacks a true equivalent, for example, of the cinematic fade-in or dissolve). In each of these arts, however, a connection between the nonintegrated material and the main diegesis potentially exists. But, as with paralipsis, it is a connection that is neither stated nor otherwise signified outright in the text and must be extrapolated by the reader or spectator.

We might consider Joyce's "Aeolus" episode as the clearest example of discontinuity arising from additive material in the narrative. Certainly it is the most visually discontinuous. The "headlines" contrast in montage fashion with the normally printed text not just typographically but also in terms of tone and diction. As in the "Cyclops," the relation between this supplementary material and the main diegesis is by no means a stable one. Sometimes the headlines act simply as labels for the contents that follow, as "IN THE HEART OF THE HIBERNIAN METROPOLIS" or "WILLIAM BRAYDEN, ESQUIRE, OF OAKLANDS, SANDYMOUNT" (pp. 116-17). In this case, while in no way furthering the diegesis, they maintain the traditional relation between title and text, between headline and story, namely, that of recapitulation or résumé. Here, in particular, though one might be tempted to go back to the explanatory titles used as chapter headings in the courtly romances and the picaresque novel, the primary function of the headline seems to be simply that of label. In fact, since journalism and Bloom's canvassing work for the newspaper are diegetically at the heart of this episode, the headlines become one of the more concrete examples of Joyce's unabashed attempts at expressive or imitative form.[7]

The headline as label set above a brief text suggests, in particular, the "vignette" characteristic of turn-of-the-century newspaper articles—characteristic as well of novels and movies of that period (cf. *Sister Carrie* and Griffith's early work). It is the covertly sensational or overtly maudlin side of naturalism that seems constantly on the point of bursting out from beneath these headlines. A great ironic tension arises precisely from the fact that what follows in the text is instead, on the whole, stylistically congruent with the writing of the preceding chapters, which is naturalistic only in its attention to sensuous detail as recorded by the Narrator or as registered by consciousness.

If, then, certain of the headlines offer a nondiegetic element or a simple label that reduplicates or summarizes the diegetic action, other headlines propound a more complex relation between narration and diegesis. In this case, the headline is not simply superfluous but also refers to an event or situation secondary to the main diegesis. As in the "Cyclops," the supplementary material, by pointing to and thus magnifying a small detail of the diegesis, significantly distorts the total narrative flow.

It is particularly interesting that the oblique headlines are generally restricted to Bloom and Stephen: first to Bloom's characteristic

7. A. Walton Litz has shown that much of the "expressive form"—a technique that "seeks to establish a direct correspondence between substance and style"—of the final version of *Ulysses*, resulted from addenda joined to the original *Little Review* publication of certain episodes in 1918. The headlines themselves, for example, are a late addition to "Aeolus." Litz suggests the term "mosaic" to describe the additive effects of these late changes, and indeed the discontinuous, zig-zag structure of montage described here is close to such a notion. *The Art of James Joyce* (London, 1961), esp. pp. 44–49.

cogitations, then to Stephen's project for a story. In each case, the headline no longer refers to the immediate external action or even to characters' spoken or quoted words (as in the long conversation about oratory), but rather to mental or imagined events. Thus, for example, the passage in which Bloom watches the old typesetter work, is headed "AND IT WAS THE FEAST OF PASSOVER" because of Bloom's mental association:

He stayed in his walk to watch a typesetter neatly distributing type. Reads it backwards first. Quickly he does it. Must require some practice that. mangiD. kcirtaP. Poor papa with his hagadah book, reading backwards with his finger to me. Pessach. Next year in Jerusalem. Dear, O dear! All that long business about that brought us out of the land of Egypt and into the house of bondage *alleluia. Shema Israel Adonai Elohenu.* No, that's the other. Then the twelve brothers, Jacob's sons. And then the lamb and the cat and the dog and the stick and the water and the butcher and then the angel of death kills the butcher and he kills the ox and the dog kills the cat. Sounds a bit silly till you come to look into it well. Justice it means but it's everybody eating everyone else. That's what life is after all. How quickly he does that job. Practice makes perfect. Seems to see with his fingers. [p. 122]

The headline leads one to expect an event specifically relating to Passover, but instead it capitalizes on Bloom's brief recollection by means of the reversed type. There are other similar examples, as in the section headed "WHAT WETHERUP SAID" (p. 126), where one expects the headline to refer to the reactions to Ned Lambert's mocking reading of Dan Dawson's speech, while in fact it refers to a detail in Bloom's mental reservation about the others' mocking. But the Passover example remains the most interesting: Bloom's seeing and reading backwards the name of his dead friend raises the problem of reversibility as it applies both to the text and to the book's thematics. Everything Bloom associates with the "backwards" Hebrew text he recalls, and with his Jewish lineage in general, is marked by the irreversible: Old Testament justice as well as the deaths of his father and son. Yet the type that the old man is setting *is* reversible: indeed, it must be in order to make sense. In the same way, Joyce's textual ordering here is more than ordinarily reversible. The oblique headlines must be returned to, out of narrative order, to make a proper collation with the main text.

Though this same basic mechanism is required in varying degrees throughout the episode, it becomes particularly crucial toward the end, when Stephen tells Professor MacHugh and the others his idea for a story to be called *A Pisgah Sight of Palestine or the Parable of the Plums*. Soon after the beginning of Stephen's account, there start to appear headlines that refer not to the men's rather uncoordinated action as they leave the newspaper offices and go to a bar, but rather to the metadiegetic[8] events of Stephen's narrative: "SOME COLUMN–THAT'S WHAT WADDLER ONE SAID," "THOSE SLIGHTLY RAMBUNCTIOUS FEMALES," and so on (pp. 147–48). A tour de force climax is reached at the end when, Stephen having finished his exposition and announced his title, the headline nonetheless cranks out a final reference to the story:

> DIMINISHED DIGITS PROVE TOO TITILLATING
> FOR FRISKY FRUMPS. ANNE WIMBLES
> FLO WANGLES–YET CAN YOU
> BLAME THEM?

–Onehanded adulterer, [the professor] said grimly. That tickles me I must say.
–Tickled the old ones too, Myles Crawford said, if the God Almighty's truth was known. [p. 150]

Though the professor and Crawford are still referring to Stephen's epithet for Nelson as embodied in the statue that, as it figures in his story, is the only material link between the diegetic and metadiegetic events here, the headline leads off on a seemingly wild tangent; the source, which is not in Stephen's own account, may be in the imagination of any of the characters who have heard the story, but the actual rendition has been characteristically transformed by the fatuous narrator of the headlines.

The transcription of consciousness and the inclusion in the text of

8. Genette: "*metanarrative* is a narrative within the narrative, *metadiegesis* is the universe of this secondary narrative in the way that *diegesis* designates . . . the universe of the primary narrative." *Figures III*, p. 239, n. 1.

secondary texts create the most interesting patterns of discontinuity in "Aeolus." These are also the prime motivators for fragments that appear elsewhere fully integrated into the main narrative. Until now we have primarily discussed instances in which discontinuity is a function, in part, of typography. In "Aeolus," the alternation between bold headline and regular text produces the effect of disjunction first on an entirely visual level. But to limit the discussion to such examples suggests a potentially high affinity between the purely physical or material properties of book and film. We know, however, that the double articulation of language prevents the literary work from attaining effects of visual configuration by any but typographical means.[9]

In fact, narrative discontinuity is by no means restricted to a ruffling of the textual surface: witness the "Cyclops." Those early twentieth-century novels that approximate most closely the discontinuous continuity of the montage process are, what is more, often marked by complete textual integration of their diverse materials. In other words, the essential transitionlessness of montage appears most clearly in the novel when graphic as well as verbal connectives are expunged.

C. *Montage of Consciousness*

The inclusion of characters' directly rendered, narratively unmediated consciousness is one of the most celebrated earmarks of modern fiction. The importance of "stream of consciousness" for this part of my study is not in any revelations of human psychology it may have operated or corroborated but rather in the radical handling of narrative that is thus introduced. After all, consciousness has always been present in fiction; what has mainly changed is its treatment. It is important, as will become clear, to consider consciousness itself as part of the diegetic universe alluded to in the narrative, on the same content level as external actions or descriptions. The various

9. On the double articulation of language, see chap. 4, n. 14. One might think of the object-poems of the Renaissance, Apollinaire's "Calligrammes," or contemporary "concrete poetry" as extreme cases of typographical configuration, i.e., where linguistic signs are used, at first, on the purely visual level, as single articulations.

means of handling this element, of combining and juxtaposing it with those other elements external to the character's consciousness, lead to techniques ultimately pertinent to the cinematic analogy.[10] In spite of its absence of narrative mediation, the new presentation of consciousness—what Humphrey calls "direct interior monologue" and Genette, "discours immédiat"—is nonetheless rigorously conventionalized by the very use of words as the vehicle of thought. Here the novel enters a diegetic realm normally closed to the cinema. The fascinating paradox is that where, substantially, the two diverge the most, compositionally they are yet very similar.

While Woolf and Joyce are the masters of the montage of consciousness, a few words should be devoted to Proust's conception of human consciousness, particularly since memory has such an important place in his novel. Throughout the *Recherche*, Proust conceives of character as a fundamentally discontinuous entity. There is a theoretically whole personality—otherwise there would be no point to characters at all—which is "our permanent self," but it is made up of "all our successive selves" (III,696). "Successive" and related words are used over and over in the *Recherche* to refer to distinct parts of a development that are sequential and yet disconnected. Thus, Marcel's sudden changes of feeling as a child at Combray teach him to distinguish "these states that follow one another within me ... contiguous, yet so external to each other, so devoid of means of communication between them, that I cannot understand or even imagine clearly to myself anymore in one state, what I desired, or feared, or accomplished in the other" (I,183). Proust's entire narrative is patterned after this discontinuous structure of noncommunicating parts which is Marcel's consciousness.[11]

10. Cf. Humphrey on "cinematic devices": *Stream of Consciousness in the Modern Novel* (Berkeley, 1968), pp. 49ff. Humphrey makes the important point that "stream of consciousness" is one type of fiction or one set of conventions for presenting human consciousness—especially at the prespeech level—and not a specific method or technique in itself (pp. 4-5).
11. Genette notes that, in the cases of Marcel's and Swann's love affairs, the use of *dès lors, depuis*, and *maintenant*, key signals of the doggedly iterative mode of these sections, has the effect of treating the diegesis "not as a chain of events tied together by causality, but as a *succession of states* endlessly substituted for one another, without any possible interrelation." *Figures III*, p. 160; his emphasis.

This discontinuity is, above all, a function of the memory, that capricious warehouse of consciousness which effects the terrible excisions and distortions of the past: "Our memory resembles those stores which, in their front window, display a certain person, one time one photo, another time another " (I,890). Through the memory, in particular, the past is cut up and compartmentalized, each unit being put away haphazardly without regard to the temporal and spatial components that are experientially contiguous to it. Any coherence we perceive in the past is illusory. "For what we believe to be our love, our jealousy, is not a single, continuous, indivisible passion. They are composed of an infinity of successive loves, of different jealousies, which are ephemeral, but which, by their uninterrupted multitude, give *the impression of continuity, the illusion of unity*" (I,372; my emphasis).

In the same way, much of the continuity of the work is illusory, particularly in the first volume, where the discontinuity of the past is reflected in the discontinuity of the narrative. It is only when the liberating power of the *mémoire involontaire* has dawned on him that Marcel conceives the secret continuity of his life and the overall continuity for his work. The continuity of disparate, fragmentary states must be imposed, and as we have seen, this special continuity-in-discontinuity through the *mémoire involontaire*, by which two isolated sense impressions are juxtaposed with one another across time and space, has in its essence a close relation to the montage process—particularly since it is reflected in the structure of the narrative itself (cf. above, chap. 6, sec. D). Thus, after the rapid sequence of revelations at the Guermantes *hôtel*, Marcel seizes on the sound of the little bell that rang when Swann would come to visit in Combray and, without a correlative sensation in the present, hears it again. "When it had rung, I existed already, and since then, for me to hear again that ringing, there had to have been no discontinuity, not one instant in which I ceased to exist, to think, to be conscious of myself . . ." (III,1047). The *Recherche* is a testament of this deeply felt but rationally uncertain retrospective imperative (there had to have been . . .) that continuity must exist, or rather, that the discontinuity of experience as stored in the memory can be forged into a continuous vision, a continuous piece of art.

In Proust, then, the discontinuity of consciousness is reflected in the narrative sequentialization but otherwise remains largely a part of the discursive content of the work. Owing in part to the complexities of the first-person narrative voices, consciousness is something talked about but that never talks itself: that is, we always have the impression that Marcel's experiencing consciousness has been carefully filtered through and rehewn by Marcel's writing consciousness. From this, in turn, proceeds the highly wrought smoothness of enunciation. In Joyce, the discontinuity of consciousness is similarly a mainspring for discontinuous narrative effects. But while Proust's discontinuity is mainly of diegetic concern, as in the slides of the magic lantern, the episodic nature of personality, and the compartmentalization of memory, Joyce's bursts into the narrative. What is mainly talked about in Proust, talks itself in Joyce. By means of a convention less ancient but just as formal as first-person narration, we have the impression that Bloom's experiencing consciousness is *not* filtered or rehewn by an intervening agent, that, at moments when this consciousness "talks," narrative and diegesis, as in direct discourse, coincide completely. And accordingly, Joyce's enunciation is all the more heteroclite and textually rough as this non-narrating voice gains direct access to the narrative.

Virginia Woolf represents a median point in this respect. There are the same effects of narrative disordering due to the vagaries of consciousness as in Proust and Joyce. But while the consciousness of characters seems to enter directly into the narrative, if only through an extensive use of *sytle indirect libre*, it is yet always shaped and molded by the narrator into what Woolf has called "ornamented processes of thought." With Woolf, it is often rather hard to say whether the narrator is talking about the characters' thoughts, or the characters are talking or thinking to themselves through the narrator. As in Proust, memory plays an important part in the diegesis. Woolf's technique, however, of introducing memory into the narrative is close to Joyce's montage of consciousness.

In the last part of *To the Lighthouse*, accordingly, one might speak of a montage of memory. Here Lily again summons up the memory of Mrs. Ramsay and links it with other remembered scenes:

She had gone one day into a Hall and heard him speaking during the war. He was denouncing something: he was condemning somebody. He was preaching brotherly love. And all she felt was how could he love his kind who did not know one picture from another, who had stood behind her smoking shag ('fivepence an ounce, Miss Briscoe') and making it his business to tell her women can't write, women can't paint, not so much that he believed it, as that for some odd reason he wished it? There he was, lean and red and raucous, preaching love from a platform (there were ants crawling about among the plantains which she disturbed with her brush—red, energetic ants, rather like Charles Tansley). She had looked at him ironically from her seat in the half-empty hall, pumping love into that chilly space, and suddenly, there was the old cask or whatever it was bobbing up and down amongst the waves and Mrs. Ramsay looking for her spectacle case among the pebbles. 'Oh dear! What a nuisance! Lost again. Don't bother, Mr. Tansley. I lose thousands every summer,' at which he pressed his chin back against his collar, as if afraid to sanction such exaggeration, but could stand it in her whom he liked, and smiled very charmingly. He must have confided in her on one of those long expeditions when people got separated and walked back alone. He was educating his little sister, Mrs. Ramsay had told her. It was immensely to his credit. Her own idea of him was grotesque, Lily knew well, stirring the plantains with her brush. [III,11; pp. 223-24]

There are five separate scenes in this passage:

1. The frame event of Lily and the plantains
2. The lecture hall during the war
3. Tansley standing behind Lily as she paints
4. The beach with Mrs. Ramsay and Tansley
5. Mrs. Ramsay confiding with Lily

They are shuttled between in a complicated manner, with Lily's consciousness, the *metteur en scène* of this sequence, weaving in and out with discursive transitions. The temporal distortion and shifts in point of view here need not be gone into at length. Let us simply note the lack of rigorous subordination of one image or scene to another, whether temporally or focally. The same lack of subordination marks the grammatical relations: for example, the lecture hall scene is introduced in the pluperfect for the first and third time, but the second time is simply in the past: "There he was. . . ."

The important thing, though, is that these scenes appear discontinuously: the lecture hall three times, the frame event twice. In between, there is really no discursive superstructure that maintains the inner relationships among these disparate sections, just other images, other scenes and thoughts. The sequence exhibits an essential discontinuity, put into motion, or "montée" in the cinematic sense, by the irregular thrusts of Lily's thought process. We get: Lily with the ants, Lily at the lecture hall, Lily on the beach with Mrs. Ramsay and Tansley—an importantly distinct but nonetheless recognizable variant of the "ideal" we postulated in James Ramsay's "foot first . . . then the wheel, and the same foot, purple, crushed."

Virginia Woolf's "ornamented processes of thought" are such that the narrative voice, except in the case of *style indirect libre*, is characteristically present to knit the patterns of consciousness into the diegetic fabric as a whole. The instances are numerous of "She thought," "She remembered," etc., as nominative introductions to a remembered image or to a random thought in the predicate; the above passage is somewhat unusual in its absence of such specific phrases, though "Lily knew well" serves a similar purpose. In those parts of *Ulysses* where the montage of consciousness is prevalent (i.e., wherever there is Stephen or Bloom, with minor exceptions, throughout the first eleven episodes), there is little or no nominative introduction of thoughts and memories, no narrative voice that links consciousness to the rest of the diegesis. Instead, according to the convention mentioned above that is patterned after that of direct discourse (where the narrator pretends to be enunciating words spoken by a character), the words in direct interior monologue are to be taken as the thoughts of the focal character.

A diegetic thought is thus its own narrative enunciation. The character's mind is the emitter of the narrative at the very moment it is the stage of (internal) events; hence the frequency of incomplete sentences, fragmentary thought-images that have no strict syntactic relation with what surrounds them. Memories, for example—to make clear the contrast with Woolf, appear without any nominative introduction, as when Bloom, speaking to Molly, remembers their earlier life together: "He smiled, glancing askance at her mocking eye. The

same young eyes. The first night after the charades. Dolphin's Barn"
(p. 64). Here the imagelike quality is evident. The latter three sentences, in grammatical suspension, are without narrative enunciation: we are obliged to supply mentally, just as in the cinema, the
temporal and spatial connectives vaguely implied—something like
"*Bloom saw in Molly* the same young eyes, *which reminded him of*
the first night after the charades *when they went to* (or simply *at?*)
Dolphin's Barn."

To get a better idea of the complexities of Joyce's montage
process, let us take up the continuation of the passage briefly
discussed above in which Bloom tries to get a look at the legs of a
woman climbing into a carriage across the street, as he carries on a
conversation with M'Coy. The passage has been cut up and cross-
referenced, as it were, for reasons that will become clear below.

[1a]—I was with Bob Doran, he's on one of his bends, and what
do you call him Bantam Lyons. Just down there in Conway's
we were.

[2a]Doran, Lyons in Conway's. [3]She raised a gloved hand to
her hair. [2a]In came Hoppy. Having a wet. [3]Drawing back his
head and gazing far from beneath his veiled eyelids he saw the
bright fawn skin shine in the glare, the braided drums. [2b]Clearly
I can see today. [2c]Moisture about gives long sight perhaps.
[2a]Talking of one thing or another. [2b]Lady's hand. [2e]Which
side will she get up?

[1b]—And he said: *sad thing about our poor friend Paddy! What
Paddy?* I said. *Poor little Paddy Dignam*, he said.

[2e]Off to the country: Broadstone probably. [2d]High brown
boots with laces dangling. Well turned foot. [2e]What is he foster-
ing over that change for? Sees me looking. Eye out for other
fellow always. Good fallback. Two strings to her bow.

[1b]—*Why?* I said. What's wrong with him? I said.

[2e]Proud: rich: [2d]silk stockings.

[1a]—Yes, [3]Mr. Bloom said.

He moved a little to the side of M'Coy's talking head. [2e]Get-
ting up in a minute.

[1b]—*What's wrong with him*? he said. *He's dead*, he said.
[1a]And, faith, he filled up. [1b]*Is it Paddy Dignam*? I said. [1a]I

couldn't believe it when I heard it. I was with him no later than Friday last or Thursday was it in the Arch. ^{1b} *Yes*, he said. *He's gone. He died on Monday, poor fellow.*

  ^{2b}Watch! Watch!   ^{2d}Silk flash rich stockings white. ^{2b}Watch!
  ³A heavy tramcar honking its gong slewed between.

  ^{2e}Lost it. Curse your noisy pugnose. Feels locked out of it. ^{2c}Paradise and the peri. Always happening like that. The very moment. Girl in Eustace street hallway. Monday was it settling her garter. Her friend covering the display of. *Esprit de corps.* Well, what are you gaping at?

  ^{1a}—Yes, yes, ³Mr. Bloom said after a dull sigh.^{1a}Another gone.
  —One of the best, ³M'Coy said.

  The tram passed. They drove off towards the Loop Line bridge, her rich gloved hand on the steel grip. ^{2d}Flicker, flicker: the laceflare of her hat in the sun: flicker, flick. [p. 74]

There are four separate scenes here:

  I. Bloom's conversation with M'Coy
  II. M'Coy's conversation with Hoppy Holohan at Conway's
  III. The unkown woman (with her escort) preparing to leave in a a carriage
  IV. Bloom catching sight of a girl doing up her garter in Eustace street

The numbers I have inserted in the text do not refer to these diverse scenes, however, but to the three distinct enunciations, or image sources, in the text:

  1 = the spoken words (direct discourse)
  2 = Bloom's consciousness (direct interior monologue)
  3 = the Narrator

Since direct discourse and direct interior monologue are the fundamental manners of diegesis reporting itself,[12] that is, of the coincidence of narrative and diegesis, the Narrator refers, in the few

12. Cf. Genette, who gives the necessary background to this issue, beginning with Plato and Aristotle, and notes "the generally ignored relation between immediate discourse [i.e., direct interior monologue] and 'direct discourse.'" *Figures III*, esp. pp. 192–94.

places he appears at all, *only* to scenes I and III, which are properly diegetic. Scenes II and IV are evoked through direct discourse and direct interior monologue alone (1 and 2) and are metadiegetic. Up to this point, then, the four scenes cut through the three enunciations in a complicated though roughly symmetrical way. Partly as a result of this broad meshing of scene and enuncation, it is necessary to distinguish among the spoken words:

la = the dialogue proper, I-you relation between M'Coy and Bloom
lb = M'Coy's reporting of his conversation with Hoppy Holohan,

though I have not bothered to distinguish further within 1b between the actual words recounted and M'Coy's own narrative "he said's": the italics take care of that. 1a, then, corresponds narratively to scene I and metadiegetically to scene II, while 1b corresponds at once narratively and diegetically to both scene I and scene II. In other words, when M'Coy recounts his and Hoppy's words, they are sounding in both scenes at once.

In the case of Bloom's consciousness, now, there is a total and characteristically uneven meshing of scene and enunciation. 2 refers intermittently and unequally to all four scenes. Bloom loses track of the conversation and follows what is going on across the street. As the result of the complexities of his silent enunciations, it is necessary to distinguish five referents for Bloom's consciousness:

2a = Bloom's interception of M'Coy's speech
2b = Bloom's commentary on himself and his relation to the immediate scene (scene I)
2c = Bloom's thoughts *not* directly related to either of the diegetic scenes (I or III)
2d = Bloom's perception of the adjacent scene (scene III)
2e = Bloom's commentary on the adjacent scene and his relation to it

Though this division may seem arbitrary, it is motivated by the text, and there is some sort of rationale behind it. 2a and 2d are alike: they are mental images produced directly by the senses—hearing in 2a, sight in 2d—and are thus both related to the perceptual framework of the double scene. Again, put simply, Bloom listens to

M'Coy as he watches the woman. But note that nowhere in the passage is this diegetic relationship stated in such grammatically subordinated terms. Every element of each scene is presented discontinuously.

2b and 2e are similarly related in that the images here (in the form of questions, assertions, suppositions) spring from Bloom's mind in reaction to what is happening. The division between these two pairs is, or course, not altogether cut and dried: The simple phrase "Lady's hand," which I have labeled as Bloom's perception, is at once a judgment on his part. We can nonetheless say, in general, that 2a and 2d are Bloom's mind passive and that 2b and 2e are Bloom's mind reacting.

2c, then, designates images that take off from the immediate scenes and posit hypothetical or analogical relations to them: "Moisture about gives long sight perhaps," "Always happening like that." These are the images of Bloom's mind in action, outside the temporal and spatial limits of the diegesis proper. We can, in sum, identify these three fundamental functions of Bloom's consciousness[13] throughout the first part of *Ulysses*: the perceptual, the cognitive, and the speculative (2a/d, 2b/e, and 2c). Again, what is most interesting here is the way these functions are broken down and spread out into fragmentary images.

At this point, I believe, the *découpage* speaks for itself. We might look further, however, into the particularities of Joyce's method. The second paragraph is transitional from the immediate scene to the adjacent scene—at least insofar as concerns Bloom's attention. As such, it presents in miniature the general movement of the passage. Bloom at first mentally repeats M'Coy's words or simply supplies the images apparently generated by the words ("In came

13. Stephen's consciousness, though no doubt analyzable according to the same more or less traditional epistemological criteria, is presented in a less distinct manner. In the Bloom episodes, consciousness is presented as a configuration of atoms visually linked and unlinked—hence more suitable to my present purposes. Stephen's consciousness, on the other hand, though generally discontinuous in relation to the rest of the diegesis, tends to incorporate, to assimilate everything it perceives. Nothing is left untouched by this scholastic mind. Every object bears its "signature" that "I am here to read": hence, an object seen is at once an object thought ("thought through my eyes") in the "ineluctable modality of the visible . . ." (p. 37).

Hoppy. Having a wet."), but then directs his attention beyond M'Coy. One might be tempted to see here a gradual penetration, 2a–2b–2d–2e, into the depths of Bloom's consciousness. Such an idea actually runs counter to the *formal* nondifferentiation among the various aspects of this consciousness: out of context, "Doran, Lyons in Conway's" and "Lady's hand" have the same linguistically fragmented properties. The dynamism of this paragraph seems instead to arise from the disparity at the beginning between Bloom's close albeit passive perception of the immediate scene and the metadiegetic content (i.e., at one remove) of this perception, as opposed to the combination, at the end, of Bloom's relaxed attention to the immediate scene with his more active perception of the scene also diegetically present but spatially at one remove.

The signal of Bloom's relaxation of attention is the phrase "Talking of one thing or another," which I have labeled 2a. In fact, it could also be (and perhaps is) 2b or 2d. That is, "Talking of one thing or another" could be the simple interception of M'Coy's words; it could be Bloom's silent commentary on the story M'Coy is recounting; or it could be Bloom's perception of the woman talking with her escort across the street. I have chosen 2a simply because hearing is throughout associated with scene I, especially as an interference with Bloom's seeing of scene III (cf. "A heavy tramcar *honking its gong* . . ."). The ambiguity of this phrase, in any case, serves to enrich the multiplicity of the montage effect.

There are other rewarding ambiguities, the most ironic one being Bloom's "Another gone," his first substantial response to M'Coy's account. As part of the dialogue, it follows from M'Coy's (or rather Holohan's) *"He's gone"* and refers to Paddy Dignam. But by simple textual contiguity—juxtaposition is, after all, the fundamental device in the montage of consciousness—the phrase is also linked to Bloom's immediately preceding thoughts ("Paradise and the peri. Always happening like that. . . .") and refers to his having missed, once again, the sight of a bit of female flesh. The two readings, which of course are simultaneous and not mutually exclusive, are reinforced by "Monday" repeated at each point in the text to which Bloom's response is syntagmatically linked. Paddy Dignam "*died on Monday*." And the girl in Eustace street, to which Bloom has just compared his present disappointment, was settling her garter "Monday was it"? Or, does Bloom suggest Monday because he has just heard "*Monday*"?

A final word on the Narrator, whom I have neglected until now. The last paragraph, which is particularly cinematic in its fragmentation and in its switches of focal distance, starts off with the Narrator. The last sentence, however, which seems to carry on the Narrator's focalization, actually reverts once more to Bloom's consciousness. The "flickers" have a complex existence with respect to the distinctions of enunciation above—as if the "flicker" flickered itself (cf. the "jingles" and "taps" of the "Sirens"); but earlier we have had Bloom's perception in just such an imagistically fragmented mode: "Silk flash rich stockings white." This phrase is a shuffling, in part, of the previous perception-commentary "Proud: rich: silk stockings" but with even less syntactic coherence. The perception is broken down into discrete images that no longer form a continuous, diachronic enunciation. As such, these images, like the less differentiated "flickers," approach in their way our "ideal" sequence of foot—wagon—foot.

In *Ulysses*, through the medium of consciousness, the literary image ultimately detaches itself from its immediate source—be it internal or external, perceptual or narrative—and is launched into a jigsaw configuration with the surrounding elements, in a kind of phenomenological free-fall. A new piece is added to the puzzle when Joyce introduces another element, such as a letter, into his text. This is an eminently literary element, a sort of ready-made for novelistic collage. Its more stable linguistic source, the written word, diametrically opposes it to the problematical, inevitably conventionalized, content of consciousness. The written word of the letter, like the spoken word of dialogue, assumes a receiver of its message. The thought word of consciousness, however—and this explains, in part, its tendency to fragment into a nondiachronic enunciation—assumes no receiver; or rather, emitter and receiver are identical. On this score, furthermore, for all their formal similarities, direct discourse and direct interior monologue part company.

The intradiegetic text throws light, retrospectively, on Joyce's montage not simply when the text appears in the midst of the main text (as a letter is quoted in any nineteenth-century novel), but when it passes back through the consciousness of the person who has read it. After Stephen leaves him in "Ithaca,"[14] Bloom looks through the drawers of a commode, one of which contains, among other things "relative to Rudolph Bloom (born Virag)," "an envelope addressed *To my Dear Son Leopold*."

> What fractions of phrases did the lecture of those five whole words evoke?
> Tomorrow will be a week that I received . . . it is no use Leopold to be . . . with your dear mother . . . that is not more to stand . . . to her . . . all for me is out . . . be kind to Athos, Leopold . . . my dear son . . . always . . . of me . . . *das Herz* . . . *Gott* . . . *dein* . . . [p. 723]

These "fractions of phrases," we realize, are Bloom's recollection of his father's suicide letter presumably contained in the envelope. They are fragments that return to Bloom's consciousness from a text that he has read some time before and that does not appear in the main text. The correspondence between the absent text and Bloom's recollection—the exactness of which, in this instance, cannot be proven—provides a convenient justification for the convention of verbalizing the content of consciousness. Seen in this light, the direct-interior-monologue convention might be said to posit consciousness not so much as another stage, as another text (cf. Mallarmé's Hamlet "reading in the book of himself"). In the present case at least, the main text is literally a *text* of consciousness.

Since Joyce's montage, then, with all its brilliant imagistic effects, is still fundamentally literary, the notion of the consciousness as

14. There is a faint montage quality to the question-and-answer alternation throughout "Ithaca." The answers are generally predicative fragments that assume the main verb of the questions. The images they produce are therefore often catalogued or juxtaposed in a discontinuous, nonsubordinated manner. But unlike the multiple narrators in the montage of consciousness, the dispensers themselves of the vast information here have little visual contact and no existential immediacy.

text further illuminates his method. Some of the most interesting examples of montage are what might be called, therefore, clashes of texts. Such is the case when, at the bookstalls, in the "Wandering Rocks," whose montage effects are generally external and of the long-range variety, Bloom takes a look at *Sweets of Sin.*

> Mr. Bloom read again: *The beautiful woman.*
> Warmth showered gently over him, cowing his flesh. Flesh yielding amid rumpled clothes. Whites of eyes swooning up. His nostrils arched themselves for prey. Melting breast ointments (*for him! For Raoul!*). Armpits' oniony sweat. Fishgluey slime (*her heaving embonpoint!*). Feel! Press! Crushed! Sulphur dung of lions!
> Young! Young!
> An elderly female, no more young, left the building of the courts of chancery, king's bench, exchequer and common pleas. . . . [p. 236]

Bloom's physical reactions, described by the Narrator's text, are juxtaposed with the text of his consciousness ("Whites of eyes swooning up") and the (italicized) text of *Sweets of Sin.* The final ironic montage effect is produced by the abrupt change of locale, the characteristic device of the "Wandering Rocks," to the courts and an "elderly female."

An even more condensed clash of texts results when Bloom rereads Martha's letter to him, "murmuring here and there a word."

> Angry tulips with you darling manflower punish your cactus if you don't please poor forgetmenot how I long violets to dear roses when we soon anemone meet all naughty nightstalk wife Martha's perfume.[p. 78] [15]

The read word, the spoken word, and the thought word of these various texts swirl together almost inextricably. The dropping of syntax produces again the effect of free-fall, suggesting the inherently nonsyntactic construction of the cinema. But, whereas in the case of "Silk flash rich stockings white" the shuffled images

15. This sentence, as well as "Language of flowers," is a late addition to the final version of *Ulysses.* Litz (see n. 7 above), p. 48.

have a clear, global referent (the woman stepping up into the carriage), here the various textual fragments are juxtaposed with Bloom's very ambiguously referential flowers ("Language of flowers"). While the montage process remains the same, the intercalated texts point, no doubt, not simply to Bloom's simultaneous reading and thinking but to a far more complex and as yet unspecified configuration of his unconscious.

Conclusion

On the surface of it, nothing might seem stranger than to suggest a theoretical or technical relation between the movies and a novel such as *A la recherche du temps perdu*.

> For anyone who hasn't the artistic sense, that is, the submission to internal reality, can be endowed with the faculty of pronouncing judgments endlessly on art. . . . Some maintained that the novel was a sort of cinematographic procession of things. This conception was absurd. Nothing could be further from what we have perceived in reality than such a cinematographic view. [III, 882-83]

Yet I have pointed out the one-sidedness of the view that cinema is nothing more than a recorder of external reality. In fact, the "cinematographic procession of things" effects temporal leaps and narrative reversals that are, with many differences as regards the multilayered texture of the *Recherche*, surprisingly comparable to the aesthetic vision conditioning Proust's "internal reality." My strategy, therefore, has been not to examine films as individual pieces of art, but rather to take stock of the cinema as a burgeoning art-form that possesses certain highly specific aesthetic tendencies, to consider the advent of the movies in 1895 as a major event in the history of perception that had concrete effects on the whole concept of artistic creation.

The creation of new artistic forms of expression—whether or not within an already highly codified medium—always involves two different activities: taking from the established canons of general or specific aesthetic perception that which is relevant to the artist's present task, and inventing, partly on the basis of this tradition and partly on the basis of the artist's unique experience of being in the world, a specialized means of expression. In this way, the movies drew on a century of technological advancement and artistic experiments that included great flops and great successes, in order to create a new means of expression that scarcely betrays a trace of these forebears. And, according to this same dialectic of creation, the "classic" modern novelists, in inventing the new, highly elastic form for the novel, drew inevitably upon their nineteenth-century predecessors but also upon recent vehicles of extraliterary aesthetic vision, of which the cinematic experience was perhaps the most powerful.

For the cinematic experience included, among its most significant effects for the novelists, a spatial configuration of the flow of time, an innate relativity and perpetual shifting of point of view, and a vivid discontinuity of the narrating material by means of montage.

Consequently, the most dynamic aspects of the new novel form were *simultaneity*, or the depiction of two separate points in space at a single instant of time, *multiperspectivism*, or the depiction of a single event from radically distinct points of view, and *montage*, or the discontinuous disposition in the narrative of diverse diegetic elements.

It is important to note that in each case the novelist has been obliged to strain the limits of his art in order to come to grips with the new vision. Simultaneity and multiperspectivism, the temporal and perceptual aspects of roughly the same sort of experimentation, are fundamentally at odds with the consecutiveness and single-effectiveness of language. In both cases, the novelist exploits the inherent sequentiality of the novel but arranges the material in a stop-start, discontinuous manner so as to suggest ubiquity and co-existence. This new disposition, in turn, by gathering together the concurrent fragments, works against the overriding continuity of language and linguistic expression as a whole.

The straining of the limits of literary expression is a sign of the indelible mark left by the cinema's spatial narration. No other art had ever before been capable of narrating so completely through images, and never before had these images corresponded so completely to the mimetic objects they were modeled on. It is this narrative space, intrinsically discontinuous yet externally timed with electric regularity, constantly in development yet essentially no more of a "procession" than a three-ring circus, that determines a pronounced tendency in the early twentieth century toward the image and elicits in the novel a decidedly visual response.

As I have argued from the beginning, the cinematic precedence need not be considered either a random choice among diverse formative influences on the classic modern novel or a unilateral determining factor. The early twentieth century is a period in which the gradual, at times subterranean, permutations of artistic forms and genres during the preceding century explode erratically into practice. It is thus the period during which the painter and the poet, the choreographer and the sculptor, the film-maker and the novelist have more to "say" to one another (even if there is no explicit verbal interchange) than ever before. It is also the period in which physics begins to confirm experimentally the relativism of time and visual perspective that previous generations had sensed but only toyed with.

Since the cinema is precisely that invented art-form whose existence is conditioned by modern technology and whose content has consistently been conditioned by prior arts and art-forms, I will conclude by asserting, now a bit more polemically, that the cinematic precedence, given the background and the practical demonstration through texts, has a particularly *privileged position* in determining and analyzing the new forms adopted by the classic modern novel. Those who insist on an even, uninterrupted development from the nineteenth- to the twentieth-century novel turn their backs not only on history but on the development as well of parallel arts which collide crucially at the turn of the century. I have tried to characterize this *coupure* in aesthetic development from many angles. Those who maintain even a clear lineage of the classic modern back to earlier masters (e.g., the Flaubertian tradition) are likely to be ignoring critical differences with regard to the boom era of monopoly capitalism and the heyday of technology and gadgetry it ushered in. I have tried to differentiate clearly between the naïve antipositivism of nineteenth-century writers and the cautious embrace of the Machine Age and its positive potentials by the moderns.

It is as though the 1910s and 1920s generated, on the basis of a sudden radical grasp of a hundred-year heritage of experimentation and iconoclasm in all disciplines, a panoply of artistic exchanges, borrowings, and raids on the self-contained, which would act as source and touchstone throughout the century for the possibilities of interaction among the arts. For this reason, it is not surprising that seminal experimenters like Eisenstein, Vertov, Joyce, and Duchamp are repeatedly invoked in discussions of the renewed breakdown of artistic and generic boundaries that has gained momentum in the 1960s and since. The twentieth-century tradition, it seems to me, is not one requiring a label such as "postmodernism" or "abstract expressionism." Those productions since World War II that really matter are consistently the ones which eschew generic categories (e.g., Godard's documentarylike fiction films or John Ashbery's "poems" that are long prose discourses) or which actively seek contagion from other arts (e.g., Yvonne Rainer's films that include motifs from dance and the photo-roman, or Larry Rivers's paintings that turn the written word back into a visually signifying material and reactivate narrative impulses that work against the static canvas). The twentieth-century tradition, if there is any pertinence to such a term, is marked fundamentally by a desire to go beyond the confines of the single art-form, to open up art to the massive influences of the modern world, from industrial architecture to the form and signification of a coat hanger.

The cinematic precedence for the classic modern novel, therefore, deserves prominence as a primary example of one art technologically ahead of its time that shocked another art into the realization of how it could align itself with the times. It was as though the cinema had become a huge magnet whose field exerted on other arts like the novel an attraction as powerful and as ineluctable as gravity. The enormous exchange of artistic energies continues and has yet to be measured definitively.

Index